America's Bachelor Uncle

AMERICAN POLITICAL THOUGHT

edited by
Wilson Carey McWilliams
and Lance Banning

WITHDRAWN

America's Bachelor Uncle

Thoreau and the American Polity

Bob Pepperman Taylor

University Press of Kansas

Published by the University Press of Kansas (Lawrence, Kansas 66049), which
was organized by the Kansas Board of Regents and is operated and funded by
Emporia State University, Fort Hays State University, Kansas State University,
Pittsburg State University, the University of Kansas, and Wichita State University

Library of Congress Cataloging-in-Publication Data

Taylor, Bob Pepperman.
    America's bachelor uncle : Henry Thoreau and the American polity /
Bob Pepperman Taylor.
       p.   cm. — (American political thought)
    Includes bibliographical references and index.
    ISBN 0-7006-0806-0 (alk. paper)
    1. Thoreau, Henry David, 1817–1862—Political and social views.
    2. Politics and literature—United States—History—19th century.
    3. National characteristics, American, in literature.   I. Title.
    II. Series.
    PS3057.P64T39   1996
    818'.309—dc20   96-22629

British Library Cataloguing in Publication Data is available.

Printed in the United States of America

10 9 8 7 6 5 4 3 2 1

FOR MY PARENTS

CONTENTS

The heart of Thoreau's revolt was his continual assertion that the only true America is that country where you are able to pursue life without encumbrances. He did not want that freedom for his private self alone. His deepest reason for disliking the pinched Yankee standardization was its starvation of the minds and spirits of the citizens. One strain of his thought that has not yet been given due attention was summed up by him thus: "To act collectively is according to the spirit of our institutions." The context of that remark in Walden *is where he is maintaining that the community is responsible for providing a more adequate cultural life, good libraries, distinguished lecturers at the lyceums, encouragement for the practice of all the arts. He was as opposed to the hoarding of our spiritual resources as he was to the lust for ownership in our rapacious economy. He believed that all great values should be as public as light.*

—F. O. Mathiessen, *American Renaissance*

The substantial body of contemporary criticism that singles out individualism as the special curse of American democracy simply flies in the face of its history. Telling Americans to improve democracy by sinking comfortably into a community, by losing themselves in a collective life, is calling into the wind. There has never been an American democracy without its powerful strand of individualism, and nothing suggests there will ever be.

—Robert H. Wiebe, *Self-Rule*

PREFACE

This study has grown out of a long, and sometimes antagonistic, relationship between myself and Henry Thoreau. I began reading Thoreau when I was a teenager, and like so many young Americans, I was drawn to his rebelliousness, his moral earnestness, and his irreverence toward his elders. When I read him as a college student, I admired his assaults on slavery and industrial capitalism as well as his love of nature, but, again like so many others, I was nervous about what I took to be his individualism and his lack of involvement in organized (oppositional or protest) politics. As I began to age, with family and job and all the other trappings and responsibilities of conventional American adulthood, I found (again like so many others) Thoreau beginning to get on my nerves. He seemed abrasive, self-righteous, arrogant. Teaching "Civil Disobedience" in courses for first- or second-year college students, I sometimes found myself giving him a thorough trashing, unfairly implying that the failure of the American Left could be traced to the smug adolescent moralizing I thought I found in Thoreau's polemic.

When I finally decided to sit down and systematically read Thoreau's work and the accompanying scholarly literature, it was more to get him out of my system, to come to some kind of understanding of my own ambivalent relationship with him, than for any more detached or scholarly purpose. Because I wanted to understand why I continued to be attracted to an author who often annoyed me, I was forced to read him more thoroughly and carefully than I ever had before. The result was unexpected and surprising. The one segment of Thoreau's work I had grown to love and accept uncritically, the "nature writings," now seemed deeply implicated in

Thoreau's overall political project. Not only that, but Thoreau's treatment of nature was actually the most troublesome component of this project. Thoreau's political thought, on the other hand, began to look much more complex, nuanced, and sophisticated than I had imagined. While I had once shared the widely held view of Thoreau as a profound nature writer but a simplistic political thinker, a polemicist without much depth or even sustained interest in politics, I have now come to believe almost exactly the opposite—that Thoreau is one of America's most important political critics and that, although he writes magnificently about the natural world, the most disturbing and least defensible element of his political project is the politically educative and equalizing influence he assigns to nature. In short, my views have been more or less turned upside down, and the following book is a report and defense of these views.

How is it that my reading of Thoreau could have changed so? I think my own experience is not idiosyncratic or uninformative for understanding more widespread and conventional attitudes toward Thoreau. First, I had always read him with an ulterior motive or an ax to grind. I read Thoreau in order to find an argument for civil disobedience or to explain the strengths or weaknesses of the American Left or to find grounds for the protection of the natural environment. In short, I had always read him with my own agenda as the overwhelming concern, and I was never terribly interested in asking what Thoreau's own agenda or concerns might have been. These, I assumed, were self-evident and not worthy of investigation. I was not alone in this, of course. Thoreau is commonly portrayed as a hero, by environmentalists or anarchists, or as a villain, by conservatives or communitarians of various stripes, but he is rarely read as a thinker with his own concerns and intellectual integrity. Thoreau is a cultural icon too frequently exploited as a symbol in our own fights and too infrequently studied as a writer with an independent message from which we can learn. As I hope will become clear from this study, Thoreau has much more to offer philosophically than we usually recognize and is a much more valuable political thinker than our sometimes flippant use of him allows us to appreciate.

Second, I had never attempted to read Thoreau's work as a whole, as a unified literary project. Rather, I would read *Walden* or *The Maine Woods* to get a good dose of nature writing, *Cape Cod* or *A Yankee in Canada* for travel literature, but if I wanted to understand Thoreau's political ideas I would confine myself to the study of "Civil Disobedience" and a small handful of other political essays. A similar pattern is found throughout the scholarly literature, with literary critics often reading one set of Thoreau's writings and political theorists another. I hope this book will persuade political theorists and students of American political thought that if we cast our net more widely and study Thoreau's political ideas in the context of his work as a whole, we will find these ideas much richer and more rewarding than has been generally recognized. In fact, I will argue that it is only by casting our nets more widely that we can come to a satisfactory understanding of even those essays commonly identified as Thoreau's "political writings."

Thanks are due to Alan Wertheimer, Lance Banning, Wilson Carey McWilliams, and especially Patrick Neal and Fran Pepperman for their thoughtful comments on the manuscript. If I were wiser, I would have found ways to take more of these readers' advice.

CHAPTER 1

Introduction

I have no private good, unless it be my peculiar ability to serve the public. This is the only individual property.

—Thoreau, *Journal*

HENRY THOREAU has never received much attention from political theorists and students of American political thought, and what attention he has received has not been very friendly. The greatest book ever written about the American political tradition, Louis Hartz's *Liberal Tradition in America,* does not mention Thoreau at all. When political theorists do take a look at Thoreau, they almost invariably become short-tempered or even peevish, as when Nancy Rosenblum declares that Thoreau's "view of political and social life" was removed "from everything concrete,"[1] or Philip Abbott claims that Thoreau's books "can be seen as pilgrimages in which America's social and political problems are treated as secondary, even epiphenomenal concerns, compared to Thoreau's egoistic obsession with self-discovery."[2] Thoreau appears either to have nothing to tell us about our public life or to hold such perverse views that he is important only as a curiosity or an illustration of a certain weakness in American political ideology.[3] Richard Ellis has recently scolded Hartz and others for ignoring Thoreau in their portraits of American political culture, arguing that Thoreau represents a "worldview that recurs throughout American history." Ellis then, however, portrays Thoreau as a "voluntary recluse or hermit."[4] If Ellis's is a fair description of Thoreau, it is not terribly surprising that other scholars conclude he has little value as a political thinker.

Thoreau's reputation among scholars might seem surprising in light of his importance in American protest politics. Everyone recognizes the contribution of "Civil Disobedience" to what Martin Luther King Jr. calls our "legacy of creative protest" (although not everyone would give it such an admiring label), and King is the greatest but certainly not the only American to be inspired in his struggle against injustice by Thoreau's prose.[5] The scholarly literature's silences about and criticisms of Thoreau, however, convey two important implications. First, Thoreau's importance in popular culture and political movements seems to have little or no correlation with judgments of the intellectual value of his political thought. Even if Thoreau has moved giants like King or Gandhi and has spoken to countless citizens at moments of political decision, the secondary literature would lead us to believe that this does not mean he actually writes shrewdly or philosophically about political life. Second, Thoreau's ideas appear in this literature to be of more interest as a symptom of a problem in the American political tradition—an extreme individualism, say, and moral subjectivism—than as a rich, powerful, and helpful resource to inspire and guide us today.[6]

This scholarly view of Thoreau's political thought has remained remarkably stable over time. Within predictable boundaries, and with a few notable exceptions, students of Thoreau's thought have fallen roughly into two categories: those who believe that the importance and quality of Thoreau's political thought are sharply limited by his intellectual and ideological commitments, and those who flatly deny his qualifications as a political thinker and social commentator altogether.

The most extreme form of the latter view rests on the claim that Thoreau was mentally unstable at best, mentally ill at worst, and that his work can thus be understood almost entirely as a reflection of psychological problems and needs. Only three years after Thoreau's death, James Russell Lowell wrote, "Mr. Thoreau had not a healthy mind. . . . His whole life was a search for the doctor."[7] Much more recently, George Hochfield, in a powerful contribution to the "anti-Thoreau" literature, suggests that Thoreau is too obsessively egoistic to be able to think clearly about other people at all, let alone evaluate society as a whole. Identifying what he believes is Thoreau's anger toward his audience, Hochfield writes: "A maggot in Thoreau's head is the source of this violence. It is an egotism so intense as to render him virtually incapable of comprehending, much less tolerating, the ordinary affairs of life as they are carried on by ordinary people."[8] C. Roland Wagner is even more explicitly psychoanalytic in his claims, arguing that in Thoreau's political essays, "the infantile wishes begin to escape all civilized limits. There Thoreau's struggle for inward identity, his rage against the ideas of passive submission and apparently arbitrary authority, almost makes him lose contact with the real world and express his fantasies only."[9] The content of Thoreau's political work need not be taken seriously, since it is the expression of a profoundly deformed personality. As Vincent Buranelli writes, "There is an excessiveness about Thoreau's personality that gives a radical distortion to his thought."[10]

A related complaint, less extreme and more common, is that Thoreau's writings are so youthful as to be immature. It is certainly true that Thoreau exhibits a young person's (and to some, annoying) rebelliousness. Emerson notes of Thoreau in his *Journal*, "He is a boy, & will be an old boy,"[11] and Henry James Sr. declares that Thoreau "was literally the most childlike, unconscious and unblushing egotist it has ever been my fortune to encounter in the ranks of manhood."[12] In our own time, Joyce Carol Oates writes that "Thoreau's appeal is to that instinct in us—adolescent, perhaps, but not merely adolescent—that resists our own gravitation toward the outer, larger, fiercely competitive world of responsibility, false courage and 'reputation.'"[13] For some critics this young quality casts a serious doubt upon Thoreau's competence as a social and political commentator. Robert Louis Stevenson disapprovingly observes that "something essentially youthful distinguishes all Thoreau's knock-down blows at current opinion."[14] George Hochfield is appalled by what he believes is the "relentless adolescent moralizing" of *Walden*,[15] and Heinz Eulau complains about Thoreau's "political immaturity."[16] As with claims about Thoreau's mental stability, the implication of these comments is that Thoreau never achieved an intellectual adulthood, and we therefore need not take the intellectual content of his work terribly seriously.

Perhaps the most common argument for dismissing Thoreau's social criticism out of hand, however, is to suggest that he was simply too inexperienced and unworldly and misanthropic to be knowledgeable about the social and public world. One contemporary reviewer of *Walden* makes the nasty suggestion that Thoreau's conception of domestic life is much too limited to allow for a useful discussion of the domestic economy: "Did he never people that bare hovel, in imagination, with a loving and beloved wife and blooming children, or did he imagine that to know what life is he must ignore its origin?"[17] John Patrick Diggins believes that Thoreau's "strategy of disassociation may have been designed to make man unfit for society, but it also rendered his ideas unfit for social philosophy."[18] Hubert

Hoeltje contends that Thoreau "cannot be accepted as a social critic" because he was simply too withdrawn from the social world to know what he was talking about.[19] James Russell Lowell, still one of Thoreau's toughest antagonists, suggests that Thoreau's thought is completely perverted by a lack of knowledge of common, everyday people and social life: "A greater familiarity with ordinary men would have done Thoreau good, by showing him how many fine qualities are common to the race."[20] Another contemporary, Walt Whitman, has said, "Thoreau's great fault was disdain—disdain for men (for Tom, Dick and Harry): inability to appreciate the average life—even the exceptional life: it seemed to me a want of imagination."[21] All these critics assume that what they believe is Thoreau's inadequate social experience and lifestyle and sympathy for other people cripples his effectiveness as a social observer. The "hermit of Walden Pond" may write knowledgeably, even profoundly, about the natural world, but he is out of his element when he speaks of society and public life.

These various beliefs about why Thoreau should be disqualified as a political writer are neither well informed nor persuasive, although their prevalence provides at least a partial explanation of why it is that Thoreau's political thought has received so little scholarly attention. There is absolutely no reason to believe that Thoreau was mentally ill; at any rate, the facts of his psychological life no more relieve us of the obligation to understand his writings on their own terms than we are relieved of the need to study *On the Social Contract* on account of Jean-Jacques Rousseau's "personal problems." Accusations of immaturity threaten to beg the question in a similar manner, and hint as well of a dogmatic conservative impatience with critics of conventional society—the sense that such criticism seems, by definition, "unrealistic" and hence "immature." Finally, it is simply not true that Thoreau was significantly withdrawn from the human community. He was deeply involved with and committed to his family throughout his life; Taylor Stoehr refers to Thoreau's "inveterate domesticity," and Henry Seidel Canby rightly notes that "the life of this so-called solitary was indeed a family life to an extent not common in modern New England."[22] He was thoroughly integrated into the village life in Concord, and was involved with abolition and other progressive politics as well.[23] There is simply no basis to the claim that Thoreau was a hermit, uninformed about public affairs, withdrawn from the world of men and women.[24] As will become clear in the following, Thoreau did seek a kind of disengagement from the common business of daily life, but this never included a literal seclusion from human society. And even if it were true that Thoreau lived a solitary life, this would by no means disqualify him as a social and political commentator. Seclusion might just as likely be a critical advantage, leading to a more dispassionate observation than is possible when one is entangled in the interests and battles of conventional affairs. As with the more extreme versions of the argument that we need not take Thoreau seriously as a social critic because of some disqualifying personal characteristic, the view that Thoreau was too ignorant about common life to be an informed critic is grossly misleading. Whatever our evaluation of Thoreau's personal life, such judgments can never relieve us of the obligation to carefully read his works if we are to provide a serious analysis of his ideas. When biography threatens to replace such a reading, the critic loses credibility.

For those who rightly assume that we need to come to some understanding of the actual content of Thoreau's views, there is a near consensus in the literature that Thoreau is committed to values that prevent him from fully appreciating and understanding the political world, or that he is intellectually or ideologically handicapped in his political thinking in some other important way. The overwhelming conventional wisdom is that Thoreau is an anarchist—as Vernon Parrington writes, "He was not political minded"[25]—and therefore rejects political life outright. This view is shared, significantly, by most of Thoreau's friends and critics alike. Emma Goldman praises Thoreau as "the greatest American Anarchist,"[26] and Henry Miller approvingly claims that Thoreau "was not interested in politics; he was the sort of person who, if there were more of his kind, would soon cause governments to become non-existent."[27] Jane Bennett, who has recently written the most extensive study of Thoreau by a political theorist, admires Thoreau as an "artist of the self," but she is nervous about what she believes is his rejection of politics and his "distaste for the identity of 'citizen.'"[28] If these friends of Thoreau's conclude that he is an anarchist, it is not surprising that a consensus emerges across the spectrum that Thoreau has nothing positive or constructive to say about public life; rather, he merely condemns it and promotes a withdrawal into privacy. Philip Abbott captures this view when he writes that "Thoreau as a political theorist is a remarkably antipolitical writer; as a reformer he is openly disdainful of reformers; as a revolutionary he refuses to accept the personal burdens of a revolutionary."[29] Thoreau's supposed anarchism appears to incapacitate him as a political thinker.

This anarchism is additionally thought to grow from an extreme individualism that further impairs Thoreau's political judgment.[30] A contemporary reviewer of *Walden* criticized Thoreau for being a member of "the class of transcendentalists who lay the greatest stress on the 'I,' and knows no limitation on the exercise of the rights of that important pronoun."[31] Francis Dedmond concludes that the result of this individualism is that "Thoreau wished to live above law, above government, above restraint. He wished to be circumscribed only by the dictates of his conscience."[32] For Richard Ellis, Thoreau's jealousy for his own autonomy produced a "haughty aloofness," a hermit's "disdain for the multitude,"[33] and Heinz Eulau claims that truth, for Thoreau, is "reduced to being a matter of individual taste."[34] Thoreau is not only a political anarchist but a moral and philosophical anarchist as well. There is no solid foundation left for a significant common life with others. As Nancy Rosenblum says, Thoreau's "militant conscience inspires self-assertion and antagonism [toward others], but inspiration is incompatible with establishment and takes no notice of justice or public order."[35]

In fact, for Rosenblum, Thoreau's individualism takes on a Nietzschean quality, in which "the noble soul is exclusive" and "enjoys no society and recognizes few peers."[36] Like Emerson, she believes that Thoreau is committed to an autonomy that experiences exhilaration only in opposition, in the discord experienced by "heroic spirits" with society at large.[37] Rosenblum's ominous suggestion is that Thoreau worshiped the struggle alone, caring for others only as opponents of his own will: "It is an anomic and amoral Nietzschean vision, and there is good reason to think he would have accepted the consequences of personal freedom gained at the expense of others."[38] Although Vincent Buranelli does not portray Thoreau as a Nietzschean amoralist,[39] he agrees with Rosenblum that Thoreau's extreme individualism can have potentially tyrannical ramifications. It produces an "unbending moralism and incorrigible self-righteousness" that tilts the "mind in the direction of fanaticism":[40]

> There is no more insidious political theory than this. When consciences conflict—and antagonism is never worse than when it involves two men each of whom is convinced that he speaks for goodness and rectitude—what then? . . . Thoreau's theory has overtones of Rousseau's Legislator who can do what he pleases with the people under his control because he alone can fathom the holy intentions of the General Will. It points forward to Lenin, the "genius theoretician" whose right it is to force a suitable class consciousness on those who do not have it, and to the horrors that resulted from Hitler's "intuition" of what was best for Germany.[41]

Buranelli is perhaps the most apoplectic of Thoreau's critics, but he is just an extreme example of the many who believe that Thoreau's individualism blinds him to any sensible understanding of a possible or a just political order. The suspicion is that it promotes at best an antipolitics and at worst a perverse and dangerous politics.[42]

Finally, there are many who simply question Thoreau's consistency or rigor as a thinker. Some critics make claims about the (in)coherence of his social and political thought, such as when Laraine Fergenson argues that "his writings, taken as a whole, are a tissue of self-contradiction,"[43] or when Buranelli holds that Thoreau's individualism is incompatible with his obvious dependencies on others, and he thus "contradicted himself . . . without realizing it."[44] Others argue that Thoreau is inconsistent in his basic political commitments, holding opposing opinions in such essays as "Civil Disobedience" and "A Plea for Captain John Brown."[45] Still others find Thoreau's use of exaggeration[46] and paradox exasperating, as when Eulau storms, "Paradox may serve the purpose of literary construction. In political theory it is self-defeating."[47] For one reason or another, many critics believe Thoreau is too extravagant and undisciplined a thinker to develop a significant political commentary.[48]

In short, a review of the literature discussing Thoreau's social and political thought leaves one with two strong impressions. First, overall the literature is quite sparse, which suggests that many students of American political thought simply do not believe Thoreau's political ideas are interesting, sophisticated, or coherent enough to bother with in the first place. Second, when Thoreau is evaluated as a political thinker, he is thought to be too anarchistic or individualistic or incoherent to be compelling. While there are a few scholars who have objected to this conventional portrait,[49] Thoreau is, on the whole, the political thinker scholars of American political thought love to either ignore or hate.

IT IS THE BURDEN of the chapters that follow to demonstrate what I think is the full range, power, and message of Thoreau's political thought and to explain why I believe our conventional understandings of Thoreau's political ideas are wildly inaccurate and misleading. When we develop a more satisfactory understanding of what Thoreau actually has to say to and about the American political community, I am convinced we will find in his work one of the strongest, most compelling, and most important voices

7

in the American political tradition. I hope to show that if we will hear him, Thoreau speaks to us as a critic whose primary concerns are the health of the democratic community we profess to value and the integrity of the citizenry upon which any decent democratic community must be built.

Before I turn to Thoreau's public writings to defend this thesis, however, consider the following passages from the *Journal* in which Thoreau discusses the tasks he sets for himself. In May 1851 Thoreau writes:

> We are enabled to criticize others only when we are different from, and in a given particular superior to, them ourselves. By our aloofness from men and their affairs we are enabled to overlook and criticize them. There are but few men who stand on the hills by the roadside. I am sane only when I have risen above my common sense, when I do not take the foolish view of things which is commonly taken, when I do not live for the low ends for which men commonly live. Wisdom is not common. To what purpose have I senses, if I am thus absorbed in affairs? My pulse must beat with nature.[50]

In this passage Thoreau is considering his chosen vocation. His concern is to find a moral space, to "stand on the hills by the roadside," so as to partially disengage himself from the conventional world. Only then will he have the distance from daily affairs required for evaluating those affairs critically and dispassionately. Finding such a moral space, however, is no small task. It requires the strength to reject the conventional temptations of society, and the discipline to find an alternative moral baseline—Thoreau finds his in the natural world, and thus his "pulse must beat with nature." By cultivating an aloofness he can cultivate a superiority not in all things but in a "given particular," to "men and their affairs." Only in this way can he earn the right and gain an appropriate perspective from which to criticize his neighbors and contemporaries. Only in this way can he become a social critic. "You might say of a philosopher that he was in this world as a spectator."[51]

There are two significant dangers in this role, however. The first is that by standing aloof, the critic may find him- or herself on hills from which no human road can be clearly seen, thereby losing sight of human affairs altogether.[52] The second is that the critic may become so preoccupied with his or her own virtue that the rest of the world may recede into insignificance, becoming something to be transcended rather than loved, embraced, and criticized. Thoreau wrestled mightily with both temptations, sometimes overcoming them, sometimes succumbing. He had written a decade earlier, "I don't like people who are too good for this world,"[53] but two months after writing the passage about cultivating an uncommon virtue, Thoreau's *Journal* finds him so preoccupied with himself that it is hard not to wonder if he is losing sight of his original project:

> That I am better fitted for a lofty society to-day than I was yesterday! To make my life a sacrament! What is nature without this lofty tumbling? May I treat myself with more and more respect and tenderness. May I not forget that I am impure and vicious. May I not cease to love purity. . . . May I so live and refine my life as fitting myself for a society ever higher than I actually enjoy. . . . May I be to myself as one is to me whom I love, a dear and cherished object. . . . The possibility of my own improvement, that is to be cherished. . . . I love and worship myself with a love which absorbs my love for the world.[54]

At this moment Thoreau's obsession with his own moral worthiness leads him to a level of self-absorption that makes him look more like a narcissist than a social critic, his claim that such self-love leads him back to the world to the contrary notwithstanding. Although it is true that he admits his moral imperfection, the passage ends on such a self-congratulatory note that we are not entirely unjustified in feeling some skepticism about the self-criticism. Here we find Thoreau at his most morally perfectionist and egoistic.

This is not the end of the story, however. Thoreau continues to fight with himself in the passages that follow. Five days after declaring his worship of himself, he remembers that the moral life cannot be "too good for this world" when he writes, "Let us not have a rabid moral virtue that will be revenged on society."[55] The task he set for himself is morally perilous, and his execution of the task is marked by human imperfection. But Thoreau never appears to have lost sight of these failures, or to fool himself for long about his own moral character.

Just as Thoreau struggles with maintaining an appropriate balance between engagement with and distance from human society, so he struggles to establish an appropriate relationship with nature, the medium within which he hopes to nurture a critical independence from social affairs. On the one hand, the retreat to the natural world must be undertaken for the sake of the human world. "It is narrow to be confined to woods and fields and grand aspects of Nature only. The greatest and wisest will still be related to man."[56] On the other hand, Thoreau's alienation from society and his sensual love for nature ("I love it as a maiden"; "All nature is my bride"[57]) constantly conspire to draw him away from human concerns. "This is a common experience in my travelling. I plod along, thinking what a miserable world this is and what miserable fellows we that inhabit it, wondering what it is tempts men to live in it; but anon I leave the towns behind and am lost in some boundless heath, and life becomes gradually more tolerable, if not even glorious."[58] When this happens for an extended period, however, Thoreau always begins to find himself dissatisfied, morally empty. "I have become sadly scientific," he writes to his sister, at a time when he is unable to consistently focus on the moral character of his naturalism.[59] Thoreau's withdrawal to nature, like his attempt to establish an aloofness from society, was a difficult balancing act. He was not always able to maintain that in-between position, apart from society but not entirely withdrawn into nonhuman nature. This was clearly, however, the position he sought and struggled to achieve.

In one of the most striking and disturbing passages in Thoreau's *Journal*, written a month after his ecstatic declaration of love for his own virtue and three months after describing his project as a social critic, we see the tensions of this balancing act erupt in a terrible spasm of pain. He begins calmly, feeling gratitude for the beauty of nature he had experienced on his walk: "I thank you God. I do not deserve anything, I am unworthy of the least regard; and yet I am made to rejoice. I am impure and worthless, and yet the world is gilded for my delight and holidays are prepared for me, and my path is strewn with flowers. . . . Oh, keep my senses pure!"[60] This sense of joy and unworthiness, however, is followed by something very different. He stops at "Nut Meadow Brook" and drinks.

> I mark that brook as if I had swallowed a water snake that would live in my stomach. I have swallowed something worth the while. The day is not what it was before I stooped to drink. Ah, I shall hear from that draught! It is not in vain that I have drunk. I have drunk an arrowhead. It flows from where all fountains rise.
>
> How many ova have I swallowed? Who knows what will be hatched within me? There were some seeds of thought, methinks, floating in that water, which are expanding in me. The man must not drink of the running streams, the living waters, who is not prepared to have all nature reborn in him,—to suckle monsters. The snake in my stomach lifts his head to my mouth at the sound of running water. When was it that I swallowed a snake? I have got rid of the snake in my stomach. I drank of stagnant waters once. That accounts for it. I caught him by the throat and drew him out, and had a well day after all. Is there not such a thing as getting rid of the snake which you have swallowed when young, when thoughtless you stooped and drank at stagnant waters, which has

worried you in your waking hours and in your sleep ever since, and appropriated the life that was yours? Will he not ascend into your mouth at the sound of running water? Then catch him boldly by the head and draw him out, though you may think his tail be curled about your vitals.[61]

There is obviously a great deal going on in this passage, some of which appears to be deeply personal and psychological; but much can be understood in light of the tensions generated by walking the moral tightrope he has placed himself on as a result of his self-assumed social role.[62] Thoreau begins these reflections with a sense of humility, unworthiness, and gratitude. He is then seduced by his life in nature. He draws nature within himself, attempting to become a natural creator himself. The initial pride and success this brings him soon turns to shame: the nature reborn in him is monstrous. It is now clear that the snake did not come from the healthy, briskly running waters but from water that is unhealthy and stagnant. Having inflated his own importance, he is captivated by the potential of his own "seeds of thought" and forgets his initial reason for turning to nature. Instead of nature's student and admirer, he tries to become nature's equal. Rather than accepting his life as a man, he attempts to become a god. When he comes to his senses and realizes that this hubris can only generate monsters, he understands that the only option is to pull the snake out, even if it threatens his "vitals." Here we see some of the complexities and dangers of Thoreau's relationship with nature. He retreats to the wild in order to establish a critical distance between himself and society, but in doing so he is tempted to forget his original purpose and worship his own creative powers.

In all these remarkable passages from the late spring and early summer of 1851, Thoreau was struggling with the implications and difficulties of his chosen vocation. These struggles grow out of and are directly related to the structural dilemmas created by his role as a social critic. It is also clear that Thoreau was deeply aware of these dilemmas and fought himself fiercely in the attempt to maintain his critical integrity as one who was both engaged and disengaged, virtuous but not perversely self-absorbed or "too good for this world." That he often failed to live up to these ideals is hardly surprising, given the moral gymnastics required to maintain an equilibrium between such opposing forces. Thoreau never claims any absolute success for himself; he insists only on the importance of his struggle and the ideals they represent.[63] What should interest us are Thoreau's successes more than his failures, and these successes are indeed impressive to consider. My contention in this book is, first, that Thoreau's social and political criticism, far from being confined to a few political essays ("Civil Disobedience," "Slavery in Massachusetts," and "A Plea for Captain John Brown"), was a lifetime project that informed virtually all his writings; and, second, that Thoreau succeeded in this criticism to a rare and largely unappreciated degree. Thoreau is one of America's most powerful and least understood critics and political thinkers.

Thoreau's understanding of his relationship to the American polity is symbolically captured in another 1851 entry to his *Journal*. He is discussing a passage from a work of natural history by Agassiz and Gould, who write, "the working bees . . . are barren females. The attributes of their sex . . . seem to consist only in their solicitude for the welfare of the new generation, of which they are the natural guardians, but not the parents." Thoreau then comments, "This phenomenon is paralleled in man by maiden aunts and bachelor uncles, who perform a similar function."[64] The imagery is striking, coming from a man who was himself childless and probably died a virgin, and who lived in a family in which none of the children married or appear to have been at all sexually active. Thoreau's chosen vocation, as critic of American society and politics, is that of a "bachelor uncle." His concern is less for his contemporaries than for the values and institutions that will nurture and mold future generations; as he writes in "Life without Principle," "It is our children's children who may perchance be really free."[65] It is the legacy of American citizenship that Thoreau ultimately aims to influence. In attempting to establish this influence, it is perhaps inevitable that he appears odd, eccentric, like a "bachelor uncle," especially to his own generation.[66] In order to appropriately evaluate Thoreau's career, it is essential to understand that his political ambitions were not defined by influencing the specific political events in his own day: Thoreau was obviously not a political activist in any recognizable sense of the word, and his impatience with such "reformers" is famous.[67] Instead, he hopes to encourage his fellow citizens to seriously consider the moral development of the nation and their own participation in this development.

When Emerson writes that Thoreau "chose, wisely no doubt for himself, to be the bachelor of thought and Nature," he encourages an understanding of Thoreau that significantly misconstrues his friend's lifelong project.[68] For Emerson, when Thoreau became the "bachelor of thought and Nature," he abandoned the human world: "I think the severity of his ideal interfered to deprive him of a healthy sufficiency of human society."[69] Emerson clucks his disapproval and claims that Thoreau lacked ambition, so "instead of engineering for all America, he was the captain of a huckle-berry-party."[70] These comments, however, reveal much more about Emerson's conventionalism than about Thoreau's relationship to America.[71] In Thoreau's view, what America needs are not social engineers but prophets, critics who force us to confront the gulf between our ideals and our practices. Thoreau embraced the role of a bachelor but not in the sense Emerson suggests.

Contrary to Emerson's evaluation, I believe there has been no writer with more ambition for America than Henry Thoreau, nor one more deeply concerned with the future moral character of our political community. As he saw it, addressing this character was his Socratic task. Before we can evaluate Thoreau's success or failure as a political thinker, it is first essential that we be open to the possibility that he was indeed a political thinker in the deepest sense of the term. In *The City of God* Augustine argues that a political community is defined by the objects loved in common within that community.[72] When Thoreau, America's "bachelor uncle," writes, he almost invariably forces us to confront our political life in this most essential and fundamental sense. Contrary to those who would understand Thoreau as little more than an egocentric individualist, a "bachelor of thought and nature," Thoreau is one of the most deeply committed political writers in our tradition. It is time to try to understand him as such.

CHAPTER 2

Founding

I cannot bear to be told to wait for good results, I pine as much for
good beginnings.

—Thoreau, "Reform and Reformers"

It is remarkable how closely the history of the apple-tree is connected with that
of man.

Thoreau, "Wild Apples"

IN HIS "DIVINITY SCHOOL ADDRESS," Emerson declares, "The old is for slaves,"[1] and in a talk delivered at Dartmouth College a month later, he claims that the "perpetual admonition of nature to us, is, 'The world is new, untried. Do not believe the past. I give you the universe a virgin today.' "[2] Emerson teaches us to turn away from what he sees as our confining traditions, customs, and histories, to make a clean break with the past, to invent a fresh, new, and free reality. This is the message of his first book, *Nature,* which concludes by encouraging the reader, "Build, therefore, your own world."[3] It is also a message of "Self-Reliance," where Emerson scolds us, saying, "I am ashamed to think how easily we capitulate to badges and names, to large societies and dead institutions."[4] The freedom Emerson seeks is a freedom beyond history because in his view history gives us only thoughtless prejudice and habit, both enemies of an authentic independence.

It is tempting to think that Thoreau shares this understanding of freedom with Emerson. In "Walking," for example, Thoreau writes, "Above

15

all, we cannot afford not to live in the present. He is blessed over all mortals who loses no moment of the passing life in remembering the past."[5] Here, as when he writes in his *Journal* that he wishes "to get the Concord, the Massachusetts, the America, out of my head and be sane a part of every day,"[6] nature appears to play the role suggested by Emerson: it is a refuge from society in the fullest sense of the word. Nature allows us to escape our daily affairs and human contacts. Indeed, it allows us to escape the human world altogether, not only our contemporaries but our predecessors and all the institutions, practices, and beliefs that bind the present to the past. The free individual who is ready for a walk is a solitary who escapes society in the shelter of nature.

Because Thoreau is commonly thought to subscribe to this Emersonian perspective, interpreters of Thoreau's political thought have predictably observed that such an orientation is less than promising for thinking about social and political life. Jane Bennett worries that "Thoreau acts as if one could exempt oneself from public life."[7] In the same vein, John Patrick Diggins writes, "Obsessed with his own salvation, Thoreau called upon others to withdraw from society and thereby become oblivious to all that is general and public."[8] Perhaps the most critical of all, C. Roland Wagner accuses Thoreau of a selfish childishness:

> Thoreau's uncompromising moral idealism, despite its occasional embodiment in sentences of supreme literary power, created an essentially child's view of political and social reality. Because his moral principles were little more than expressions of his quest for purity and of hostility to any civilized interference with the absolute attainment of his wishes, he was unable to discriminate between better and worse in the real world.[9]

Bennett, Diggins, and Wagner, and many others like them, are right to believe that *if* Thoreau holds an understanding of nature and freedom similar to that found in Emerson's writings, we cannot expect a social and political commentary of any real sophistication or significance. In this event, it is easy to think that Thoreau is little more than a self-absorbed egoist.

There are good reasons to believe, however, that Thoreau's views are significantly different than Emerson's on these matters. In fact, these differences can be dramatically illustrated by looking at Thoreau's first book, *A Week on the Concord and Merrimack Rivers*. In this work Thoreau immerses himself in American colonial history, specifically investigating the relationship between Indian and European settler. Far from encouraging us to escape our past, to cut ourselves off from our social legacies and the determinative facts of our collective lives, Thoreau provides us with a tough, revealing look at the historical events and conditions and struggles that have given birth to contemporary American society. When Thoreau and his brother travel up the Concord and Merrimack Rivers, nature does not give them "the universe a virgin." On the contrary, they find a social world within this nature that is filled with crime, violence, heroism, and the tragedy resulting from the conflict of dissimilar social orders.

A Week has rarely been taken seriously (or considered at all) by those interested in Thoreau's political ideas. It is often viewed, by Thoreau's admirers and critics alike, as a rather tedious series of seemingly unrelated observations, thoughts, and ideas all tied together by a young, preachy, self-preoccupied Thoreau. Herman Melville, who thought it was a terrible and self–indulgent book, wrote to Hawthorne that he planned to satirize it with a work entitled "A Week on a Work-Bench in a Barn."[10] One of Thoreau's friendliest biographers, Henry Salt, concludes that the book is "vague, disjointed, and discursive; and is, moreover, almost arrogant in its transcendental egoism."[11] What could such an unbearably "transcendental" book have to do with politics? Even those (mainly literary) critics who are friendly toward the work describe it as primarily concerned about private issues, such as Thoreau's response to his brother's death.[12]

One recent biographer, Robert D. Richardson, breaks with these common views when he writes, "*A Week* has strong, if frequently overlooked, social themes: friendship, settlement, Indian life, oriental law."[13] I agree but would make the case even more forcefully: what is thought of as a painfully personal and apolitical book is actually a sophisticated meditation on the realities and consequences of the American founding. Once we are in a position to appreciate the degree to which Thoreau, unlike Emerson, accepts the necessity of locating our choices and freedoms within social contexts and historical time, we have taken the first step toward a reevaluation of the quality and significance of Thoreau's political thought as a whole.

THOREAU BEGINS his book with the following sentence: "THE MUSKETAQUID, or Grass-ground River, though probably as old as the Nile or Euphrates, did not begin to have a place in civilized history, until the fame of its grassy meadows and its fish attracted settlers out of England in 1635, when it received the other but kindred name of CONCORD from the first plantation on its banks, which appears to have been commenced in a spirit of peace and harmony."[14] Out of respect for historical chronology, Thoreau presents the Indian before the English name for the river. The river itself and, by implication, the native inhabitants are of ancient lineage, while "Concord" and the people responsible for this name are relative newcomers.[15] In the second sentence of text, Thoreau explains that the Indian name is actually superior to the English, since it will remain descriptively accurate as long as "grass grows and water runs here," while Concord is accurate only "while men lead peaceable lives on its banks"—something obviously much less permanent than the grass and flowing water. In fact, the third sentence indicates that "Concord" has already failed to live up to its name, since the Indians are now an "extinct race."[16] Thoreau wastes no time in pointing out that regardless of the "spirit of peace and harmony" that first moved the whites to establish a plantation on this river, relations between the natives and the settlers soon exhibited very little concord indeed.

In these opening sentences Thoreau presents us with an indication of a primary problem motivating his trip down the Concord and Merrimack Rivers: he hopes to probe the nature of the relationship between Indian and white societies and to consider the importance of this relationship for understanding our America.[17] Joan Burbick, one of the few to recognize the primacy of the political theme underlying Thoreau's voyage, writes that in this book Thoreau "tries to forge the uncivil history of America."[18] We know the end of the story already: one "race" annihilates the other. Part of Thoreau's intention is to not let us forget this critical truth about our society, to remind us that our founding is as bloody and unjust as any, try as we may to put this fact out of sight and tell alternative tales about our past. As the story progresses throughout the book, however, we see that another intention is to explain the complexity and ambiguity of the historical processes that led to and beyond this bloody founding. The history Thoreau presents is "uncivil" in two senses: first, and most obviously, it is about violent, brutal, uncivil acts; second, it is not the official or common self-understanding that the nation wants to hold.[19] Thoreau's journey is not only aimed at personal self-discovery, despite the obvious importance of that theme for the book. On the contrary, the opening sentences and the problems they pose suggest that Thoreau is first and foremost interested in a project of discovery for the nation as a whole, the success of which will depend upon looking carefully at the relationship between settler and native. The project of self-discovery is to be accomplished within the context of this larger social history. Thoreau's personal and more private ruminations are set quite literally between ongoing discussions of events from the colonial life of New England. We are never allowed to forget for very long that our contemporary private lives are bounded by, in some crucial sense defined within, the possibilities created by this earlier drama of Indian and colonist.

When Thoreau and his brother cast off from Concord on Saturday afternoon, a number of friends are present along the riverbank to wish them well. The two brothers, however, refuse to return the waves and shouts: "We, having already performed those shore rites, with excusable reserve, as befits those who are embarked on unusual enterprises, who behold but speak not, silently glided past the firm lands of Concord."[20] There is a noticeable silence throughout this book, marked by the complete absence of dialogue. The narration is entirely reflective and contemplative, and when human interactions are recorded, even those between Thoreau and his brother, they are presented impersonally, as if by a detached observer. Once on the river, Thoreau is not so much relaying a series of personal events and interpersonal interactions—such would be best conveyed by talk among individuals—as he is interested in gaining a distance from the intensely personal in order to assume the appropriate position from which he will be able to observe and tell the stories of the larger society. His is an "unusual enterprise," and an ambitious one, precisely because it requires a subordination of the intensely personal nature of his experience to a greater project of social discovery and evaluation. The brothers, in fact, immediately and symbolically assume the role of their forebears. Although they refuse to return the greetings of their friends, they "did unbend so far as to let our guns speak for us, when at length we had swept out of sight."[21] This military salute is only appropriate, as they move from the established Concord of their generation back in time to the original settlement of the region, in that they now let their guns do their speaking for them.[22]

The first landmark they pass is the remains of the "North Bridge," at which the first battle of the Revolution was fought. Thoreau pauses long enough to give a poem or two and to remind the citizens of Concord that the Revolution was fought and won by patriots of greater courage than is now routinely exhibited in Concord.

> Ah, 't is in vain the peaceful din
> That wakes the ignoble town,
> Not thus did braver spirits win
> A patriot's renown.[23]

This, however, is not the end but the beginning of their journey of discovery of America's origins. The Revolution, with its heroes, principles, noble deeds, and ideals, is the story we like to tell of our founding. But Thoreau floats by the remains of this event, and he and his brother are off to more remote but more revealing regions and times.

It is not until the next day that they have enough distance from the America of the Revolution to return to the theme of the settlement of New England by Europeans. On Sunday morning they find themselves in sparsely populated country: "For long reaches we could see neither house nor cultivated field, nor any sign of the vicinity of man."[24] They are now far enough from the world of contemporary America that it is possible for them to discover earlier times when the fate of the new civilization was still unsettled, when white settlements were themselves new, untested, and unsure of their future. Thoreau introduces these white incursions into the "howling wilderness"[25] quite gently, much as the whites themselves might want them portrayed. He and his brother pass the village of Billerica, a town of "ancient" character that is "now in its dotage."[26] It is a living illustration of a European village that has experienced an almost complete life cycle and is thus useful as a representative of its kind. With the initial settlement came the bells to call the faithful to worship on the Sabbath; these bells can still be heard, sometimes as far away as Concord. Thoreau thus equates the founding and perpetuation of this colonial town with the attractive, pastoral symbol of church bells. But Thoreau refuses to move on without hinting at the very different reality these bells represent for the Indian. They ring so loud that it is "no wonder that such a sound startled the dreaming Indian, and frightened his game, when the first bells were swung on trees, and sounded through the forest beyond the plantations of the white man."[27] This comment is brief and understated, but Thoreau rightly suggests that even something as seemingly innocent and pious as the church bells of the white settlers represents an ominous development for the native. The noise is new to the landscape, unusual, and startling. It apparently will have significant material consequences as well, since it is capable of "frightening" the Indian's game and thus threatening the economic foundations of his mode of life. There has as yet been no overt violence, nor, as far as we know, evil intentions on the part of the new settlers. But even if we grant that the first "plantation" along the river was "commenced with a spirit of peace and harmony," the seemingly innocuous religious habits of the white settlers will themselves threaten the foundations of the Indian's world.

We see, then, that the interaction between whites and Indians does not have to be self-consciously or overtly hostile in order for the consequences to be dramatic, harmful, even murderous to the Indians. The whites bring their religion and their economic institutions as well. The white "buys the Indian's moccasins and baskets, then buys his hunting-grounds, and at length forgets where he is buried and ploughs up his bones."[28] Even if the economic transactions between the white and the Indian are "consensual" and contain no threats or fraud, the result is disastrous. The Indian's entire social order is undermined through its contact with the white forms of property ownership and commerce. The end is annihilation and, what is perhaps the worst consequence of such an annihilation, the loss of memory. When the Indians die, we do not even remember, or care to remember, where they are buried.[29]

The compulsion of white society is to continually plow more and more of the land, and the memory of a dying people will not be allowed to intrude upon economic progress. "The white man's mullein soon reigned in Indian cornfields, and sweet-scented English grasses clothed the new soil. Where, then, could the Red Man set his foot?"[30] Nowhere, of course. It does not require individually and personally malicious behavior in order to threaten the survival of a people. What is at work here is the clash between dramatically different and incompatible modes of life. The forces are impersonal and deadly. "We talk of civilizing the Indian, but that is not the name for his improvement." His "improvement" was possible only in his traditional life, in which he engaged in an "intercourse with Nature" that admitted "of the greatest independence of each."[31] This life is simply not available once the wilderness has been tamed by European agriculture. "If we could listen but for an instant to the chant of the Indian muse, we should understand why he will not exchange his savageness for civilization. Nations are not whimsical. Steel and blankets are strong temptations; but the Indian does well to continue Indian."[32] But if he does remain an Indian, where is he to "set his foot"? To retain his identity is to face a certain death. Thoreau's observations here are similar to William Cronon's in his ecological history of New England: "A people who loved property little had been overwhelmed by a people who loved it much."[33] As agriculture replaces hunting, the hunter becomes obsolete, irrelevant, extinct. As

Thoreau writes in his *Journal*, "A race of hunters can never withstand the inroads of a race of husbandmen."[34]

In the remainder of "Sunday" two significant passages address the relationship of white settlers and Indians. In the first, Thoreau quotes extensively from Gookin regarding John Eliot's conversion of Indians at a place on the Merrimack were the natives traditionally gathered to fish.[35] Eliot succeeds in converting a sachem named Wannalancet (concerning whom Thoreau will have more to say later), among others. The final paragraph of this passage simply observes that "Pawtucket and Wamesit, where the Indians resorted in the fishing season, are now Lowell, the city of Spindles and Manchester of America, which sends its cotton cloth round the globe."[36] For Thoreau the conversion of these Indians is clearly just a step in the process of displacing and destroying them, replacing them with manufacturing towns and economic development.

The final discussion of white–Indian relations in "Sunday" moves again from religion to economics. Thoreau tells the story of Wicasuck Island, a large and desirable island owned by the Indians. On or around the year 1663, the son of an Indian chief was jailed for a debt owed to one John Tinker. The jailed man's brother, Wannalancet (who was not yet a Christian), arranged for the sale of Wicasuck Island in order to raise the revenue needed to pay the debt. The General Court, apparently feeling that the sale took place under some sort of duress or coercion, voided the transaction and returned the island to the Indians in 1665. Later, Thoreau tells us, the land was granted to a white man, Jonathan Tyng, as a reward for maintaining a garrison against the Indians during King Philip's War. This took place "after the departure of the Indians in 1683."[37]

There are a number of interesting elements in this story. First, it appears as though the Indians were the recipients of something fairly close to justice when the General Court returned the island to them. This alone gives a somewhat hopeful quality to the tale. Yes, certain whites unscrupulously attempted to take the land from the Indians, but they were foiled, at least in this case, by the independence and integrity of the white judicial system. Second, however, overt hostilities between Indians and colonists broke out in 1675 with King Philip's War. We learn later[38] that Wannalancet, on the advice of his father, Pasaconaway, refused to participate in this war and withdrew from the region. Thoreau tells us that the Indians did not leave the island until 1683; this is important since it suggests that when they did leave it was for reasons other than military hostilities, since King Philip's War was concluded by 1678. It apparently was not the overt threat of arms that drove the Indians from this land (land that quickly became a prize for a white Indian fighter). On the contrary, it appears to have been something very much like the social processes generated by the religious and economic differences Thoreau has discussed throughout the chapter that make it impossible for the Indian to find a place to "set his foot." Even while a certain kind of justice had been granted the Indians, they were still unable to retain their grip on the land. Not even religious conversion (Wannalancet was converted by Eliot in 1674) was able to produce a lasting accommodation between the two communities. Christians or not, Wannalancet and his people were forced from a favored place. "Sunday" thus ends with a very pessimistic assessment of the compatibility of two radically different ways of life, and the conflict and misery that appears to be the inevitable result when such social orders crash against one another.[39]

Although these processes of conflict and struggle may (and, Thoreau seems to be saying, let us assume for the sake of argument that they do) begin, as it were, "on the sabbath"—in an environment in which there are good intentions on the part of all the players—it is just a matter of time before they spill over into overt acts of violence. And this is exactly what happens in the next chapter, "Monday," which begins with an account of the "famous Captain Lovewell," a man of mythic and heroic reputation who is said to be the son of "an ensign in the army of Oliver Cromwell" and who lived in this country a life of biblical span, dying finally at the age of 120 at the hands of the Indians he fought continuously during his life in the New World.[40] In his final raid Lovewell leads a small group of men into a successful engagement with a far more numerous enemy, but the price of this victory is very high. Most of Thoreau's discussion of the event is a gruesome account of the fate and agonies of the wounded white survivors.

Although the details of the physical suffering experienced by these men as they attempt to find their way back home are horrific, Thoreau presents them in such a manner that we are not allowed to forget the context in which they suffered. He quotes a ballad, for example, that praises the "wounded good young Frye, Who was our English Chaplin." The ballad continues, "He many Indians slew, And some of them he scalped while bullets round him flew."[41] Thoreau lets us know that this Chaplin Frye, who would be left by his fellows to die of his wounds alone in the wilderness,[42] is a fierce, even vicious enough, character to risk his life in order to scalp his victims. Barbarism and savagery are certainly not absent from the colonists' ranks. As Thoreau would write in his *Journal* years later, "Savage meets savage, and the white man's only distinction is that he is the chief."[43] Similarly, after telling of the suffering of the men after the battle, Thoreau observes that there is no record of the wounded Indians and how they suffered in their attempt to return home.[44] The fight with the Indians has taken a terrible toll on these white men, but at least we have a memory of their suffering, unlike that of their native counterparts. Finally, Thoreau suggests that not only the bodies of these soldiers have been tormented and crippled. As the example of the scalping chaplin suggests, the soldiers' hatred of Indians has disfigured their moral characters as well. Their leader, Captain Lovewell, is himself the embodiment of hatred for the Indian: "It is stated in the History of Dunstable, that just before his last march, Lovewell was warned to beware of the ambuscades of the enemy, but he replied, 'that he did not care for them,' and bending down a small elm beside which he was standing into a bow, declared 'that he would treat the Indians in the same way.' This elm is still standing, a venerable and magnificent tree."[45] The ironically named Lovewell is consumed by this hatred, while the elm flourishes.

Thoreau's understanding of these events is complex and ambivalent. There is a good deal of dry criticism in his discussion, but there is real sympathy as well. We are left thinking, on the one hand, that these men get roughly what they deserve and, on the other, that no human beings deserve the torments they experience. But even more pointed is Thoreau's contrast between these men of Lovewell's generation and Thoreau's own contemporaries: "Our brave forefathers have exterminated all the Indians, and their degenerate children no longer dwell in garrisoned houses nor hear any war-whoop in their path. It would be well, perchance, if many an 'English Chaplin' in these days could exhibit as unquestionable trophies of his valor as did 'good young Frye.' "[46] There are two crucial points here. First, although the hatred these men felt and the crimes they committed were enormous, it is simply not true that they were without moral virtues. They were loyal and brave to a degree that few of our contemporaries even aspire to. Second, all the descendants of these white settlers enjoy a peace and stability that is taken for granted and that is the direct result of the actions of these early colonists. Thoreau's casual journey down the Concord and Merrimack Rivers would be unimaginable in an earlier age, when peace was not possible between whites and Indians. Thoreau's reflections, this very book and the criticisms it includes of American society, are utterly dependent upon these original murderous acts of founding. Far from exempting himself from the implications of the story he tells, Thoreau situates himself right in the middle of it. He is nothing if not the offspring of these "brave forefathers."[47]

Thoreau returns to Lovewell later in "Monday," repeating the story of his long life but this time saying that it was Lovewell himself, not his father, who had served in Oliver Cromwell's army—thus providing even more potent heroic credentials for him.[48] And if this is not enough, Thoreau explains that during the various Indian wars, the Indians spared him "on account of his kindness to them."[49] Lovewell's death in battle would not come until 1725, but prior to this he apparently led a charmed life, the life of a noble soldier respected even by his enemies. Thoreau uses Lovewell as the mythic thread to tie other stories and characters together. He mentions that it was Lovewell's house that "Mrs. Dustan" reaches while fleeing from her Indian captors[50]—a story he will not tell in full until "Thursday," late in the book. It is through Lovewell that we first learn about Farwell (he was present at Lovewell's final battle), and it is to Farwell that Thoreau now turns. A year before his death, Farwell is involved in a campaign to rescue two settlers who are captured by Indians and taken to Canada. Soon after their capture, a party of ten rescuers rushes foolishly into an ambush. Only one, Farwell—the only member of the rescue party to warn against this method of pursuit—survives.[51] Farwell lives another year, only to die from wounds received while fighting with Lovewell.

Thoreau concludes this passage with the following comments:

> These battles sound incredible to us. I think that posterity will doubt if such things ever were; if our bold ancestors who settled this land were not struggling rather with the forest shadows, and not with a copper-colored race of men. They were vapors, fever and ague of the unsettled woods. Now, only a few arrow-heads are turned up by the plough. In the Pelasgic, the Etruscan, or the British story, there is nothing so shadowy and unreal.[52]

Again, Thoreau is contrasting our current reality with the historical realities upon which it is built. The destruction of the Indians makes their original existence hard to imagine, and the deeds of the settlers in response to the presence of the Indians are thus equally incredible. But even though these brutal facts seem shadowy and unreal to us, Thoreau reminds us that they are nonetheless the facts of our collective life. As distant as such fear, violence, and killing seem from our everyday experiences, Thoreau does not let us forget that they were once all present in plenty along the banks of our rivers.

In "Sunday" Thoreau discusses some of the original sources of conflict between the Indians and the settlers, and in "Monday" we find these conflicts bursting into brutal, genocidal violence. There is violence in the stories Thoreau is yet to tell, but in the remaining days of the week Thoreau will, on the whole, dwell less on it. Most of the remaining references to the relationship between Indian and settler are brief comments, intended primarily to reinforce what has already been detailed in "Sunday" and "Monday." Thus, for example, in "Tuesday" Thoreau points to a wood where Farwell escaped from Indians. Thoreau's point is only to remind the reader of the contrast between the present and the past: "It did not look as if men had ever had to run for their lives on this now open and peaceful interval."[53] And again, at the beginning of "Wednesday," Thoreau juxtaposes the success of the town of Bedford, famous for its "hops and for its fine domestic manufactures," with "some graves of the aborigines."[54] In a longer and poignant passage in "Wednesday," Thoreau contrasts the fate of Pasaconaway and his son Wannalancet with that of a local white hero, John Stark. Thoreau tells us that Pasaconaway is believed to have lived 120 years, implying that he (Pasaconaway) is as deserving of heroic status as is the 120-year-old Lovewell. Thoreau also praises Stark, a hero in the French and Indian Wars as well as the Revolution, and suggests that he is deserving of the monument built for him in Manchester, overlooking the Merrimack: "Who is most dead,—a hero by whose monument you stand, or his descendants of whom you have never heard?" But Thoreau ends the passage by reminding us of Pasaconaway and Wannalancet: "The graves of Pasaconaway and Wannalancet are marked by no monument on the bank of their native river."[55] In passages like this, the discussion of the relationship between Indians and colonists is a reminder of issues Thoreau has already explored, ambivalence he has already expressed, rather than presentations of new issues or ideas.

Some of the remaining stories, however, introduce new complexities into our understanding of these relationships. In "Tuesday" Thoreau tells of three violent incidents between Penacook and Mohawk Indians along the Merrimack, occurring between 1670 and 1685.[56] It is clear that, even though hostilities between these two tribes may or may not have ancient roots, these specific events take place in a context in which the Penacooks are increasingly aligned with the colonists: we learn later that Pasaconaway, Wannalancet's father, had advised his Penacooks as early as 1660 to make peace with the white settlers;[57] and two of these three confrontations, one of which is an assault on Wannalancet's son by a group of Mohawks,[58] occur after Wannalancet's conversion to Christianity. Thus, the white settlement of the land not only produces the obvious conflicts with native peoples, but the indigenous people are themselves increasingly divided by the white presence. And, lest we forget, the Indians are just as capable of fratricide as the whites.

Or consider the story of the friendship between Wawatam and Henry the fur trader found in Thoreau's long discourse on friendship in "Wednesday." Thoreau uses this as an illustration, first, of how friendship can transcend the barriers of tribe and culture. "If Wawatam would taste the 'white man's milk' with his tribe, or take his bowl of human broth made of the trader's fellow-countrymen, he first finds a place of safety for his Friend, whom he has rescued from a similar fate."[59] After escaping many dangers, Henry and Wawatam eventually manage to spend a happy winter together. But Henry is forced in the spring to leave his friend in order to "avoid his enemies," that is, Indians who continue to hate him for being English, and who wish to kill and consume him in order to gain courage for future battles with the colonists. The friends never meet again. So the second message is clearly that even this ideal friendship is at last limited by the broader sets of relationships within which these individuals live. It may transcend the cultural gulf between Indian and white, but it is ultimately unable to overcome the contemporary context of warfare between the English and Chipeway societies.

The last and perhaps most powerful of the major tales of Indians and colonists is the Hannah Dustan odyssey in "Thursday." Dustan is taken from childbed by attacking Indians, sees "her infant's brains dashed out against an apple-tree," and is held captive with her nurse, Mary Neff, and an English boy, Samuel Lennardson. She is told that she and her nurse will be taken to an Indian settlement where they will be forced to "run the gauntlet naked." To avoid this fate, Dustan instructs the boy to ask one of the men how to best kill an enemy and take a scalp. The man obliges, and that night Dustan, Neff, and Lennardson use this information to kill all the Indians, except a "favorite boy, and one squaw who fled wounded with him to the woods"—the victims are two men, two women, and six children. They then scuttle all the canoes except the one needed for their escape. They flee, only to return soon thereafter to scalp the dead as proof of the ordeal. They then manage to paddle the sixty or so miles to John Lovewell's house and are rescued. The General Court pays them fifty pounds as bounty for the ten scalps, and Dustan is reunited with her family, all of whom, except the infant, have survived the attack. Thoreau ends the story by telling us that "there have been many who in later times have lived to say that they had eaten of the fruit of that apple-tree," the tree upon which Dustan's child was murdered.[60]

Striking as it is, many of the themes of this story are repetitive of what has come before, a powerful return to the material from the opening chapters, primarily the violence in "Monday." Thus, Thoreau starkly conveys the grotesque violence on both sides of the conflict, and he concludes here, as he does earlier, that we are the beneficiaries, even the products, of these terrible events—it is we, of course, who have "eaten of the fruit of that apple-tree."

But this story is different too. Most obviously, it is a story in which women and children, traditional noncombatants, play a crucial role. The brutality in the Lovewell campaigns is between men who voluntarily assume the roles of warrior and soldier. The brutality in the Dustan story is aimed primarily at those who are most innocent, children. And this brutality, like that among male combatants, is not confined to one side. The Indians murder Dustan's infant, but she, in turn, methodically kills six children and attempts to kill the seventh (the "favorite boy" was a favorite within his family, not to Dustan). In addition, this murder of children is conducted not only by men but by women and children as well. The violence and hostility between Indian and settler have reached a point at which all traditional restraints have vanished, where the weakest are fair game and all members of the community are combatants. Here, not in the Revolution, is the climax of the American founding. In this climax all colonists and Indians, even women and children, are implicated, and the entire family of Indians, not just the male warriors, is systematically killed off. This frenzy of violence, of escalating atrocity and counteratrocity, of total war, is the natural culmination of the processes Thoreau has been describing throughout the book. The Dustan story represents the victory of the colonists and the final destruction of the Indians. Thoreau is returning down the river to his own home, as Dustan had to hers 142 years earlier. His investigation into the nature of the American founding, his "uncivil history," is mainly complete.

The image of the apple tree returns in "Friday" at two critical points. First, Thoreau tells of Elisha, a "friendly Indian" in the service of Jonathan Tyng (the recipient, you will recall, of Wicasuck Island), who was killed "by his own race in one of the Indian wars."[61] Although the exact location of his grave has been forgotten—as with all the Indians Thoreau tells us of—a great flood in 1785 left an indentation in the earth that was believed to mark the spot. This place, too, has since been forgotten, but there is an apple tree—"Elisha's apple tree"—that stands in the neighborhood of where the grave must be. Elisha, like Dustan's infant, died at the foot of an apple tree and is remembered by the fruit the tree continues to bear. Not only white blood has borne fruit.

Second, Thoreau directs our attention back to these stories in the final sentences of the book, the last of which, describing Henry and John's landing at Concord, reads: "And we leaped gladly on shore, drawing it up, and fastening it to the wild apple-tree, whose stem still bore the mark which its chain had worn in the chafing of the spring freshets."[62] In case we need yet another reminder, the tree that has grown out of the violence and conflict described throughout the book is the tree in our own hometown, to which we anchor our own peaceful, mundane, and unheroic lives.

In November 1851, more than two years after the publication of *A Week*, Thoreau declared in his *Journal*, "And this is my home, my native soil; and I am a New-Englander."[63] Thoreau was acutely aware of his rootedness in New England culture and society and the impossibility of separating his own battles and concerns from the human environment that produced him. This alone should make us skeptical of Quentin Anderson's claim that Thoreau was with Emerson and Whitman in denying "the shaping character of the past," that he, like they, did not wish to see his life as a story in which other people figured.[64] And Thoreau's first book confirms this skepticism by clearly illustrating Thoreau's break with the Emersonian understanding of moral self-reliance. While Anderson's claims about Emerson have a great deal of power, Thoreau, in contrast, is plainly insisting that we cannot escape our society and our past. In *A Week* Thoreau is not so much a disciple of Emerson as he is assuming the decidedly un-Emersonian role of an American Machiavelli. He is unafraid to look honestly at the terror and inhumanity of our political founding; he understands and conveys this terror clearly. But this does not lead him to a simple moral revulsion or paralysis or denial of the degree to which he, too, is implicated in this history. On the contrary, the point is made again and again that for better or for worse our collective fates are played out within the context of this founding drama: "Our fates at least are social. Our courses do not diverge;

but as the web of destiny is woven it is fulled, and we are cast more and more into the centre."[65]

Consider Thoreau's use of the Hannah Dustan story as the climax of a historical process set in motion by the collision of incompatible societies. He is appalled by the events, but he also understands that they are the culmination of huge political conflicts that are greater than the individual players. It is instructive to contrast this analysis with Cotton Mather's simple praise of Dustan as a colonial heroine and with Nathaniel Hawthorne's shrieking condemnation of her when he calls her "this awful woman," "a raging tigress," and "a bloody old hag" on account of her victims being primarily children.[66] Thoreau's analysis is considerably more shrewd than either Mather's or Hawthorne's, and Thoreau resists the temptation of either of these simpler and much less satisfactory moral responses.

Thoreau's conclusion about our political interconnectedness is built upon a hard-boiled and realistic political analysis combined with a notable moral subtlety. As we have seen, Thoreau believes that the forms of life represented by Indian and colonist are simply and irrevocably incompatible; the structure of each requires a mode of production and a social organization that make it impossible to accommodate the other. This argument is compelling, but, more importantly, it illustrates the degree to which critics like John Patrick Diggins are mistaken when they accuse Thoreau of being "innocent of the nature of power, ignorant of the realities of social change, and indifferent at times to the spectacle of human suffering."[67] Much of the story Thoreau tells in *A Week* is an impersonal and terrible one in which individuals are swept up into a much greater flow and brutality of history. There is room for heroism and virtue within this story, but the hero's freedom is nonetheless limited by the historical cards he or she has been dealt. Pasaconaway is forced by the superiority of colonial power to seek peace with the whites, but he is also a heroic, inspired, and wise leader of his people. Lovewell is a courageous soldier who rightly deserves our admiration for his martial heroism, but he is also a man obviously twisted by the hatreds engendered, nurtured, and inflamed by the struggle between white and Indian. Both of these men are caught in a whirlwind of conflict, hatred, and violence that eventually runs out of control (as represented in the frantic and indiscriminate violence of the Hannah Dustan story). But both retain an essential human freedom and dignity within this struggle they do not really control. Far from having, in Jane Bennett's phrase, an "aversion to thinking about power,"[68] Thoreau presents in *A Week* a meditation on the nature, extent, and limitations of such power. Thoreau's conclusions resist both a heroic denial of impersonal power and a fatalistic submission to it. Instead, he suggests a more sophisticated understanding of the possibilities and limitations of human freedom in the face of power.

Throughout his writings, Thoreau is committed to a view of human nature that transcends, in essential ways, the limitations of history. Thus, he is devoted to classical literature (as he argues in *A Week*, the *Iliad* is among the greatest books ever written)[69] and firmly believes that truth, heroism, and virtue are universal attributes found in great individuals in all historical settings. But we also know, in light of the conflict between Indian and colonist, that different social orders produce significant, sometimes unbridgeable, gulfs between people.[70] Even when individuals are able to overcome cultural differences and experience each other as related and equal human beings, such as the friends Henry and Wawatam, it is not surprising that great social pressures sometimes intervene to pull them apart.[71] Despite such profound barriers, however, Thoreau succeeds in suggesting the common failures and virtues of the players in these stories. White settlers could be as vicious as the "savage," and frequently were (remember that the only two episodes of scalping in the book are performed, first, by a white chaplin and, second, by white women and a child). And just as there is an inclination toward evil in both communities, so is there a common possibility for virtue. Thoreau insists on the heroic status of the Indian: Lovewell is not the only hero to live, like Moses, 120 years, and Pasaconaway is just as deserving of a monument as John Starks. Despite the differences between the white and the Indian ways of life, the virtues of courage, loyalty, and humanity are recognizable as "natural," as containing essential qualities and potentials for members of both communities, the foundations of a universal humanity. "All men are children, and of one family. The same tale sends them all to bed, and wakes them in the morning."[72] Thoreau is committed to this overriding humanism and the moral freedom it implies, but in no way does this blind him to the power of culture and different modes of life, and the complexities cultural differences raise for his view.

Rejecting any historical determinism that would deny our freedom and thus our moral responsibility, and also rejecting an extreme Emersonian libertarianism that denies the realities of history, Thoreau rightly promotes an understanding of our moral choice that is bounded and constrained by our social inheritance. In this context Thoreau observes early in *A Week* that "conscience really does not, and ought not to monopolize the whole of our lives, any more than the heart or the head. It is as liable to disease as any other part."[73] This comment may be surprising to those who have looked for Thoreau's political ideas only in "Civil Disobedience," where conscience appears to hold a privileged and solitary authority.[74] But here Thoreau is well aware of the potential pitfalls of conscience, a radically individualized sensibility and will. An absolute and untempered appeal to conscience is just as dangerous as untempered appeals to love or reason, and any satisfactory morality will have to appeal to all three. The project of *A Week* is, in large part, to provide some of the knowledge we need in order to develop an appropriate moral relationship with our nation. Such a relationship must be based upon a love that is not blind to the harsh realities of our history. It must be based upon a reasonable evaluation of the possibilities available to us.[75] And we must not allow our consciences, in response to the evil we find in our own social—and personal—fabric, to prevent us from making a kind of peace with the world we are a part of. "It is not worth the while to let our imperfections disturb us always."[76] This is not a call for moral blindness, fatalism, or disinterest. On the contrary, it is a call for a moral realism that nonetheless maintains a sharp and critical eye on the society around it. Thoreau's argument is a rejection of any simplistic moralism that appeals to only one side of our understanding, one way of knowing. Instead, he is promoting a morality that appeals to our reason, our conscience, and our love, and critically embraces the world despite its flaws.

A number of passages in *A Week* are similar to those found in Thoreau's more familiar political works. He alludes to his night in jail and says, "I do not wish, it happens, to be associated with Massachusetts, either in holding slaves or in conquering Mexico. I am a little better than herself in these respects."[77] He says that he loves mankind but hates the "institutions of the dead un-kind."[78] He satirizes a soldier he and his brother pass while hiking: "Poor man! He actually shivered like a reed in his thin military pants, and by the time we had got up with him, all the sternness that becomes the soldier had forsaken his face, and he skulked past as if he were driving his father's sheep under a sword-proof helmet."[79] And, as we have seen earlier, he doubts the courage and heroism of his own generation, fearing that "generally speaking, the land is now . . . very barren of men."[80] All of these comments are similar to those found in "Civil Disobedience" and elsewhere, but in the context of the rest of *A Week*, we are able to appreciate the degree to which they do not represent the simple moral arrogance of an antisocial egoist. Thoreau knows very well the limitations history places upon us. But he also believes, as we have seen, that we are nonetheless left a healthy space for moral freedom and action, and it is this freedom that he believes American citizens have abandoned. The soldiers he criticizes here and in "Civil Disobedience" are morally repugnant not because they are soldiers but because they are soldiers who appear to have no martial virtue.[81] Such virtue has limits and moral blindness, but it at least has moral courage and commitment. Likewise, the Indian and white men who struggled so terribly with one another at the nation's founding were, for all their excesses, individuals who took their moral characters seriously, unlike the increasingly complacent contemporary state and society upon which it is built. Thoreau wants us to be both appalled and inspired by the history he tells. Only then will we break the cycle of moral cowardice and lethargy from which he believes we suffer.[82]

In "Concord River," the first chapter of *A Week*, Thoreau says that along the banks of the Concord you will find "greater men than Homer, or Chaucer, or Shakespeare, only they never got time to say so; they never took to the way of writing."[83] The story he tells is both real and mythic, an attempt to capture in our American setting truths akin to those found in that greatest of books, the *Iliad*, since "Our own country furnishes antiquities as ancient and durable, and as useful, as any."[84] *A Week* is written to inspire us to two heroic tasks: to face up to the truths of our past, and to recapture a moral inspiration from that past upon which we can build the courage and commitment to reform our contemporary society. It is not that we should become modern Indian fighters; rather, we must discover the moral resolve that inspired the founders, and direct this resolve toward combating current moral evils, such as slavery and imperialism. The problem facing the nation, Thoreau is suggesting, is not primarily moral error. On the contrary, it is moral fear and indifference.[85] Our "Iliad," the founding that Thoreau presents, is an attack on what he sees as our moral deterioration. "The past is only so heroic as we see it."[86] Thoreau's "uncivil history," paradoxically, functions as both shocking revelation and moral inspiration.

Nancy Rosenblum claims that "Thoreau declared his country lost."[87] In reality, however, Thoreau was deeply involved in exploring what he thought were the possibilities before the nation. Far from abandoning hope, Thoreau was committed to considering the ways in which New England and all of America might be reformed to develop a more vigorous and respectable moral character. In the chapters that follow, it will become clear that Thoreau's investigation of the real American founding in *A Week* was only a first step in a critical analysis of the American political community. In Thoreau's major mature writings, he continues to study what he understands to be America's shaping environments, precedents, and values, with the aim of encouraging and directing the growth of a more legitimate and admirable polity, and reclaiming what he takes to be the promise of American political life.

CHAPTER 3

Frontier

To live in relations of truth and sincerity with men is to dwell in a frontier country. What a wild and unfrequented country that would be.

—Thoreau, *Journal*

Our wild apple is wild only like myself, perchance, who belong not to the aboriginal race here, but have strayed into the woods from the cultivated stock.

The era of the Wild Apple will soon be past. It is a fruit which will probably become extinct in New England.

—Thoreau, "Wild Apples"

AT THE END of "Natural History of Massachusetts," Thoreau writes, "The natural history of man himself is still being gradually written."[1] While the whole of Thoreau's work can be viewed as an extended contribution to this project—aiming to understand the history of the human experience within the context of the natural world[2]—there is no work for which this is more true than *The Maine Woods.* This book is usually thought to focus primarily on nature and, to a lesser extent, Indians. Thoreau certainly has much to say about both of these topics in this work, yet I will suggest in this chapter that a main concern is with pioneers, the whites of European extraction who settle the American frontier. Ultimately, we can think of the book as a commentary on two ideal-typical Americans: the defeated Indian, a hunter whose present has been degraded and whose future looks bleak; and the white frontiersman, who hunts for more than wild game, turning first to logging and then to agricultural settlement and clearing the way for a qualitative transformation of the environment. Thoreau's confrontation with nature in Maine is a study of the relationship between human society and the natural environment. His intention is to present a "natural history of man himself," for which he believes the American natural and social environment is well suited. Thoreau's goal is to investigate, through this "natural history," some of the personal and social options available to Americans, and to evaluate some of the likely developments facing the American political community.

MODERN ENVIRONMENTALISTS frequently interpret Thoreau as a forebear of radical contemporary environmentalism, claiming the mantle of a great writer as a cloak of legitimacy for their own biocentrism.[3] Donald Worster calls Thoreau "a seeker of the primitive forest," arguing that his romanticism is "fundamentally biocentric."[4] Max Oelschlaeger claims that Thoreau sought to discover the truths of premodern peoples through the experience of wilderness unmediated by modern society: "The seeker of Indian wisdom is clearly not a classicist imposing timeless Virgilian and Homeric categories on nature. Rather the search is for presocial meaning through primary experience in the wilderness, through encounter with a nonhuman other outside the domain of conventional wisdom. . . . Thoreau's goal . . . is to rekindle a primitive (savage, Paleolithic, archaic, or Indian) awareness of the Magna Mater."[5] Most recently, Lawrence Buell admits that Thoreau's biocentrism is not consistent, but he chooses to read this as a case in which a prophet is unable to fully grasp and develop his own idea. Although Thoreau "could not get past the Emersonian axiom that 'nature must be viewed humanly to be viewed at all,'"[6] Buell presumes that Thoreau should have gotten beyond that axiom, and that his own ideas in fact lead in that direction. As "Thoreau became less interested in himself . . . he became more interested in nature," and "appearances of self-contradiction notwithstanding, the development of Thoreau's thinking about nature seems pretty clearly to move along a path from homocentrism toward biocentrism."[7] Thoreau is an early, if confused, biocentrist, and we can appreciate the degree to which his ideas at least opened the door for what Buell believes is our more consistent and enlightened biocentric environmentalism today.[8]

These environmentalist interpreters are part of a broader tradition that detaches Thoreau's "nature writings" from his writings about social and political life.[9] Henry Seidel Canby, for example, suggests that Thoreau "had sold his heart to nature, as Faust sold his soul to the devil, and it was hard for him afterwards to turn back to the needs of the town."[10] And when Emerson comments, in his eulogy for Thoreau, that "his visits to Maine were chiefly for love of the Indian,"[11] the implication is that this was another of Thoreau's eccentric excursions into the natural world (of which the Indian was a part) and that this purpose reflected no general concern about American society at large. These comments suggest that nature (and the Indian in nature) is a private and even antisocial interest of Thoreau's. Perhaps the extreme version of this perspective is the claim that Thoreau's concern with nature can be explained away as sublimated sexuality.[12] In one form or another, it is common to think of Thoreau's writings about nature as reflecting a more or less private (artistic or philosophical or sexual) interest.

The view that Thoreau's involvement in nature is fundamentally biocentric, antihumanist, private, or apolitical stands in the sharpest contrast with the best of the previous generation of Thoreau scholarship. Sherman Paul, in what is perhaps the foremost intellectual biography of Thoreau, writes that "Thoreau's love of man was always greater than his love of nature; he loved nature for its human possibilities—it was the bulwark against the 'shivered heavens' of the city, and the lamentable depersonalization."[13] For Paul, "Nature was not Thoreau's final goal, but rather the place of renewal, and out of it, as his own utopian descriptions of ideal human relations and communities revealed, he hoped would come a higher, a spiritually or inwardly formed—that is, an organic—society."[14] Leo Stoller, too, argues that "it was humanized nature that provided the only adequate natural environment for civilized man."[15] Far from the biocentrism described by Worster and Buell, Paul and Stoller find not only a deeply humanist link with nature in Thoreau's work but even a link with a broader social and political project.

The Maine Woods is central to these interpretative debates since it is the major work that most completely captures the seemingly conflicting tensions of Thoreau's views of nature. It is, in fact, a microcosm of the development of his thinking about the proper moral relationship between nature and human communities. Although there are significantly biocentric moments in this text, it is clear, as the book develops, that Thoreau's interest is less in defending a biocentrism than in exploring the nature of some of the major options facing American society. Far from demonstrating an interest in nature divorced from social and political issues, *The Maine Woods* nicely illustrates the degree to which the natural world provided Thoreau with the springboard for evaluating the character and possibilities of American national life. Thoreau never loses for long his fundamentally humanist and political concerns.

When Thoreau went to Maine, in 1846, 1853, and 1857, he was visiting what he took to be a true wilderness, a natural environment that could perhaps literally qualify as a "state of nature." "This was what you might call a bran-new country; the only roads were of Nature's making, and the few houses were camps. Here, then, one could no longer accuse institutions and society, but must front the true source of evil."[16] Thoreau begins "Ktaadn," the first essay in the book, by claiming that the forest in Maine is more "primitive, . . . more interesting, perhaps, on all accounts," than what can be found a thousand miles to the west,[17] and he ends the chapter making the same point: "And there still waves the virgin forest of the New World."[18] The Maine he discovers is America in its infancy. "Can you well go further back in history than this?"[19] Thoreau is "reminded" by his trip "of how exceedingly new this country still is." We have still "discovered only the shores of America. While the republic has already acquired a history world-wide, America is still unsettled and unexplored."[20] Maine represents for Thoreau something absolutely central to the character of America: the frontier, the American roots in wild nature.[21]

Thoreau certainly does not mean to imply that this wilderness is unpeopled. He thinks of the Maine woods as largely wild and natural not because it is without a human presence but because people have done little to alter the natural landscape. Until very recently, Maine was populated primarily with hunters, Indians. Such people, in Thoreau's view, live with and accept nature on its own terms.[22] Thoreau also does not intend to suggest, contrary to the insights of *A Week on the Concord and Merrimack Rivers*, that this is a land literally prior to history. He makes clear in his descriptions of Indians and whites that the current conditions in Maine are very much the aftermath of war; the Indians have been beaten into submission, the whites are just beginning to exploit the conditions of their victory (as we will see later). This state of nature is not a state of innocence. In fact, as we saw in chapter 2, it is a state that has witnessed awesome virtue and appalling vice. But this drama has in itself left the natural world relatively unchanged. The rivers Thoreau travels in Maine are wild, but they are no longer the scenes of warfare. The American frontier is the natural world encountered by the pioneer after the native population has been "pacified."

Despite the vicious and violent American founding, the frontier that remains is Edenic. In "Walking" Thoreau writes, "As a true patriot, I should be ashamed to think that Adam in paradise was more favorably situated on the whole than the backwoodsman in this country."[23] The message in *The Maine Woods* is the same. Regarding the food he enjoys in a camp he visits, he observes, "Everything here was in profusion, and the best of its kind."[24] He claims that any poor person could move to these woods and live cheaply, living "life as Adam did."[25] This wild nature is abundant and friendly.

> Who shall describe the inexpressible tenderness and immortal life of the grim forest, where Nature, though it be mid-winter, is ever in her spring, where the moss-grown and decaying trees are not old, but seem to enjoy a perpetual youth; and blissful, innocent Nature, like a serene infant, is too happy to make a noise, except by a few tinkling, lisping birds and trickling rills? What a place to live, what a place to die and be buried in![26]

This may be a postlapsarian Eden, one in which death and injustice are present, but it is nonetheless without scarcity. Even among its dead and decaying elements it promotes a sense of youth and well-being. "My nature grows ever more young / The primitive pines among."[27]

One of the apparent consequences of Thoreau's experience of this wild frontier is his increasingly biocentric attitude toward the natural world. The wild elements of this world have a heightened independence and integrity for him, and he is impressed by how his own moral essence appears to lose any special claim in this environment: "A pine cut down, a dead pine, is no more a pine than a dead human carcass is a man. . . . Every creature is better alive than dead, men and moose and pine-trees, and he who understands it aright will rather preserve its life than destroy it." The pine "is as immortal as I am, and perchance will go to as high a heaven, there to tower above me still."[28] While in most of his works nature is primarily "a canvas to our imaginations,"[29] in *The Maine Woods* Thoreau finds a nature that is wild enough to have a more independent character than the pastoral world he usually inhabits. It is still the resource for his imaginative life, but it has in addition a more obvious independent integrity than it does in much of Thoreau's work.[30]

As nature becomes increasingly independent, however, Thoreau becomes increasingly sober in his assessment of the abundance and friendliness of the wild. He observes that the forest "is even more grim and wild than you had anticipated."[31] Most famously, he journeys to the very heart of this wilderness, the summit of Mt. Ktaadn, where he finds "an undone extremity of the globe."[32] He is the only member of his party to make it to the top of the mountain, and what he finds there is a radical contrast to the nature he usually inhabits. In this environment nature "does not smile" on people "as in the plains." On the contrary, "She seems to say sternly, why came ye here before your time? This ground is not prepared for you. Is it not enough that I smile in the valleys?"[33] Upon descending, Thoreau reflects on how indifferent, if not hostile, this brute nature is:

> Nature was here something savage and awful, though beautiful. I looked with awe at the ground I trod on, to see what the Powers had made there, the form and fashion and material of their work. This was the Earth of which we have heard, made out of Chaos and Old Night. Here was no man's garden, but the unhandselled globe. It was not lawn, nor pasture, nor mead, nor woodland, nor lea, nor arable, nor waste-land. It was the fresh and natural surface of the planet Earth, as it was made for ever and ever,—to be the dwelling of man, we say,— so Nature made it, and man may use it if he can. Man was not to be associated with it. It was Matter, vast, terrific,—not his Mother Earth that we have heard of, not for him to tread on, or be buried in,—no, it were being too familiar even to let his bones lie there,—the home, this, of Necessity and Fate. There was there felt the presence of a force not bound to be kind to man. It was a place for heathenism and superstitious rites,—to be inhabited by men nearer of kin to the rocks and to wild animals than we.[34]

The friendliness of the forest below is completely absent, and this wildest of natural places is not even an appropriate environment for a man or woman to become lost in and die. At its very wildest, nature is no place for people. Beneath, or rather above, the benign nature Thoreau so commonly praises is an awesome, beautiful, "titanic," and radically inhuman core to the natural world.

This does not mean that such a nature has no value for Thoreau. On the contrary, one night when he finds some phosphorous wood, Thoreau is extremely excited, and the event symbolizes the treasures to be found in the wild. "I little thought that there was such a light shining in the darkness of the wilderness for me."[35] He argues that at least the poet can understand the biocentric value of nonhuman nature and thereby "sympathize" with it and enjoy the love of it on nature's own terms.[36]

Nonetheless, Thoreau does appear to change his perspective on this wilderness as the book progresses. Initially, his enthusiasm for wild nature spills over into an enthusiasm for the human life lived within it. By the end of the second essay, "Chesuncook," he no longer appears as sure of this. His respect for the independent integrity of the wilderness makes him disgusted with the ways in which the frontier is being subdued—for example, he mentions with horror a machine invented to chop his beloved huckleberry bushes for fuel.[37] For all of his aversion to the civilized world's lack of respect for wild nature, however, he admits that "it was a relief to get back to our smooth, but still varied landscape"—pastoral New England: "For a permanent residence, it seemed to me that there could be no comparison between this and the wilderness, necessary as the latter is for a resource and a background, the raw material of all our civilization. The wilderness is simple, almost to barrenness. The partially cultivated country it is which chiefly has inspired, and will continue to inspire, the strains of poets, such as compose the mass of any literature."[38] Thoreau now suggests that wilderness is less the central home for our civilization, a place in which to live, like Adam, in abundance and youthful pleasure, than it is the periphery that supplies the pastoral center with its necessities. His understanding of what constitutes necessities is, of course, more expansive than those who would use it only for lumber and other raw materials. Such wilderness is needed mainly for "inspiration and our own true re-creation."[39] But the idea here is to protect the wild frontier as a park rather than as a home. A truly wild nature is a place to visit, not a place to live.

Without the protection of these wild places, Thoreau understands clearly that white settlement threatens a complete transformation of the environment. "But Maine, perhaps, will soon be where Massachusetts is."[40] This is unambiguously tragic for Thoreau, but when he admits his preference for "partially cultivated country," he has come a long way from his initial buoyant enthusiasm for wilderness in "Ktaadn." His respect for wilderness is deep and unshakable, but his main interest is not really in those parts of nature that are alien to the human experience; such wilderness is "simple, almost to barrenness." Those who privatize Thoreau's interest in nature, or who portray it only as an early version of contemporary biocentrism, have significantly distorted our ability to fully appreciate works like *The Maine Woods*, in which Thoreau is exploring his "natural history of man himself." Although biocentric elements can clearly be found here and throughout Thoreau's works, it is the human drama he is most interested in.[41] This drama, in Maine and throughout the country, is one that takes the wilderness and makes it a frontier. As in *A Week*, it is the drama between Indian and white that continually attracts Thoreau's attention in Maine. For better or worse, he believes, this drama holds a key to understanding the future development of American civilization.

IN CHAPTER 2 I argued that the Hannah Dustin story in *A Week* represented for Thoreau the final destruction of the Indians at the hands of the white settlers. Recall, however, that the slaughter was not complete; a "favorite boy" and a wounded woman escaped the massacre. Thoreau refers, in *The Maine Woods*, to the Indian's "extinction," even while observing living Indians.[42] His initial view, and the one that appears to hold throughout the book (although it is significantly modified by his experience with Joseph Polis on his last visit in 1857), is that the remnants of earlier Indian societies are now so beaten, ravaged, and controlled by white society as to have lost their native character. "These were once a powerful tribe," he observes of the Indians he describes in the opening pages of the book. "Politics are all the rage with them now."[43]

In "Ktaadn" Thoreau has very little to say about the Indian. His attention is focused primarily on the wilderness and the white people he finds there. His assumption at this point is that Indians have been so far removed from their natural conditions that they are no longer of positive interest or usefulness to him. He is grateful for his luck in securing white boatmen to take him into the interior, since he accepts the opinion that Indian guides are "less to be relied on, and more disposed to sulks and whims."[44] He concludes near the end of the chapter that the oppression of the Indian has caused them to lose all their distinctive qualities as a people. All they are left with is a common, but sadly degraded, humanity. "There is . . . a remarkable and unexpected resemblance between the degraded savage and the lowest classes in a great city. The one is no more a child of nature than the other. In the progress of degradation the distinction of races is soon lost."[45] The "race" is extinct, even if individuals descending from that community can still be found.

On his second trip to Maine, Thoreau "employed an Indian mainly that I might have an opportunity to study his ways."[46] This guide does not seem, on the whole, to have disabused Thoreau of his initial view of Indians. Joe Aitteon had worked in a lumber camp, where he had learned his English slang and songs like "O Susanna," and his socialization into white society appears to have left him unable to live independently in the woods.[47] Thoreau has serious doubts about Joe's abilities as a tracker and a hunter; he is not skilled in his tracking of a wounded moose, and at another time he gets very excited and yells "bear" when in fact the animal before them is only a hedgehog.[48]

Thoreau's discussion of moose hunting illustrates his doubts not only about Joe but about the traditional hunting life of Indians generally. When Thoreau's party spots and kills a moose, Thoreau is disgusted and ashamed: "This afternoon's experience suggested to me how base or coarse are the motives which commonly carry men into the wilderness."[49] His initial criticism is aimed at sport hunting. He imagines that if he lived as a "hunter in the woods, fishing and hunting, just enough to sustain myself," this would be "next to living like a philosopher on the fruits of the earth which you had raised, which also attracts me." What he had witnessed was something very different, the slaughter of an animal for no purpose outside of the pleasure of the hunt itself. Such killing, which presents no risk to the hunter and is tied to no necessities of life, "is too much like going out by night to some wood-side pasture and shooting your neighbor's horses."[50] What Thoreau says next, however, is surprising. We would suspect, given his initial suggesting that hunting is at least close to the philosophical life under appropriate conditions, that the Indian in his traditional lifestyle would be exempt from criticism. On the contrary, Thoreau explicitly equates the Indian with sport hunters as he continues to reflect on the killing: "What a coarse and imperfect use Indians and hunters make of Nature! No wonder that their race is so soon exterminated."[51] Thoreau's lack of respect for Joe has spilled over at this point into his assessment of Indians as a hunting people. Killing a magnificent animal like a moose is always a lesser life than the "philosophical" life of raising one's own food. Later in the book, when Joseph Polis kills a moose, Thoreau holds his tongue and goes fishing rather than dwell on the issue, and he even makes what appear to be positive remarks about eating the meat.[52] This response, however, seems to grow more out of respect for Polis as an individual than out of a change of heart about the hunting life.

On this second Maine trip Thoreau does spend a night camping with Indians who impress him as much more representative of traditional native life than Joe Aitteon. Their camp, he says, was "as savage a sight as was ever witnessed."[53] Although he is squeamish about how dirty it is,[54] he is happy to have the opportunity to spend time listening to the men speak their native language and go about their business: "I felt that I stood, or rather lay, as near to the primitive man of America, that night, as any of its discoverers ever did."[55] But even though these individuals seem to Thoreau less corrupted by white civilization than his guide, he expresses his old skepticism about the future that awaits them. "Alas for the Hunter Race! the white man has driven off their game, and substituted a cent in its place."[56] Even though he still finds vestiges of the traditional native life in the Maine woods, there is no way, in the long run, for this life to remain unchanged by the economic and social structures of white society.

Joseph Polis, Thoreau's guide on his third trip to Maine, is the one Indian who gains the full measure of Thoreau's respect and analysis. This is not to say that Thoreau does not make critical or stereotypical observations about Polis: he is very critical of his storytelling abilities (he finds that Polis makes much of nothing and adds insult to injury by being long-winded about it);[57] although he enjoys Polis's singing, saying there was a "beautiful simplicity about it," he also finds it "mild and infantile";[58] he is critical of Polis's Protestantism and his qualms about traveling on the Sabbath;[59] and, using an image raised earlier in the book, he suggests that, like the Irish, Polis complains too much about being sick.[60] And, because Polis cannot (or chooses not to) explain all the techniques he uses to find his way in the woods, Thoreau at one point reduces this skill to mere animal instinct.[61] Despite these comments, however, it is clear that Polis is for Thoreau a heroic figure. He is deeply impressed by Polis's solitary travels in the wilderness. "Here was traveling of the old heroic kind over the unaltered face of nature," in "Places where he might live and die and never hear of the United States, which make such a noise in the world,—never hear of America, so called from the name of a European gentleman."[62] Polis is a perfectly independent man, capable of living an entirely self-sufficient and solitary life. Thoreau greatly admires Polis's claim that "it makes no difference to me where I am."[63] Polis is, for Thoreau, a remarkable individual who understands a great deal about living successfully and freely. This is symbolized by Polis's woodcraft, which Thoreau takes to be the standard against which he measures himself: Thoreau thus boasts of his success in locating an outlet to a lake that had eluded Polis,[64] and he is extremely flattered at the end of the trip when Polis compliments his ability with a canoe, coaches him to improve his skills, and gives him an Indian name that means "great paddler."[65] With the exception of John Brown, there is no contemporary figure in Thoreau's work who receives a more respectful treatment than Joseph Polis.

There is even some evidence that Thoreau finds Polis's heroic personality more demanding than he himself can live up to. Polis has a brother who failed to return from a hunting trip the previous year, but Polis appears to have accepted this turn of affairs stoically, and Thoreau writes as if it is something of a natural event toward which it is inappropriate to express any emotion.[66] When a companion gets separated from Thoreau and Polis, however, Thoreau displays a significant level of panic and fear. Now that it is his friend who is apparently lost in the wilderness, his stoicism quickly dissolves. Polis is more annoyed than frightened about losing a member of his party, and when, after spending a night lost, the companion is spotted working his way along the river, Polis peevishly tells Thoreau that the lost man has heard their cries and it is unnecessary to continue yelling.[67] This incident shows Polis maintaining his composure in a manner that Thoreau does not even attempt.[68]

But Polis is far from representing only a stoic fatalism. On the contrary, he is a fully emotive and charming personality. One of the most amusing and attractive passages in the book is a playful scene in which Polis challenges Thoreau to a footrace across a portage—Polis, significantly, bearing the much heavier load (the boat) across the carry. Upon finishing the race, Polis laughs at his cut feet and exclaims, "O, me love to play sometimes."[69] Thoreau thoroughly enjoys it too, and it is obvious that this playful quality makes Polis even more appealing in Thoreau's eyes. It certainly helps to make him a more complex and developed personality than any of the other Indians portrayed in the book.

There is another sense in which Polis is more complex than the other Indians described by Thoreau. As in *A Week,* in *The Maine Woods* Thoreau generally assumes that the Indian and the white ways of living are mutually exclusive. Polis's genius is, however, at least partly the result of his ability to exploit both ways of life to his advantage. He is a native hunter but is perfectly willing to exploit the technologies of white society, "proving himself the more successful hunter for it."[70] Thoreau admires Polis's quickness in learning "anything in his line,"[71] and he never suggests that drawing on the resources of white society in any way compromises Polis's integrity as an Indian. In this sense Polis is both unusual and something of an inspiration for Thoreau, an individual who manages to live as an Indian in the modern world. He is an exceptional individual who learns to live his own life in a world that is obviously none too supportive of people like himself. We can think of Polis as Thoreau's Indian counterpart.

It is clear, however, that the heroism and independence of such individuals is significantly constrained by social conditions. Thoreau is sensitive to the indignities suffered by Indians, even by a man as remarkable as Polis. In the opening pages of "The Allegash and East Branch" we see Polis lying to a white man, saying he has no pipe, simply to distance himself from the caste of individuals that represent such an obvious threat to him.[72] Even more poignant is Thoreau's description of Polis's encounter with Daniel Webster. Polis had heard Webster deliver the "Bunker Hill Oration" in Boston. The next day Polis called on him in the hope of paying his respects. After waiting unsuccessfully, he went away and returned another day. After a second long wait, Webster came to him and gruffly asked what Polis wanted. Webster was so gruff, in fact, that Polis was afraid Webster was going to strike him. Polis declares that he does not believe an Indian would have treated him in such a rude manner, and that he did not like Webster very well. Thoreau and his companion dryly "suggested that probably Mr. Webster was very busy, and had a great many visitors just then."[73] The contrast between a famous, admired, and powerful American statesman and an obscure Indian tends much to the disadvantage of the former. Ours is truly a world that fails to understand genuine virtue, and Polis is undeniably at a grave disadvantage in the world as it is currently constituted.

The potential and limitations of Polis's virtue are vividly illustrated by one of the final stories Thoreau tells of him. Thoreau explains at two points in the book that the Indian community in Maine is divided between two "parties," those who support modern education for their children and those who do not. The party opposed to schooling is, significantly, led by the Catholic priest. Those supporting schooling, led by Governor Neptune (the Indian leader of the community), believe that modern education represents the best chance for Indians to compete in the modern world. As Governor Neptune's son-in-law tells Thoreau, "If Indians got learning, they would keep their money."[74] Polis shared this view and emerged as a leader of the pro-school, anti-priest faction. The priest decided to find an opportunity to have his followers cut down the "liberty pole," which within the community symbolized the struggle for education. Polis prevented this from happening by taking a group of "fifteen or twenty stout young men, 'stript 'em naked, and painted 'em like old times.' " Thus transformed, they braced to frighten those who would attack the liberty pole. Polis assured his followers that the opposition would surrender without a fight, and so it proved. When the priest's men came to cut the liberty pole, Polis and his warriors rushed them. "There was a great uproar, and they were about coming to blows, but the priest interfered, saying, 'No war, no war,' and so the pole stands, and the school goes on still."[75]

Thoreau and his companion are impressed by Polis's shrewd tactics and assessment of the opposition. "We thought that it showed a good deal of tact in him, to seize this occasion and take his stand on it; proving how well he understood those with whom he had to deal."[76] Polis understands not only the priest but the general situation confronting him in America. He uses traditional war garb to terrorize his opponents, ironically employing traditional tactics to promote nontraditional ends. But even though Polis is clever enough to make the best of a bad situation, he is powerless to transform the bad situation itself. To the degree that Indian children are taught in schools, they will no longer be educated in the folkways of traditional Indian society. Polis is probably right to believe that, given contemporary conditions, the future of the Indian community will be best served by European-style schools and education. But in pursuing this end, the community is also maximizing the degree to which future generations will be alienated from their traditional culture. And this is the tragic decision confronting them. To reject white ways and retain as much of their traditional society as possible is to knowingly disadvantage the community in the contemporary world. To cultivate the types of knowledge needed for this new world is to abandon much of their native culture. Either choice appears to assure the destruction of the traditional Indian world.

Herein we see the limits placed upon even the most virtuous and heroic of Indians. Thoreau is inspired by the example of Joseph Polis. But even though Polis achieves a great deal of personal independence, and thus deserves a full measure of respect, his example simply cannot function as a model for all to follow. The social and political structures at play are too overwhelming and powerful, and will ultimately destroy even this remnant of the Indian community, virtuous and talented and farsighted individuals to the contrary notwithstanding. Polis's own son is receiving his education in a school shared with white students rather than at his father's side in the wild.[77] Thoreau's assessment of the Indian's future is more nuanced and subtle in *The Maine Woods* than in *A Week,* but the conclusion is essentially the same: for better or worse, the future of society in America lies with the white settlers. The native Indian represents one American life that is no longer realistically available within the context of our social and political realities.

THE TRANSFORMATION of the American wilderness into the American frontier, the movement from a hunting community to an agricultural and commercial community, from Indian to white, is thus at this point in our history the inevitable development of the "natural history of man" in North America. The problem, for Thoreau, is that this community embodies a set of virtues he admires and promotes, but only in a form that is highly unstable. In the final analysis, the frontier Thoreau admires undermines itself and creates a world hostile to those very qualities it initially encourages.

Thoreau's praise for the white settlers in the back country is based upon the independence and simplicity of such a life. The solitary hunter

> is comparatively an independent and successful man, getting his living in a way that he likes, without disturbing his human neighbors. How much more respectable also is the life of the solitary pioneer or settler in these, or any woods,—having real difficulties, not of his own creation, drawing his subsistence directly from nature,—than that of the helpless multitudes in the towns who depend on gratifying the extremely artificial wants of society and are thrown out of employment by hard times![78]

On the frontier is found a life that is more natural, more authentic, less corrupted by the artificial influences of and desires created by the more complex societies of our towns and cities. In this environment the distinctions between rich and poor dissolve, and with them the antagonisms of social class.[79] The frontier is the most free and equal of American social environments.

In addition, Thoreau suggests that the frontier encourages the most rewarding and extensive uses of human capabilities, the most attractive development of human intelligence.

> In fact, the deeper you penetrate into the woods, the more intelligent, and, in one sense, less countrified do you find the inhabitants; for always the pioneer has been a traveller, and, to some extent, a man of the world; and, as the distances with which he is familiar are greater, so is his information more general and far reaching than the villager's. If I were to look for a narrow, uninformed, and countrified mind, as opposed to the intelligence and refinement which are thought to emanate from cities, it would be among the rusty inhabitants of an old-settled country, on farms all run out and gone to seed with life-everlasting, in the towns about Boston, even on the high-road in Concord, and not in the backwoods of Maine.[80]

It is the backwoods of newly settled land, surprisingly, that encourages an openness, a cosmopolitanism, even a tolerant and liberal intelligence, in contrast to the prejudices and habits found in older communities. Thoreau notes that in a lumber camp he visits he finds reading material that includes Emerson's essay on West Indian emancipation. This literature apparently *"had made two converts to the Liberty Party here."*[81] Far from being isolating and narrowing, the frontier is an environment for expanding human personality.

Thoreau's models for frontiersmen are the guides he hires on his first visit to Maine. They are brilliant navigators of the very difficult rivers and streams of the back country—much superior to the Indians[82]—and Thoreau is impressed not only by their individual skills but by the silent unity with which they work together. After climbing a series of rapids no one, to the best of their knowledge, had ever climbed before, Thoreau says, "I could not sufficiently admire the skill and coolness with which they performed this feat, never speaking to each other."[83]

In a posthumous essay, Thoreau praises the "wild apple." Such apples, he argues, are partly civilized and partly wild. The appeal of this wild apple is that it "is wild only like myself, perchance, who belong not to the aboriginal race here, but have strayed into the woods from the cultivated stock."[84] He claims that the wild apple is hardier than the native crabapple, and they are the apples he is most interested in: "These are the ones whose story we have to tell."[85] The symbol of the frontiersmen's achievement in *The Maine Woods* is their boat, or "batteau," an object with exactly the same character as the wild apple; Thoreau describes it as "a sort of mongrel between the canoe and the boat."[86] These guides (and their boat) are cut from the same cloth as Thoreau himself. They come from civilization but have "strayed" back into the woods, away "from the cultivated stock," and have become "semi-civilized."[87] It is their story that interests him the most and is the focus of his tale (in fact, of most all his tales). They represent a possible and desirable future for the people of North America, one that combines the most attractive qualities of "civilization" (that is, white society) and "nature" (or, life lived in close contact with the natural world). Just as their bateaux are superior to both the native canoes and the more refined boats of "civilization," so is the pioneer superior to both the Indian and those who dwell in the center of white society.

Thoreau comments that the pioneers in Maine face a more pristine frontier than those in the West, since "there is a greater interval of time at least between him and the army which is to follow."[88] Pioneers, it seems, are like advanced soldiers at an outpost. "It is a sort of ranger service. Arnold's expedition is a daily experience with these settlers. They can prove that they were out at almost any time; and I think that all the first generation of them deserve a pension more than any that went to the Mexican war."[89] But herein lies the dilemma for Thoreau. He is obviously respectful of the lives and characters of these frontier dwellers, but it is equally obvious that it is the nature of such dwellers to radically and irreparably transform the frontier itself, and thereby remove the conditions that encourage their own virtues. "The civilized man not only clears the land permanently to a great extent, and cultivates open fields, but he tames and cultivates to a certain extent the forest itself. By his mere presence, almost, he changes the nature of the trees as no other creature does."[90] Once this process is set in motion, once Maine is well along the path of becoming like Massachusetts, the resources of the wilderness are in danger of extinction. When they are gone, "We shall be reduced to gnaw the very crust of the earth for nutriment."[91] The virtue of the pioneer is, apparently, a self-defeating virtue.

In fact, when we look at all that Thoreau has to say about the early frontiersmen and settlers in Maine, we see that his hope that such individuals will embody the virtue of the "wild apple" is frequently disappointed. It appears not only that these individuals clear the way for future, more civilized, migrations to the area but that they themselves are much more "civilized" than Thoreau would like; they are frequently less free of the spirit of commerce that infects civilization than the previously quoted passages about the simplicity and independence of backwoods folk suggests. It does not take Thoreau long, for example, to observe that the logging industry in Maine threatens to destroy the forest altogether: "The mission of men there seems to be, like so many busy demons, to drive the forest all out of the country, from every solitary beaver-swamp and mountain-side, as soon as possible."[92] The initial purposes that lure these individuals into the forest are too strong to be completely altered by the simple experience of being in the wild, and thus they are prevented from experiencing the frontier as it might be experienced, as a liberating and equalizing natural environment. Instead, the environment is commodified, and alternative experiences of nature become unimaginable.

> The character of the logger's admiration [for the forest] is betrayed by his very mode of expressing it. If he told all that was in his mind, he would say, it was so big that I cut it down and then a yoke of oxen could stand on its stump. He admires the log, the carcass or corpse, more than the tree. Why, my dear sir, the tree might have stood on its own stump, and a great deal more comfortably and firmly than a yoke of oxen can, if you had not cut it down. What right have you to celebrate the virtues of the man you murdered?[93]

The logger "ignorantly erases mythological tablets in order to print his handbills and town-meeting warrants on them." He is unable to see the "beautiful but mystic lore of the wilderness" and instead can only understand money and commerce and the utility of natural resources.[94]

It might be suggested that the logger is a different sort of individual for Thoreau than the pioneer. The former is a hired hand, one who ventures into the wild for a limited purpose and then beats a hasty retreat back to civilization. The latter, in contrast, builds his home on the frontier and becomes a permanent fixture in the landscape. The distinction is real enough, but Thoreau does not believe it is enough to get the pioneer off the hook. Remember that he holds that the "civilized man" "tames and cultivates . . . the forest itself," like "no other creature," simply by being on the frontier. The white settler, no less than the logger, alters the natural environment, shaping and pacifying it, and thus sets himself apart from the Indian. Thoreau writes in "Walking":

> The weapons with which we have gained our most important victories, which should be handed down as heirlooms from father to son, are not the sword and the lance, but the bushwack, the turf-cutter, the spade, and the boghoe, rusted with the blood of many a meadow, and begrimed with the dust of many a hard-fought field. The very winds blew the Indian's corn-field into the meadow, and pointed out the way which he had not the skill to follow.[95]

Rather than partially returning to wild nature, like the wild apple, the frontier dweller, even if flirting with the wild, represents domestication when all is said and done—not only in future generations but in his own current values and impulses.[96]

We saw earlier that Thoreau ultimately preferred the pastoral landscape to the wilderness, and this preference is reflected in his generally higher regard for the white frontier dweller than the Indian (even taking into account the exception of Polis). Thoreau's hope for the frontier is obviously not an unusual hope in America, but his early optimism fades as his reflections develop. It is clear in this book, especially in the enthusiasm of "Ktaadn," that Thoreau was toying with the notion that the frontier represents an answer to the corruptions of American civilization. Although he deeply and genuinely admires a number of the individuals he finds in Maine, Indian and white, his final judgment is disappointing to him. Not only does the wildness of the frontier make it an inhospitable home; this inhospitality requires the destruction of the wildness that makes the frontier environment attractive in the first place. Individuals may reap the benefits of living on the frontier, like Thoreau's guides to Ktaadn, but once the door is opened to white settlement, it is just a matter of time before the wilderness is tamed and there is no longer a nature capable of enforcing the independent life Thoreau admires. As Steven Fink says, "Thoreau fears that the wild apple, which in its very toughness and durability represented the fruits of democracy, available to even the humblest, will be replaced by the cultivated apple available only in the marketplace."[97] The frontier appears powerless, by itself, to resist this pressure.

IF THE "NATURAL HISTORY OF MAN" in North America suggests the "extinction" of Indians and their replacement by white settlers and frontiersmen, Thoreau believes that this first wave of whites will be under tremendous pressure, both because of their own impulses and because of the demands of the greater white society, to give way to the village, town, and city dwellers who are sure to follow. As mentioned earlier, the most we can hope for from the frontier is to preserve as much of it as possible in a pristine state as a type of park for us to enjoy; perhaps it can then provide at least a minimal counterbalance to the values of commercial society.

> The kings of England formerly had their forests "to hold the king's game," for sport or food, sometimes destroying villages to create or extend them; and I think that they were impelled by a true instinct. Why should not we, who have renounced the king's authority, have our national preserves, where no villages need be destroyed, in which the bear and panther, and some even of the hunter race, may still exist, and not be "civilized off the face of the earth,"—our forests, not to hold the king's game merely, but to hold and preserve the king himself also, the lord of creation,—not for idle sport or food, but for inspiration and our own true re-creation? or shall we, like villains, grub them all up, poaching on our own national domains?[98]

When Thoreau promotes the frontier as a park, he is actually settling for a much less ambitious project than he had initially imagined. The woods of Maine, or the wilds of the frontier in general, are simply not going to offer an alternative life to any significant number of American citizens. Thoreau never gave up completely on his dreams for the frontier, as we know from the famous declaration in "Walking" that "the West of which I speak is but another name for the Wild; and what I have been preparing to say is, that in Wildness is the preservation of the world."[99] But the thrust of the discussion in *The Maine Woods* suggests that Thoreau will have to look for new sources of inspiration if he is to discover a way for Americans in general to become "wild apples," capable of resisting and challenging the undesirable seductions of contemporary society. When all is said and done, the pioneer represents the future of a free and attractive America no more than does the Indian. Such is the sobering natural history lesson Thoreau received in the Maine woods.

CHAPTER 4

Fraternity

The chief want, in every State I have been into, was a high and earnest purpose in its inhabitants.

—Thoreau, "Life without Principle"

THOREAU EXPLORES a third American type, the member of a morally committed community, in his book *Cape Cod*. If *The Maine Woods* investigates the Indian and the white pioneer at the periphery of American society, *Cape Cod* considers the Pilgrim, the citizen of the small, intimate community built around shared and deeply held ideals. Toward the end of the book, Thoreau says, "It must be confessed that the Pilgrims possessed but few of the qualities of the modern pioneer. They were not the ancestors of the American backwoodsman. They did not go at once into the woods with their axes. They were a family and church, and were more anxious to keep together, though it were on the sand, than to explore and colonize a New World."[1] Although the character of the Pilgrim differs significantly from that of the pioneer, this church-based community is nonetheless, of course, a foundational element in the history of the country. Thoreau says of the Cape, in the final sentence of the book, "A man may stand there and put all America behind him."[2] America has produced Indians and pioneers and, as I will discuss in the next chapter, entrepreneurs and business types, but the fates of all have in important ways been shaped by the successes and, more often, failures of these idealistic, communal villagers. If the founding frontiersman and the pioneer are always ahead of, or escaping from, the center of white American society, the Pilgrims represent the original heart of this society.

55

On the opening page of *Cape Cod* Thoreau says, "I did not see why I might not make a book on Cape Cod, as well as my neighbor on 'Human Culture.' It is but another name for the same thing."[3] The problem of this book, and of a number of Thoreau's other travel, or "excursion," writings, is the problem of human solidarity. How it is that human beings are, or might be, held together in coherent, meaningful, and morally respectable community? In light of its history, and since contemporary residents of the Cape "are said to be more purely the descendants of the Pilgrims than the inhabitants of any other part of the State,"[4] this is an ideal setting for evaluating the nature and character of a social fabric. As I hope will become clear in this chapter, Thoreau is by no means an enemy of fraternity and human community. On the contrary, he is a critic, sometimes respectful but critical nonetheless, of the forms that such fraternity and community have taken in America.[5]

This problem of human community can first be approached negatively: What are the forces that threaten the shared experiences and commitments essential to any healthy community? In *Cape Cod* Thoreau considers in some detail two of the most privatizing elements of human life, death and the yearning for personal salvation (or, in more general and secular language, for an independent moral integrity),[6] and the problems they pose for human solidarity. Thoreau severely criticizes three major responses to these forces within the American experience, all of which represent attempts to prevent the dissolution of common life: charity, our historical narratives, and religious intolerance. But we know from other writings, most importantly *A Yankee in Canada,* that he is even more critical of societies that do not even aspire to civic concern or moral consensus, societies that are built only and self-consciously upon brute political force. For Thoreau, we desperately need a moral community, but the models that exist for such communities in the American tradition are significantly flawed.

"THE SEA-SHORE," says Thoreau, "is a sort of neutral ground, a most advantageous point from which to contemplate this world." Part of the reason it is so ideal is that it is a place where nature is at its roughest, wildest, least hospitable.

> It is a wild, rank place, and there is no flattery in it. Strewn with crabs, horse-shoes, and razor clams, and whatever the sea casts up,—a vast *morgue*, where

famished dogs may range in packs, and crows come daily to glean the pittance which the tide leaves them. The carcasses of men and beasts together lie stately up upon its shelf, rotting and bleaching in the sun and waves, and each tide turns them in their beds, and tucks fresh sand under them. There is naked Nature,—inhumanly sincere, wasting no thought on man, nibbling at the cliffy shore where gulls wheel amid the spray.[7]

Cape Cod represents for Thoreau the force of nature and necessity at the margins of habitability.[8] He is continually noting how unfertile the land is, how it is amazing that the residents manage to grow anything at all. "As for the interior, if the elevated sand-bar in the midst of the ocean can be said to have any interior, it was an exceedingly desolate landscape, with rarely a cultivated or cultivable field in sight."[9] At the extremity of the Cape, nature is not only stingy but presents the unrelenting threat of death. "The annals of this voracious beach! who could write them, unless it were a shipwrecked sailor? . . . Think of the amount of suffering which a single strand has witnessed. The ancients would have represented it as a sea-monster with open jaws, more terrible than Scylla and Charybdis."[10] Thoreau wants to observe the ocean, "that seashore where man's works are wrecked,"[11] precisely because it represents such a threat to all we make, to our very lives. The Cape is a morgue and the ocean a voracious monster. Here men and women are continually facing the facts of life at their most basic and elemental.[12]

Any successful society must, of course, control the threatening forces of nature enough to allow its members to subsist and reproduce. But Thoreau's concern in this book is not economic (as it is in *Walden* or "Life without Principle"). He is here interested in the impact that nature and death have on the forces of social integration, on the relationships between citizens and individuals. And what he finds is terribly disturbing. The book begins with a shipwreck of a boat full of Irish immigrants at Cohasset in which 145 people have died. Thoreau visits the scene and is both moved and appalled. He is moved by the story of a woman awaiting the arrival of her infant daughter and sister, only to find them both dead and sharing a casket, dying herself of grief three days later.[13] He is appalled to find the citizens of Cohasset ignoring the tragedy and concentrating instead on the harvest of seaweed thrown on the beach by the storm.

In the very midst of the crowd about this wreck, there were men with carts busily collecting the sea-weed which the storm had cast up, and conveying it

beyond the reach of the tide, though they were often obliged to separate frag-
ments of clothing from it, and they might at any moment have found a human
body under it. Drown who might, they did not forget that this weed was a valuable manure. This shipwreck had not produced a visible vibration in the fabric
of society.[14]

Although the grieving Irishwoman suggests that love and compassion can
be found in at least isolated doses, the overwhelming thrust of the scene
indicates that such a response to human suffering is much less common
than we might expect or desire. The residents gather seaweed, the surviv-
ing mate of the wrecked boat, the *St. John,* is questioned heartlessly by curious bystanders,[15] and Thoreau observes among those on the beach "no
signs of grief, but there was a sober dispatch of business which was affect-
ing."[16] On the whole, the remarkable fact about the scene is this lack of
grief and compassion, even if we ignore the downright heartless behavior
of some.[17]

This leads Thoreau to consider generally the relationship of the dead
to the living. What overwhelms his discussion is the gulf between the two,
a gulf that seems so radical and complete as to threaten any and all sense
of connectedness between them. "Why care for these dead bodies? They
really have no friends but the worms or fishes. Their owners were coming to the New World, as Columbus and the Pilgrims did,—they were
within a mile of its shores; but, before they could reach it, they emigrated
to a newer world than ever Columbus dreamed of, yet one of whose existence we believe that there is far more universal and convincing evidence . . . than Columbus had of his."[18] In a sense, we are all in the same
position as the Wellfleet Oysterman who, later in the book, tells Thoreau
about having witnessed the sinking of another boat, the *Franklin,* the previous spring. A boy fetches him early in the morning to tell him that the
vessel is in distress. Being an old man, the Oysterman takes his time, eats
his breakfast, walks to the top of the hill from where he has a good view
of the wreck, and finds a comfortable place to sit and watch the drama
unfold. Although the boat is on a sandbar only a quarter mile from him,
there is nothing he can do but watch and bear witness to the event. His
description of the struggles and deaths of the passengers and crew, as conveyed by Thoreau, is dispassionate, detached. These people are not only
beyond the Oysterman's ability to help. Their situation is such that there
is an unbridgeable chasm between his own experience and theirs, a chasm
over which a meaningful empathy or compassion appears unable to cross.

He is more interested, even entertained, than traumatized or emotionally wrenched by the event.[19]

Thoreau is himself emotionally numbed by the magnitude of the disaster of the wrecked *St. John*. He sees that as the number of corpses grows, the identity of the victims is dissolved in the brute impersonality of death. "I saw that corpses might be multiplied, as on the field of battle, till they no longer affected us in any degree, as exceptions to the common lot of humanity. Take all the graveyards together, they are always the majority. It is the individual and private that demands our sympathy. A man can attend but one funeral in the course of his life, can behold but one corpse."[20] Just as dying is perhaps the most private of all experiences, so is death, paradoxically, the least individuating of acts. We are all equal in death, equally reduced to natural elements and processes, and the unique and defining qualities of personality disappear. If that personal spirit lives, it lives in a world (at least seemingly) unrelated to our own. The living are left alone with memories of the dead in life. The extreme grief Thoreau endured when his brother died of lockjaw in 1842 manifested itself not only in depression but also in intense sympathetic symptoms of his brother's illness. Thoreau was well acquainted with the overwhelming frustration the living may face in properly relating to, sympathizing with, and grieving for the dead. Death threatens the stability of community not only in an economic or material sense but in an emotional, affective sense as well. It strains and threatens to rend the foundations of individualized concern upon which meaningful community is built.

Just as necessity threatens community through the extraordinarily personal nature of suffering and the extraordinary impersonality of death, so nature threatens to rob the living of even a clear and proper memory of those who have died. Thoreau returns to the Cohasset shore during a later visit and finds the sea calm and inviting. The swimming from Cohasset Rocks is "perfect." "The water was purer and more transparent than any I had ever seen. There was not a particle of mud or slime about it."[21] There is absolutely no evidence of the wreck or the human suffering related to it. "Not a vestige of a wreck was visible, nor could I believe that the bones of many a shipwrecked man were buried in that pure sand."[22] Nature erases all signs of our existence with the same indifference with which it takes our lives.

The residents of Cape Cod (and America as a whole) have responded to these two threats from nature—the threat of isolation in our struggle with necessity, and the threat to the memory of our lives—by, among other things, practicing charity and writing history. The former aims not only to protect us from extremity but also to institutionalize compassion and concern and a willingness to sacrifice for one another; the latter places us in a human narrative that meaningfully connects the generations. At their best, both charity and the stories we tell of our collective life that constitutes the historical record are expected to teach our interrelatedness, to mitigate the isolating effects of nature. When Thoreau looks closely at the actual practices of charity and history on the Cape, however, he finds a situation far removed from the ideal. Instead of teaching compassion and fraternity, our charity is radically insufficient, cold, even cruel. And the history we tell is distorted, biased, and crudely self-serving, masking rather than illuminating the realities of our collective experience.

The primary symbols of charity in *Cape Cod* are the "charity houses" or "humane houses" that are scattered along the shore as emergency shelters for shipwrecked sailors. The charity house Thoreau and his companion discover on their walk is not only in disrepair (it "had neither window nor sliding shutter, nor clapboards, nor paint")[23] and lacking emergency supplies; the door is actually nailed shut. Instead of standing as a humane protection against the perils of shipwreck, the house is itself a sort of wreck. "Indeed, it was the wreck of all cosmical beauty there within."[24] The closest Thoreau and his companion come to the interior of the house is a view through a knothole in the door.

> Turning our backs on the outward world, we thus looked through the knot-hole into the Humane house, into the very bowels of mercy; and for bread we found a stone. It was literally a great cry (of sea-mews outside), and a little wool. However, we were glad to sit outside, under the lee of the Humane house, to escape the piercing wind; and there we thought how cold is charity! how inhumane humanity! This, then, is what charity hides![25]

Peering through the hole in the door is an act of introspection, seeing into the depths of our charity. What he finds is a far cry from the warmth of human solidarity. Rather, this house is perhaps a worse insult than if there were no pretense of charity at all. As it is, the person in need is lured to the house, led to believe that there is help offered by others, only to be shut out and left to die on the steps. To Thoreau, the charity houses "appeared but a stage to the grave,"[26] a mere pretense, a lie about the humanity of our own community.

This is not the only example of such hypocrisy that Thoreau finds on the Cape. The lighthouse keepers, he discovers, are handicapped by the unwillingness of the government to buy winter-grade oils to burn in their lamps. As a result, it is extremely difficult to keep the lights burning in cold weather, and even when they do burn they burn less brightly than they ought. "A government lighting the mariners on its wintery coast with summer-strained oil, to save expenses! That were certainly a summer-strained mercy."[27] The whole citizenry of the nation, not only the residents of the Cape, is implicated here. We share a collective responsibility for the inhumanity represented in shuttered charity houses and insufficient lighthouses. It is not only lives that are lost as a consequence of our "inhumane humanity"; our character as neighbors, citizens, fellow human beings is compromised.

Thoreau is so disgusted with what he finds at the charity house that he comically suggests that this must not be a charity house at all but a cottage "belonging to some of the family of Night or Chaos, where they spent their summers by the sea, for the sake of the sea-breeze, and that it was not proper for us to be prying into their concerns."[28] It is hard to imagine that such an insult could be the work of normal people; it would be much more comforting to assign the blame to a "family of Night or Chaos." Thoreau also takes this opportunity to gently defend himself from the charge that he cares little for others. It is the society at large, not himself, that is hard-hearted and unconcerned with the needs of those who suffer. "My companion had declared before this that I had not a particle of sentiment, in rather absolute terms, to my astonishment; but I suspect he meant that my legs did not ache just then, though I am not wholly a stranger to that sentiment."[29] It is impertinent, in the light of the cruel charity Thoreau has described, to accuse Thoreau of inhumanity. Additionally, what is commonly mistaken for compassion is nothing other than the aching of our own legs, a symptom of our own needs and desire for moral justification in our own eyes or in the eyes of the community, rather than a genuine concern for the welfare of others. How else can we explain the hardness and hypocrisy of our charity?

Thoreau finds "wreckers" (those who profit by gathering the debris from shipwrecks) on the Cape, seaweed rakers amid the bodies and debris of the St. John, a charity house nailed shut, and inadequate lighthouses. This is certainly a damning body of evidence with which to make a case against the nature of the compassion, charity, and cooperation practiced by our society. But Thoreau is himself humbled when he realizes, as he walks the beach, that a ship at sea is sending messages that he and his companion do not understand. For all he knows the ship may be in distress. Could the captain believe that Thoreau and his companion are "cold-hearted wreckers who turned our backs on him"?[30] Our moral failure to care for others is not only due to bad intentions and underdeveloped moral sensibilities, although these problems are real enough. Our failures are also partly the result of the difficulty of understanding the needs of others, of simply being able to make a sufficient level of genuine human contact to have a satisfactory handle on what it is they are trying to say to us. There are times when necessities can draw us together; Thoreau jokes that his illness from eating a giant clam was just the same as that experienced by the Pilgrims when they ate the same creature, and knowing this brought him closer to his ancestors.[31] But more often, natural needs separate and privatize us, much as the ocean separates Thoreau from the captain of the ship and thus makes it impossible for him to understand what, if anything, is being asked of him.

Even accounting for these difficulties of human solidarity, however, Thoreau does not find the mercy, compassion, and charity of our society to be equal to the task of even beginning to bind us together into a community of shared concern. On the contrary, our acts of charity, when we make efforts in this direction at all, are frequently cruel and harmful, suggesting a serious failure on the part of our community. "Our charitable institutions are an insult to humanity," Thoreau writes in his *Journal*. Ours is, at best, "a charity which dispenses the crumbs that fall from its overloaded tables, which are left after its feasts!"[32]

Thoreau is equally critical of the stories we have told about our past, the history we claim, admire, teach, and pass on to future generations. When he examines the history of the Cape, he finds that the English historians completely ignore the contribution of the French, who had been the early explorers of the New England coast and beyond, and had settled Nova Scotia fifteen years before the Pilgrims landed.[33] "Indeed, the Englishman's history of *New* England commences, only when it ceased to be, *New* France."[34] The history we tell is therefore false, as are the claims to the right of possession that this false history has been used to justify.[35] When Thoreau considers not only the exploits of the French but the much earlier adventures of Icelandic explorers,[36] he is struck by the partisanship of our historical narratives. If we impartially survey the historical record, we become hard-pressed to recognize our conventional historical wisdom. "I believe that, if I were to live the life of mankind over again myself, (which I would not be hired to do,) with the Universal History in my hands, I should not be able to tell what was what."[37] On the whole, history tends to be little more than the "story agreed on by posterity."[38] And this agreement more often than not merely celebrates the victors rather than seriously considering the nature of our past and how it influences our present and future.

Although Thoreau is critical of our charity and the histories we tell, these attempts to tie ourselves together in the face of the powerful threats represented by nature, it is important to remember that Thoreau is not Nietzsche. In no way does his criticism imply that human compassion is always or necessarily hypocrisy and cruelty,[39] or that there is no possibility for honesty in the stories we tell about our common life. Thoreau writes in *Walden*, "Do not stay to be an overseer of the poor, but endeavor to become one of the worthies of the world."[40] There is always a demeaning, patronizing element to the charity we practice, since it is premised upon the existence of gross and probably unjustifiable inequalities. This should not, however, make us think that Thoreau has no interest in promoting a compassionate society. John C. Broderick pointed out many years ago that Thoreau's specific proposals for legislation, scattered primarily throughout the *Journal*, "suggest Thoreau's acceptance of the principle of governmental activity, legislation for human welfare, so long as increased, abusive authority over the individual is not its inevitable companion."[41] As we will see in chapter 5, even the best human communities cannot and should not escape the need for mutual aid, neighborliness, and civic interdependence. But such communities will be egalitarian enough to make charity, in its current degrading forms, obsolete. It is such a world that the "worthies of the world" work to promote.[42] As for telling our common stories honestly, Thoreau's own history of the Cape suggests his faith in at least the possibility of such a project. Thoreau's task in *Cape Cod* is not simply to debunk our charity and our histories but to suggest the need for reform and transformation. His message is that in our society fraternity is underdeveloped and unfulfilled, not that the value is itself a fraud.

THE PROBLEM of salvation is twofold. First, it is not an easy thing for us to concentrate on the concerns of the moral and spiritual life when the material life continuously and so effectively distracts us. Thoreau observes that the interiors of the Provincetown houses are elegant and luxurious. "As for the interior of the inhabitants I am still in the dark about it."[43] It is the easiest thing in the world to become preoccupied with the interiors of our houses and to ignore our own "interiors." This is obviously one of the oldest stories we know, probably best illustrated by Socrates' rather annoying role as a "stinging fly" to the Athenian polity, and one that Thoreau continually harps on in almost all his works.[44] But Thoreau's comment about the interior of the inhabitants of Provincetown also suggests a second (and also ancient) problem: the difficulty of one person knowing the actual spiritual or moral state of another. Such information is never entirely hidden from us, but it is always partly hidden, and this is enough to make our judgments about others uncertain. This is just another way of acknowledging a profoundly private side of the moral life. "How alone must our life be lived!" exclaims Thoreau in the very first volume of his *Journal*.[45]

Not only is the interior life of others always at least a partial mystery to us. When individuals do commit themselves to the moral or spiritual life, two significant problems can emerge. First, they may (and probably will) find themselves in some tension with, and perhaps active hostility to, the society around them. Socrates' relationship to Athens is always and inevitably ambiguous, as the stinging fly is both a pest and (we want to believe) a blessing. To be interested in truths beyond the common or conventional makes us appear alien to the community at large.

> Nothing remarkable was ever accomplished in a prosaic mood. The heroes and discoverers have found true more than was previously believed, only when they were expecting and dreaming of something more than their contemporaries dreamed of, or even themselves discovered, that is, when they were in a frame of mind fitted to behold the truth. Referred to the world's standards, they are always insane.[46]

But the flaws are not all with the greater community. A second, and equally troubling, problem is that morally serious individuals may be tempted to cultivate this alienation for its own sake, allowing their initial concern for the moral life to be deflected or perverted into a more general self-righteousness and vanity. This is the tone that slips into Thoreau's prose in passages like the following:

> I was glad to have got out of the towns, where I am wont to feel unspeakably mean and disgraced,—to have left behind me for a season the barrooms of

Massachusetts, where the full-grown are not weaned from savage and filthy habits,—still sucking a cigar. My spirits rose in proportion to the outward dreariness. The towns need to be ventilated. The gods would be pleased to see some pure flames from their altars. They are not to be appeased with cigar-smoke.[47]

Just as material life threatens to undermine our moral lives, so our moral lives threaten to make us self-centered and self-righteous and cut off from our society. The promotion of the moral life is obviously fraught with obstacles and danger, not only concerning our relationship with society as a whole but also regarding our understanding of and honesty with ourselves. We are threatened by isolation from without, narcissism from within.

Early New England society attempted to solve these problems by building a uniform and intolerant religious community. It is not unreasonable to suppose that an imposed religious doctrine and code of conduct may serve to create a higher level of moral seriousness among a citizenry than we find in a society without such an imposition. A minimum of religious uniformity may also mitigate the arrogance moral seriousness can breed. Thoreau, however, is unimpressed by the success of these New England experiments in religious piety. Some of his criticisms are fairly standard and unexceptional. For example, he observes how ungenerous many of the parishes were in paying the clergy, suggesting the hypocrisy of what was supposed to be Christian love and generosity.[48] He attacks the notion that religious piety can be taught by corporal punishment: "Think of a man being whipped on a spring morning, till he was constrained to confess that the Scriptures were true!"[49] Finally, Thoreau has nothing but scorn for the fire-and-brimstone method of teaching people religious truth. After presenting the text of a terrifying sermon, Thoreau mentions an account of how this minister, Mr. Treat, had so frightened a "comparatively innocent young man" that he then had to "exert himself to make hell seem somewhat cooler to him."[50] To impose religious doctrine through the power of law and the terror of threatened divine retribution, Thoreau suggests, is both inhumane and ineffective.

Thoreau adds to these common complaints two additional observations. First, not only does an imposed religion encourage hypocrisy and deception, thus undermining the religious life it is supposed to encourage; in addition, there is reason to believe that even if we ignore all evidence of hypocrisy, this policy fails to teach the doctrine it takes so seriously. The story Thoreau tells of Mr. Treat and his father-in-law, Mr. Willard, speaks to this point. Mr. Treat was known for his fearful sermons delivered in an "unhappy manner." Mr. Willard was a much more genial man, who "possessed a graceful delivery, a masculine and harmonious voice." Unlike Mr. Treat, Mr. Willard was "generally admired." Mr. Treat occasionally gave guest sermons in his father-in-law's church. On one occasion, in which he delivered "one of his best discourses," Mr. Willard's congregation complained vigorously and requested that Mr. Treat never be invited to preach to them again. Mr. Willard delivered the very same sermon, "without alteration," a few weeks later. The congregation "ran to Mr. Willard and requested a copy for the press," claiming that it proved his superiority to his son-in-law, that he could preach such a wonderful sermon on the same text that Mr. Treat had botched so. Thoreau ends the story by quoting Phaedrus, " 'En hic declarat, quales sitis judices,' That shows what sort of judges you are."[51] For all the emphasis placed on teaching proper Christian doctrine, the example of Mr. Treat and Mr. Willard suggests there is no reason to suppose that this doctrine was what was being effectively communicated to the laity. It was the personality and behavior of the clergy, not their formal teachings, that influenced this congregation.

A second story is of Rev. Samuel Osborn, and it suggests that the New England clergy was not only ineffectual but also so bogged down in the minutiae of doctrine that it lost sight of common sense and simple moral truths. Despite being well respected, Osborn was excommunicated for holding Arminian doctrines, such as his view that obedience to Christ can contribute to a person's "justification," or salvation. After reviewing the charges against him, Thoreau dryly comments, "And many the like distinctions they made, such as some of my readers, probably, are more familiar than I am. So, far in the East, among the Yezidis, or Worshippers of the Devil, so-called, the Chaldaeans, and others, according to the testimony of travellers, you may still hear these remarkable disputations on doctrinal points going on."[52] As far as Thoreau is concerned, Osborn was "fully justified" by the work he did in teaching his parishioners to produce and use peat in their farming, even aside from his overtly religious labors.[53] In imposing doctrinal uniformity, the clerical court had lost sight entirely of the important works Osborn actually performed. Like the worship of the devil, doctrinal nitpicking destroys our ability to properly evaluate the moral life.

Thoreau's criticism of the old Puritan clergy is balanced by a grudging respect, despite his inability to feel any kinship with its theology. "Let no one think that I do not love the old ministers. They were, probably, the best men of their generation, and they deserve that their biographies should fill the pages of the town histories. If I could but hear the 'glad tidings' of which they tell, and which, perchance, they heard, I might write in a worthier strain than this."[54] Thoreau's criticisms are aimed at the content of the moral views promoted by these ministers and the policies used to institute these views in their society. He does not suggest that their desire to build a virtuous community is itself mistaken. On the contrary, the reason he considers them the "best men of their generation" is precisely because they lived morally serious lives and did what they thought they could to promote such lives within their society.[55]

In *A Yankee in Canada* Thoreau is extremely critical of the omnipresence and power of the Catholic Church in Quebec. He insults the priests and nuns,[56] criticizes the stultifying influence of the church on the education of children,[57] and doubts "if there are any more simple and unsophisticated Catholics anywhere."[58] For all this, however, he admits that these Catholics have two significant advantages over contemporary Yankees. Despite their provincialism and lack of sophistication, the Canadians have a religious sensibility no longer found in New England.

> It is true, these Roman Catholics, priests and all, impress me as a people who have fallen far behind the significance of their symbols. It is as if an ox had strayed into a church and were trying to bethink himself. Nevertheless, they are capable of reverence; but we Yankees are a people in whom this sentiment has nearly died out, and in this respect we cannot bethink ourselves even as oxen.[59]

In addition to this sense of reverence, the Canadians enjoy a social equality and intimacy Thoreau finds appealing and missing from his own experience.

> There was apparently a greater equality of condition among the habitants of Montmorenci County than in New England. They are an almost exclusively agricultural, and so far independent population, each family producing nearly all the necessaries of life for itself. If the Canadian wants energy, perchance he possesses those virtues, social and others, which the Yankee lacks, in which case he cannot be regarded as a poor man.[60]

Although it is true that the Catholic Church stifles the "energy" and independence Thoreau admires, good Yankee that he is, it cannot be denied that it has encouraged a social order in which the pleasures of human solidarity are enjoyed to a much greater extent than they are in the bustling world of New England. Thoreau is attracted by the civility of the Canadians. Some Yankees, for example, believe the Canadians' habit of touching their hats in greeting is a sign of servility, but Thoreau believes such views only illustrate how crass New England has become: "It would, indeed, be a serious bore to be obliged to touch your hat several times a day. A Yankee has not the leisure for it."[61]

Just as Thoreau criticizes the nature of our charity and the history we like to tell about ourselves, so he criticizes colonial New England's great social experiment in promoting religious and moral virtue. But this does not mean he is opposed to the public promotion of the moral life any more than he is opposed to charity or history. In his *Journal* Thoreau writes, "Every man, and the woodchopper among the rest, should love his work as much as the poet does his. All good political arraignments proceed on this supposition."[62] A good polity is one that is deeply involved in the promotion of a morally satisfying life for all citizens in all walks of life. Compassion, an honest understanding of history, and moral virtue are all necessary elements of any society that intends to bind its citizens together in a meaningful and respectable unity. Thoreau's insistence is that we get these projects right, not that we abandon them. When we abandon them, we seriously compromise any opportunity to overcome the privatizing elements of nature and the moral life, and we forgo the opportunity to promote human fraternity.

IT IS NOT SURPRISING that Thoreau's most patriotic work is *A Yankee in Canada*, his only travel narrative that takes as its subject another country (traveling to Canada was Thoreau's only venture outside the United States). Because he is a critic of his own society, we can see most clearly Thoreau's positive evaluations of his native land only when it is contrasted with another nation. Although, as we have seen, Thoreau's criticism of the Catholic Church in Canada retained an element of respect, there is no such qualification of his evaluation of the military presence he finds there. Quebec is an armed camp, and Thoreau thinks it is simply intolerable. "What makes the United States government, on the whole, more tolerable,—I mean for us lucky white men,—is the fact that there is so much less of government with us. . . . [I]n Canada you are reminded of the government every day. It parades itself before you. It is not content to be the servant, but will be the master."[63] What Thoreau sees in Canada is blatant political oppression: an attempt by the English to create a political community through the frank imposition of physical force.

In *Cape Cod* Thoreau concludes that religious imposition is a flawed method of creating social solidarity, that our telling of history is incomplete and dishonest, and that our charity is a thin and hypocritical fraternal gruel. But his observations in Canada demonstrate to him that brute force is the most cynical method of all for imposing a sense of social unity. This is illustrated by the way in which a tyrannical military robs its own soldiers of their manhood. "It is impossible to give the soldier a good education, without making him a deserter. His natural foe is the government that drills him."[64] The very means of making these soldiers requires that all "originality and independence" be drilled out of them.[65] Part of the process of losing their independence is losing the opportunity to put their human qualities to work in some useful labor. "They reminded me of the men who are paid for piling up bricks and then throwing them down again."[66]

The sacrifice of men like these soldiers for some necessary social good might be at least arguably justifiable under certain circumstances, but as far as Thoreau can tell the martial pretenses of the government are altogether fraudulent. He dryly notices that bullets tend to fall almost entirely upon fortresses: "It is a remarkable meteorological and psychological fact, that it is rarely known to rain lead with much violence, except on places so constructed."[67] When he considers the motto of the Quebec government—"In time of peace prepare for war"—he observes that he "saw no preparations for peace; she was plainly an uninvited guest."[68] The purpose of this army is simply to promote its own interests and oppress the citizenry. It is an entirely self-validating institution: "Of course, if they had no wall, they would not need to have any sentinels."[69] The government's only real claim to rule is its overwhelming power. For Thoreau, it has no moral legitimacy whatsoever.

But again, Thoreau's criticism is aimed at the methods and nature of the community he finds in Canada. By no means is he criticizing the project of creating a legitimate social union, or throwing up his hands in despair over the possibility of ever finding such a thing in the world as we know it. On the contrary, his claim is once more that what is needed is a genuine human solidarity, not its abandonment. Watching the soldiers in Montreal, Thoreau writes:

> It was one of the most interesting sights which I saw in Canada. The problem appeared to be how to smooth down all individual protuberances or idiosyncracies, and make a thousand men move as one man, animated by one central will; and there was some approach to success. . . . If men could combine thus earnestly, and patiently, and harmoniously to some really worthy end, what might they not accomplish? They now put their hands, and partially perchance their heads together, and the result is that they are the imperfect tools of an

imperfect and tyrannical government. But if they could put their hands and heads and hearts and all together, such a cooperation and harmony would be the very end and success for which government now exists in vain,—a government, as it were, not only with tools, but stock to trade with.[70]

We see here that Thoreau is no anarchist. When he imagines "a government . . . not only with tools, but stock to trade with," he is imagining a legitimate government and a just political community. His observation of these Canadian soldiers also promotes the critical knowledge required for distinguishing such a government from tyranny. Thoreau writes in his *Journal* that "all nations are remiss in their duties and fall short of their standards."[71] As true as this observation certainly is, it does not suggest that there are no recognizable and meaningful distinctions between regimes, or that political reform is necessarily meaningless or illusory. Nancy Rosenblum is therefore unconvincing when she claims that Thoreau "admitted no alternative idea of the state to Leviathan."[72] Thoreau does not ignore the moral distinctions to be drawn between different states, nor does he deny the need to develop the moral sense to recognize these distinctions. What Thoreau observes in Canada is a significantly less legitimate attempt at political community than what he discovers on Cape Cod, even though both are flawed and deserving of criticism and reform.[73]

I MENTIONED at the beginning of this chapter that the residents of Cape Cod are for Thoreau a direct link between his own and previous American generations, being "more purely the descendants of the Pilgrims" than people found anywhere else in New England. It is important to note that for all his criticism of these folks, he liked them and found them interesting and friendly: "They were particularly downright and good humored."[74] There are vices and flaws in this community, but there are obviously virtues as well, which Thoreau appreciates.

The "representative man" of the Cape is the Wellfleet Oysterman, a talkative and jolly old man. "This was the merriest old man that we had ever seen, and one of the best preserved."[75] Since his company usually consists of ministers, the Oysterman is glad to have the opportunity for looser conversation with Thoreau and his companion, Channing. Thoreau admires his intellectual and moral independence, noting that the Oysterman loves his Bible and knows it well but has always resisted joining a Christian sect.[76] Most significant for Thoreau, however, is the way the Oysterman spans the generations, tying the present to what, for Thoreau, seems a distant past. His grandfather was an original settler from England, and he himself was fourteen years old at the outbreak of the Revolution. "There was a strange mingling of past and present in his conversation, for he had lived under King George, and might have remembered when Napoleon and the moderns generally were born."[77] The Oysterman remembers having seen George Washington riding through the streets of Boston, and he even provides a demonstration of how Washington looked.[78] But even as the Oysterman links Thoreau directly with the founding era, the link serves to illustrate the distance, as well as the continuity, between the generations. Thoreau humorously relates that the old man asks him and Channing where they had been at the time of the Concord and Bunker Hill battles. "We were obliged to confess that we were not in the fight."[79] By Thoreau's time, the excitement, demands, and commitments of the Revolution are distant and irretrievable. It is also clear that a shared history is not in itself sufficient for building a complete understanding between individuals. To know where a person comes from is to know a lot, and to come from the same background as another is a significant bond. But these facts are not enough to fully explain a person's values or intentions. When Thoreau and Channing go to bed, the Oysterman's wife locks them in their room to assure that they will not rob the house during the night.[80] Later, when the Oysterman hears of a bank robbery in Provincetown, he suspects that Thoreau and Channing are the robbers.[81] For all the pleasure the Oysterman gains from their company, there is no reason for him to trust Thoreau and Channing before he has more information about their characters, before he has confidence in his knowledge about the things they love and worry about. The different values held by their respective generations make this task of understanding all the more difficult.

Human solidarity is, for Thoreau, not only a matter of sociology or history. It is most importantly a moral problem. If *Cape Cod* explores a number of the obstacles to fraternity, the most significant is implied in the story of the Wellfleet Oysterman: how to build a common moral bond among free individuals. If we, like the Oysterman, reject the authority of a particular religious sect and allow all individuals to pursue truth as they best see fit, this raises obvious problems for finding a common moral sensibility as the basis of our community. Far from simply rejecting, in the abstract, the notion of a moral community, Thoreau is interested in understanding such a community.[82] Once we recognize this, the famous passage from Walden about our collective traditions in the United States will no longer seem as puzzling as it has to so many interpreters who think of Thoreau as a mere anarchist.[83]

> To act collectively is according to the spirit of our institutions; and I am confident that, as our circumstances are more flourishing, our means are greater than the nobleman's. New England can hire all the wise men in the world to come and teach her, and board them round the while, and not be provincial at all. That is the *uncommon* school we want. Instead of noblemen, let us have noble villages of men. If it is necessary, omit one bridge over the river, go round a little there, and throw one arch at least over the darker gulf of ignorance which surrounds us.[84]

These comments from "Reading" constitute an argument for raising the level of public support for intellectual culture. Instead of being an anomaly or a contradiction with his general view of public life, this passage is in harmony with the views developed in *Cape Cod*. The issue is not to give up on collective life but to reform and perfect it. As Wilson Carey McWilliams writes, Thoreau's desire is "to redirect the state and its citizens, to shift the goal of politics from the purpose of commerce and the machine to the goal of human development."[85] Such a reformation requires the encouragement of a respectable and common moral life, while rejecting all methods of blunt moral imposition.

In a letter to his English friend, Thomas Cholmondeley, Thoreau considers the moral health of the American polity as it lurches toward civil war:

> While war has given place to peace on your side, perhaps a more serious war still is breaking out here. I seem to hear its distant mutterings, though it may be long before the bolt will fall in our midst. There has not been anything which you could call union between the North and South in this country for many years, and there cannot be so long as slavery is in the way. I only wish that Northern—that any men—were better material, or that I for one had more skill to deal with them; that the north had more spirit and would settle the question at once, and here instead of struggling feebly and protractedly away off on the plains of Kansas. They are on the eve of a Presidential election, as perhaps you know, and all good people are praying that of the three candidates Fremount may be the man; but in my opinion the issue is quite doubtful. As far as I have observed, the worst man stands the best chance in this country. But as for politics, what I most admire now-a-days, is not the regular governments but the irregular primitive ones, like the Vigilance committee in California and even the free state men in Kansas. They are the most divine.[86]

These comments are astute and revealing. Thoreau's contention is that the North and South are committed to incompatible values and, as such, are incapable of any meaningful union. The government is thus placed in an impossible situation in which it can only find itself corrupted by the dishonesty required by imposing order on an illegitimate union. Significantly, Thoreau assumes a degree of personal responsibility for being unable to convince the North to resolve this problem, to abolish slavery and thereby clear the way for a legitimate political unity. Established political institutions roll along in this unprincipled and inevitably disastrous direction. Thoreau's admiration is reserved for those informal, "irregular" political organizations, unified by a legitimate moral commitment, and functioning to achieve a morally desirable political outcome (in this case, a political community without slavery). These organizations are the most "divine" precisely because an admirable human solidarity must be built upon a defensible moral principle, to which the members of the community agree and willingly submit.

The fundamental political question for Thoreau is always, therefore, the nature of the moral commitments that bind a community. Without such commitments, the community deteriorates, and such a deterioration is a terrible human loss. *Cape Cod,* however, warns us to beware that our concern for fraternity not lead us in the direction of trying to authoritatively impose a moral life on society, like the Pilgrims before us. Thoreau's warning about this temptation is not that it is foolish or misguided to worry about building a moral community. Rather, it is that such methods will produce hypocrisy and failure. In contrast to the Pilgrims, who suspected that individual freedom and communal solidarity are incompatible, Thoreau holds that the most praiseworthy and meaningful solidarity will grow naturally among free and independent men and women. He writes in *Walden,* "Sell your cloths and keep your thoughts. God will see that you do not want society."[87] In order to defend this view, Thoreau is required to explain what he takes to be the true nature of human freedom and why this will help to build, rather than dissolve, community. This is the task undertaken in Thoreau's greatest work, *Walden.*

CHAPTER 5

Independence

Do we call this the land of the free? What is it to be free from King George and continue the slaves of King Prejudice? What is it to be born free and not to live free? What is the value of any political freedom, but as a means to moral freedom? Is it a freedom to be slaves, or a freedom to be free, of which we boast?
—Thoreau, "Life without Principle"

Beauty and true wealth are always thus cheap and despised. Heaven might be defined as the place which men avoid.
—Thoreau, "Autumnal Tints"

The question is whether you can bear freedom.
—Thoreau, *Journal*

POST-REVOLUTIONARY AMERICA was a nation turning its attention almost single-mindedly toward trade, commerce, and the love of wealth. Joyce Appleby refers to the early part of the nineteenth century as a period when "materialism and morality fused" together,[1] and Gordon Wood writes about how the Revolution, contrary to the wishes of the founding generation, unleashed a society increasingly committed to private affairs and interests.[2] Thoreau captures the spirit of this society at the end of *Cape Cod*. On a boat from Provincetown to Boston, a timber merchant turns to Thoreau and says, "This is a great country,"[3] his patriotism swelled by his sense of the boundless business opportunities in the young nation. Thoreau is less celebratory of these opportunities, but he certainly does not deny them; he comments soon thereafter that it is trade and trade alone that builds our cities: "The more barrels, the more Boston. The museums and scientific societies and libraries are accidental."[4] Even on the Cape, the descendants of the Pilgrims spend the bulk of their lives worrying about nothing but their economic condition, and in this sense they are indistinguishable from the citizens in the rest of the country.[5]

It is the new "economic man" of Thoreau's own generation who constitutes the fourth ideal-typical American that Thoreau investigates, most importantly in his greatest work, *Walden*. The Indian has become "extinct," the white frontiersman simply paves the way for villages and towns, and the moral community that functioned as a "family and a church" has given way, even on its native soil of Cape Cod, to the seductions of commerce. Thoreau's central quarrel with America is with its emerging capitalist economy and the manner in which this economy functions to define the parameters and provide the content of American freedom.[6] *Walden* insists on an alternative understanding of America's promise and encourages Thoreau's fellow citizens to demand a more authentic and humanly satisfying independence.

IN ONE OF HIS TALES, Rabbi Nahman of Bratslav tells of a *Baal Tefilla*, a master of prayer, who is confronted by a city whose citizens love only money. The *Baal Tefilla* speaks with the people and tries to convince them that they are "living in great error" and that chasing money is "not the purpose of life at all," that the purpose of life is "to be engaged in Torah and prayer."[7] While it may seem obvious to some that there are more important things in life than the pursuit of money, the response of the people to the *Baal Tefilla*'s teachings is significant. "And they considered him mad, because all the people of that country were so immersed in money, and had become so foolish because of it that whoever spoke against their folly was considered a madman."[8] To those for whom money becomes a consuming passion, who simply do not believe in other loves or higher values, the *Baal Tefilla* speaks of things that are literally incredible, unbelievable. The *Baal Tefilla* must either be cynical, hiding his own commonplace loves (for his own hidden purposes) behind a fancy but meaningless rhetoric, or, more likely, he is crazy, out of touch with the "real world" of normal men and women. The citizens of this city will respond to those who teach of prayer, or serving God, or living for any higher moral purpose, with either overt hostility or a patronizing condescension, depending on how threatened they feel. Their moral equipment is so limited as to make it almost impossible for them to hear those who speak of a moral life beyond their own experience.

Nahman's story is only one particularly powerful version of a story that is as old as philosophy itself; we might even think of it as the founding story of political philosophy. Plato is only slightly more optimistic than Nahman when he presents Socrates before the Athenian court. Like the citizens of Nahman's city, the Athenians simply do not believe in the religious foundation of Socrates' mission, or that he is only interested in convincing them of the superiority of the moral life to all others.[9] On the contrary, most assume that he is driven by the same passions as they are. His unusual behavior, therefore, must be a lie, self-serving, heretical, and subversive. Socrates is surprised that the court convicts by a margin of only 30 (out of 501) votes, and he hints that if he had had more time he would have been able to sway a majority in his favor.[10] But time runs out, and Socrates' conviction is the damning fact that is only slightly mitigated by the hope that philosophers will have "more time," and therefore more success, in the future.

Walden is Thoreau's major Socratic work, his most rigorous, detailed, and hopeful attempt to convince his fellow citizens that they need to significantly readjust their moral compasses. Much of what he has to say in this book has been so commonly repeated within the Socratic legacy as to sound banal at this point, such as when he writes, "Rather than love, than money, than fame, give me truth."[11] But Thoreau does not claim originality in his philosophy. On the contrary, *Walden* is an attempt to call America to truths that Thoreau holds to be ancient and universal, and if they sometimes sound banal, this certainly is not because we embrace them in our daily lives.

The parallels between *Walden* and the story of Socrates are striking. Although Socrates professes to teach universal truths, it is Athenian citizens he is interested in talking to. Thoreau similarly stresses his connection with his immediate New England political community: "I would fain say something, not so much concerning the Chinese and Sandwich Islanders as you who read these pages, who are said to live in New England; something about your condition, especially your outward condition or circumstances in this world, in this town, what it is, whether it is necessary that it be as bad as it is, whether it cannot be improved as well as not."[12] If the Socratic project is an implicit attack on the moral status of traditional beliefs, Thoreau explicitly (even obnoxiously) declares that he finds no necessary correlation between convention and truth: "I have lived some thirty years on this planet, and I have yet to hear the first syllable of valuable or even earnest advice from my seniors."[13] For all his criticism, however, Thoreau is no more tempted than Socrates to actively revolutionize against the political order. Instead, he cultivates a Socratic independence, letting the state decide for itself how to relate to him.[14] Thoreau encourages a Socratic poverty and simplicity of lifestyle, as when he claims that "my greatest skill has been to want but little."[15] He distances himself from the "sophists" of his own day by distinguishing between "professors of philosophy," those who may have "subtle thoughts" and even found philosophical schools, and true philosophers, who are committed to solving "some of the problems of life, not only theoretically, but practically."[16] He promotes a Platonic distinction between what he takes to be the shadowy illusion of our commonsense world and the sharp, clear, beautiful reality of truth:

> Shams and delusions are esteemed for soundest truths, while reality is fabulous. If men would steadily observe realities only, and not allow themselves to be deluded, life, to compare it with such things as we know, would be like a fairy tale and the Arabian Nights' Entertainments. . . . I perceive that we inhabitants of New England live this mean life that we do because our vision does not penetrate the surface of things. We think that that *is* which *appears* to be.[17]

Like Socrates, Thoreau assumes that we desire to know what is real and true, even if we are frequently confused and misguided about it.[18] In the chapter on "Visitors," Thoreau assumes his most Socratic incarnation by questioning, even interrogating, the visitors to his cabin. In predictable Socratic form, he champions the authentic and honest retarded man over most of the others who come his way.[19]

But perhaps the most significant Socratic element of Thoreau's persona in *Walden* is the peculiar hubris he embodies. Like Socrates, he appears to have a special relationship with the gods. "Sometimes, when I compare myself with other men, it seems as if I were more favored by the gods than they, beyond any deserts that I am conscious of; as if I had a warrant and surety at their hands which my fellows have not, and were especially guided and guarded."[20] This special relationship, however, does not consist in actually knowing the truth. Rather, it involves understanding the need to respect and pursue the truth above all else. Writing about the "higher laws" and their transcendence of sensuality, Thoreau says, "I hesitate to say these things, but it is not because of the subject,—I care not how obscene my *words* are,—but because I cannot speak of them without betraying my impurity."[21] Thoreau, like Socrates, may claim a superiority to his contemporaries, but it is a superiority only in a limited sense. They both claim a commitment to philosophy, while denying that they themselves are successful philosophers. Their ambition is to get others to share their commitments and thus experience what they take to be the full capacity of life, rather than to promote themselves as somehow deserving of special privilege, status, or recognition. "If I seem to boast more than is becoming," writes Thoreau, "my excuse is that I brag for humanity rather than for myself; and my shortcomings and inconsistencies do not affect the truth of my statement."[22]

For all its similarities with the traditional Socratic story, however, *Walden* has its unique qualities as well. The most significant departure from the classical message is Thoreau's Yankee optimism, a habit of mind he is seemingly powerless to break regardless of how disgusted he becomes with his society.[23] When Thoreau declares that he does "not propose to write an ode to dejection, but to brag as lustily as chanticleer in the morning, standing on his roost, if only to wake my neighbors up,"[24] he presumes that his neighbors are capable of such an awakening. And this presumption is the motor that drives the entire book. Thoreau is not only an optimist in the manner of Socrates, one who is cheerful and seemingly content even while being scorned and murdered. Thoreau's optimism rejects the fatalism implied by Socrates' death. His hope for democracy is certainly greater than Plato's, since *Walden* is committed to the project of teaching an entire citizenry, while Socrates must apparently settle for persuading the talented and potentially virtuous few, like Glaucon and Adeimantus in the *Republic*. Put another way, Thoreau appears to believe that the time has come when philosophy *will* have enough time to win over the hearts not just of a minority but of a democratic majority. There is nothing inevitable or necessary about his, but Thoreau apparently believes that his fellow New Englanders at least are in a position to be persuaded. At the very end of the book he notes, "We think that we can change our clothes only."[25] Everything up to this point has aimed to convince every reader that such a belief is wrong, that "it is never too late to give up our prejudices,"[26] and that all of us are capable of such a transformation.[27] He assures us that his message is not for the few but for the many.[28]

> I do not mean to prescribe rules to strong and valiant natures, who will mind their own affairs whether in heaven or hell. . . . I do not speak to those who are well employed, in whatever circumstances, and they know whether they are

well employed or not;—but mainly to the mass of men who are discontented, and idly complaining of the hardness of their lot or of the times, when they might improve them. There are some who complain most energetically and inconsolably of any, because they are, as they say, doing their duty. I also have in mind that seemingly wealthy, but most terribly impoverished class of all, who have accumulated dross, but know not how to use it, or get rid of it, and thus have forged their own golden or silver fetters.[29]

While the Socratic story is born of a tragic conflict between philosophy and democracy, Thoreau's version of the story in *Walden* holds out a greater promise for a resolution of these two values. When Thoreau writes, "I know of no more encouraging fact than the unquestionable ability of man to elevate his life by conscious endeavor,"[30] he is writing about the ability of all members of a democratic society.

Going to Walden Pond, Thoreau symbolically assumes the role of an outsider, even an outcast. The details he gives of the former inhabitants—slaves, freed slaves, a murderer, a potter who never escaped debt, an old soldier reduced to digging ditches, poverty, sickness, and a lonely death—assure that we understand his marginal social status.[31] Although he cultivates the margins, however, Thoreau's intention is never to live the life of the hermit, to completely shut himself off from social affairs: "I think that I love society as much as most, and am ready enough to fasten myself like a bloodsucker for the time to any full-blooded man that comes in my way. I am naturally no hermit."[32] His hope is that by standing on the periphery he will gain a critical distance from which to view his society. *Walden* is not about the supposed virtues of social isolation. Rather, Thoreau's is a Socratic message about the importance and nature of moral independence, a lesson of the greatest importance for participants in a democracy. As Stanley Cavell writes, *Walden* is a tract of "political education" for American citizens.[33] Thoreau's distance from the village symbolizes the independence of a responsible citizen rather than the seclusion of a solitary.[34]

Thoreau's project has three primary elements. First, he explains why he believes we must "give up our prejudices" in order to live freely and independently. Second, he tells us how we might go about giving up our prejudices once we are convinced of the need to do so. And third, he tells us something about what he believes a more independent America would look like.

* * *

THOREAU EXPLAINS that he went to live at Walden Pond in order to reduce his life to essentials, and thus understand it better and experience it more vigorously.

> I went to the woods because I wished to live deliberately, to front only the essential facts of life, and see if I could not learn what it had to teach, and not, when I came to die, discover that I had not lived. I did not wish to live what was not life, living is so dear; nor did I wish to practice resignation, unless it was quite necessary. I wanted to live deep and suck all the marrow of life, to live so sturdily and Spartan-like as to put to rout all that was not life.[35]

What is important to note here is Thoreau's assumption that he is, in some crucial sense, a representative man. He is not writing about an esoteric experience that is reserved for an elite or an elect. Thoreau is thoroughly Protestant in his presuppositions.[36] The life he searches for is the life available to all ordinary people, all the citizens of New England who constitute his intended audience. If there is a moral arrogance here, it is in the presumptuousness of speaking for others, of assuming that his needs, potentials, and failings share certain universal, democratically distributed qualities with the needs, potentials, and failings of others.[37] Thoreau's loss of his hound, bay horse, and turtledove, three precious and irreplaceable objects of love, serves to illustrate not only his unique story but his representativeness as well, as one who has experienced the pain of such misfortune.[38] Thoreau may have a special relationship with the gods, a Harvard education that allows him to read the classics in their ancient languages, and a discipline and independence in his own life that sets him apart from others, but none of this intrudes upon the fundamental assumption of *Walden*, that his experience is generalizable in all its essentials. *Walden* is a Protestant sermon written by a sinner for all the sinners in the congregation.[39]

This democratic egalitarianism allows Thoreau to assume the authority to speak to the various ailments suffered by other representative men and women. Thoreau's criticism of our daily lives and affairs is famous and powerful. His extensive "travels" in Concord have shown him a citizenry that appears to be "doing penance in a thousand remarkable ways."[40] We labor intensely, only to be denied the comforts and pleasures of leisure. The market conditions of our labor alienate us from others and even from our work itself.

> Most men, even in this comparatively free country, . . . are so occupied with the factitious cares and superfluously coarse labors of life that its finer fruits can-

not be plucked by them. Their fingers, from excessive toil, are too clumsy and tremble too much for that. Actually, the laboring man has not leisure for a true integrity day by day; he cannot afford to sustain the manliest relations to men; his labor would be depreciated in the market. He has no time to be any thing but a machine.[41]

We have forgotten that the necessities of life are means to higher goods, and have begun to treat them as ends in themselves.[42] In the process of creating a fantastically wealthy society, we complicate our economy beyond our ability to control it. "The farmer is endeavoring to solve the problem of a livelihood by a formula more complicated than the problem itself."[43] We have become enslaved to the process that is intended to liberate us from nature. "But lo! men have become the tools of their tools."[44] "We do not ride on the railroad; it rides upon us."[45] We have become so preoccupied with our material life that we have forgotten to attend to our moral and spiritual lives. "Why concern ourselves so much about our beans for seed, and not be concerned at all about a new generation of men?"[46] In short, the modern economy has distorted our lives in dramatic ways, promising riches but burdening us with excessive labor, increased individual helplessness, and moral deterioration.[47]

These problems reflect, for Thoreau, a confusion deep in the heart of the productive process. As we increasingly move toward a market economy and factory production, the economy loses its moral bearings.[48] Instead of aiming to provide the necessities of life in the easiest, most rational manner, modern production aims at generating profits. Thoreau sees no reason to think that the interests of capital will solve, as a sort of magical by-product, our economic needs in the most humane and desirable manner.

> I cannot believe that our factory system is the best mode by which men may get clothing. The condition of the operatives is becoming every day more like that of the English; and it cannot be wondered at, since, as far as I have heard or observed, the principle object is, not that mankind may be well and honestly clad, but, unquestionably, that the corporations may be enriched. In the long run men hit only what they aim at. Therefore, though they should fail immediately, they had better aim at something high.[49]

Mass production and the extreme division of labor will certainly generate increasing material wealth, but it takes a certain moral obtuseness to think that this fact settles the issue of whether or not these economic developments are desirable. "Where is this division of labor to end? and what object does it finally serve? No doubt another *may* also think for me; but it is not therefore desirable that he should do so to the exclusion of my thinking for myself."[50] To evaluate an economy only in terms of a narrowly defined economic efficiency is to completely ignore moral questions about the aims and processes of production, to say nothing of the overall purposes of economic life. As Thoreau writes in a letter to his friend H. G. O. Blake, "It is not enough to be industrious; so are the ants. What are you industrious about?"[51]

So modern production distorts our private lives and our political economy. It also produces an inappropriate relationship between ourselves and the natural environment. Nature becomes property, and property is merely a tool to be employed in the relentless pursuit of wealth. "By avarice and selfishness, and a grovelling habit, from which none of us is free, of regarding the soil as property, or the means of acquiring property chiefly, the landscape is deformed, husbandry is degraded with us, and the farmer leads the meanest of lives. He knows Nature but as a robber."[52] The contemporary farmer is only an illustration here, since the structure of the modern economy requires all of us to approach nature as nothing more than raw materials to be exploited in the productive process. "Nature has no human inhabitant who appreciates her. The birds with their plumage and their notes are in harmony with the flowers, but what youth or maiden conspires with the wild luxuriant beauty of Nature? She flourishes most alone, far from the towns where they reside. Talk of heaven! ye disgrace earth."[53] None of us, not Thoreau or any other modern man or woman, is able to live gracefully and harmoniously with the earth.[54]

Finally, the emerging American economy is the source of significant injustice. Thoreau imagines Irishmen asking if the railroad they built is not good. "Yes, I answer, *comparatively* good, that is, you might have done worse; but I wish, as you are brothers of mine, that you could have spent your time better than digging in this dirt."[55] As we generate wealth, much labor is reduced to drudgery, and society is torn by grotesque material inequality, social class divisions, even crime. "I am convinced, that if all men were to live as simply as I then did, thieving and robbery would be unknown. These take place only in communities where some have got more than is sufficient while others have not enough."[56] Thoreau reminds us that a necessary consequence of the railroads is the shanties of the "degraded poor" who provide the labor that drives our economic progress. "The luxury of one class is counterbalanced by the indigence of another."[57] For all our technological innovation and economic development, Thoreau sees our economic life as a new incarnation of an old attempt by nations to assure their place in history by building monuments to themselves, the "insane ambition to perpetuate the memory of themselves by the amount of hammered stone they leave."[58] The oppression and exploitation required by our massive industrial undertakings is not qualitatively different than that required for building the ancient pyramids, and is equally deserving of condemnation.[59] Thoreau refuses to grant the desirability of our economic development. While it creates wealth, it also creates poverty and exploitation, and it robs American citizens of their independence and personal integrity.

All of these elements of Thoreau's criticism of the American economy are famous and familiar. What is important to recognize, however, is that he is not simply describing what he takes to be a given state of affairs. His point is not only that these are recognizable facts about our economic life; he also contends that they are not necessary or natural or inevitable. It is one thing to notice how hard, unfair, or unhappy life is. It is quite another to think that life can be anything other than hard, unfair, or unhappy. One of the most frequently quoted comments from *Walden* is Thoreau's claim that "the mass of men lead lives of quite desperation." The next sentence, "What is called resignation is confirmed desperation," is much less frequently noted but critical to Thoreau's argument.[60] Many of us are resigned to our "desperation," thinking it the most natural thing in the world. But Thoreau's claim is that it is not natural at all, that our resignation is a sign of desperation instead of a realistic assessment of the nature of things. Although we frequently recognize the problems that Thoreau so powerfully discusses, we are much less likely to believe there is a desirable alternative. Until we are convinced of the possibility of such an alternative, there is no reason to even imagine what it might be or to question the legitimacy of the world as we find it.

Thoreau's contention is that "men labor under a mistake"; as he writes in his *Journal*: "There is nothing but confusion in our New England life. The hogs are in the parlor."[61] It is not true that there are no alternatives to the contemporary economy. Thoreau's experiment at Walden illustrates, if nothing else, that it is possible to live a satisfactory life, even a most desirable life, with significantly less wealth and labor than most people believe necessary. And it is not true that the contemporary economy is justified by its own merits, that it is the best possible economy available in the real world. To argue this would be to simply admit moral defeat, to hold that all the symptoms Thoreau describes are of less importance than the gain in material wealth modern production promises. Such an argument assumes the narrowest imaginable conception of human potential. It also implicitly assumes that an extremely limited conception of utility constitutes the whole of legitimate moral evaluation. The former assumption amounts to fatalism, and the latter to cynicism, and one or the other appears to be behind the generally favorable view that most citizens have of the emerging American economy. This is why Thoreau finds that the "greater part of what my neighbors call good I believe in my soul to be bad."[62] Fatalism and cynicism may be impervious to any absolute logical refutation, but they are certainly not defensible in light of the evidence of Thoreau's own experience and the faith that rightly grows from experience.[63] To approve of the modern economy is to approve of injustice and settle for an "incredible dulness."[64] Most importantly, it is to fail in our pursuit of individual liberty, the freedom we claim to hold so dear. It is a mistake, Thoreau claims, to think that the market economy and modern production will deliver independence to the American citizen. On the contrary, it robs us of our independence by making us dependent on employment by others, on the whims of the market, and by creating social structures that produce a radically inegalitarian distribution of social and economic power.

Why does Thoreau believe we should "give up our prejudices" about the contemporary political economy? Because this economy is morally and politically unnecessary and undesirable. Most importantly, because it does not do what it promises. Instead of nurturing freedom, it produces only wealth. When Thoreau says he believes that most of what his neighbors think is good is actually bad, he is criticizing their methods for achieving independence, not the goal of independence itself. Thoreau's rejection of the market economy is not a result of a rebellion against the values he finds in the American society. It is the seriousness with which he embraces these values that leads to his radical political economy. "This town is said to have the largest houses for oxen and cows and horses thereabouts, and it is not behindhand in its public buildings; but there are very few halls for free worship or free speech in this country."[65] Thoreau's assumption in *Walden* is that he shares with his audience a commitment to individual freedom.

As Martin Bickman writes, "*Walden* . . . is most thoroughly American in its heartbreaking awareness of the gap between American ideals and the immediate social and political realities betraying that ideal at every turn."[66] Thoreau's negative task is complete when he explains why and how American society fails to honor this commitment, and why this failure is unnecessary. His positive task is to explain how we might approach a more satisfactory freedom.[67]

WE SHOULD NOT be misled by Thoreau's claim, mentioned earlier, that he knows "of no more encouraging fact than the unquestionable ability of man to elevate his life by a conscious endeavor."[68] Reform, for Thoreau, is not only a matter of human will, the simple desire to "elevate" our life. Thoreau's "transcendentalism" has a hard materialist edge to it. The desire for individual freedom must be combined with a realistic method for working toward this independence. We cannot simply "will" ourselves free; our desire must be combined with a conviction that freedom is possible and a practical program of action. As we have seen, Thoreau criticizes all philosophy that is merely theoretical and fails to be practical in the sense of being able to guide an actual human life. *Walden* aspires to be a practical philosophy for independence.[69]

The chapter on "Reading" suggests one method for gaining this independence: studying and experiencing classical literature. The *Iliad* is the only book Thoreau keeps on his table at Walden, and it represents for him, more than any other work, the universality of classical wisdom. When we read such a book, we discover the "noblest recorded thoughts of man"[70] and experience a kind of immortality. "In accumulating property for ourselves or our posterity, in founding a family or a state, or acquiring fame even, we are mortal; but in dealing with truth we are immortal, and need fear no change nor accident."[71] Upon a pile of great books "we may hope to scale heaven at last."[72] Classical learning is an effective teacher of independence because it provides us with examples of individuals who solved their moral problems, achieved and maintained their own independence and moral integrity, in ways that are beyond the vision of our common imagination and conversation. "We should be as good as the worthies of antiquity, but partly by first knowing how good they were."[73] The classics provide us with examples and inspiration and thereby assure us that the conventions of our own society are not the only options imaginable. Our moral independence is encouraged by thus looking beyond our everyday "prejudices."

Thoreau is so committed to the moral power of classical learning that he suggests that local communities take an active and vigorous role in encouraging all higher culture: "In this country, the village should in some respects take the place of the noblemen of Europe. It should be the patron of the fine arts."[74] With the proper commitment, villages could become "universities, and their elder inhabitants the fellows of universities, with leisure—if they are indeed so well off—to pursue liberal studies the rest of their lives."[75] Thoreau believes such a program is well within the means of any prosperous New England town, and would represent a commitment to the moral, and not merely economic, development of the community. As we saw in chapter 4, he appeals to our sense of collective responsibility to provide for these "uncommon schools," to "throw one arch at least over the darker gulf of ignorance which surrounds us."[76] For Thoreau, it is a legitimate function of democratic government, as the ensurer of liberty, to provide public authority and resources in the service of classical learning, since this learning opens the door to uncommon thoughts and moral independence.

Yet, for all his enthusiasm about "reading" and classical learning, Thoreau has a clear understanding of its limitations as a universal tool for his readership. Thoreau argues, for example, that we need a knowledge of ancient languages in order to understand the history of the world.[77] It is obvious that this knowledge will always be confined to the scholarly and intellectual elite. Thoreau does not pretend that all citizens will become classical scholars in some future democratic society. Thoreau calls the woodchopper, Theron, a "Homeric" man, and he respects his independence and character tremendously, but he never expects him to be able to read Homer in the original Greek.[78] Such an expectation would be nothing more than academic snobbery. The classics provide one road to freedom, but it is a road that is unavailable to the democratic citizenry as a whole. Democratic society must provide a haven for classical learning but never be fooled into believing that such learning is a necessary precondition for, the only road to, the moral independence required by a democratic citizen.

It is significant that immediately following "Reading" and all this highfalutin talk about the classics, Thoreau comments that on his first summer at Walden he did not read at all. Instead he hoed beans.[79] As was pointed out in chapter 3, the bean field, like the wild apple, represents for Thoreau the unity of nature and civilization, "the connecting link between wild and cultivated fields; as some states are civilized, and others half-civilized, and others savage or barbarous, so my field was, though not in a bad sense, a half-cultivated field."[80] Thoreau brought his copy of the *Iliad* to his cabin, but he did not move to Walden to read the classics. He came, instead, to experience nature, to submerge himself in the natural world so that his own highly civilized personality could become wilder, less cultivated, more like his bean field than the fields of the surrounding farms.

Thoreau's second and more democratic method for cultivating independence is represented by this experience of nature, the nature symbolized by Walden itself. In nature we find a medicine for our ails, the "pill" that cures the symptoms of our unhappy political economy.

> What is the pill which will keep us well, serene, contented? Not my or thy great-grandfather's, but our great-grandmother Nature's universal, vegetable, botanic medicines, by which she has kept herself young always, outlived so many old Parrs in her day, and fed her health with their decaying fatness. For my panacea, instead of one of those quack vials of a mixture dipped from Acheron and the Dead Sea, which come out of those long shallow black-schooner looking wagons which we sometimes see made to carry bottles, let me have a draught of undiluted morning air.[81]

While Thoreau feels obliged to mention that his beloved classics are a source of moral strength, inspiration, and independence, it is nature that is the heart of *Walden,* and potentially conveys all these virtues to all members of a democratic society. "The setting sun is reflected from the windows of the alms-house as brightly as from the rich man's abode; the snow melts before its door as early in the spring."[82] Nature speaks in a powerful and egalitarian voice, and the primary aim of *Walden* is to teach us to hear it.

And what is it that nature says if we listen? First, it teaches "solitude," a sense of being alone yet secure. "I have, as it were, my own sun and moon and stars, and a little world all to myself." Being in nature gives us distance from society and allows us to construct a sense of ourselves independent from others. Nature tells us to "do without the society of our gossips a little," in order to establish a stronger sense of our own personality.[83] Society can become "wearisome and dissipating" if we have no sense of ourselves except in relationship with others; we become "dissipated," scattered, spread too thin to recognize and develop our unique identity, overly susceptible to prejudice and the tyranny of public opinion. Nature does not provide for Thoreau an isolation from society but rather a distance, a buffer between ourselves and the intrusions of society. There are visitors aplenty at Walden, whom Thoreau welcomes and enjoys, and Thoreau tells us that he frequently travels to the village. He even welcomes the gossip in town as long as he does not get too much of it at once: "Taken in homoeopathic doses, [gossip] was really as refreshing in its way as the rustle of leaves and the peeping of frogs."[84] But without the experience of privacy and solitude that nature provides, society threatens to overwhelm us. In this sense nature "disorients" us, and Thoreau speaks in favor of being "lost" in nature as a method of providing a critical perspective on our own views and commitments. "Not till we are lost, in other words, not till we have lost the world, do we begin to find ourselves, and realize where we are and the infinite extent of our relations."[85] Like the classics, nature provides the distance from society that our independence requires, but unlike the classics, this experience is potentially and realistically available to all.

Nature also teaches an appropriate understanding of human potential and human limitations. Contemporary society is in a paradoxical situation. On the one hand, we are committed to an unlimited transformation of the material and natural world for the sake of "obtaining gross necessaries and comforts merely."[86] On the other, even while we see no limitations on our economic development, we have very little hope in the possibility of moral improvement: "But man's capacities have never been measured; nor are we to judge of what he can do by any precedents, so little has been tried."[87] We believe in a never-ending material progress at the same time that we are complete moral fatalists. For Thoreau, these commitments are perversely reversed from their proper order. Instead of using nature as a resource for living a fully human life, we turn our talents and concerns and energy toward the mastery and domination of nature, even at the risk of pillaging it beyond recognition.[88] Rather than use our talents to develop our moral characters, we assume there is little that can be done in this sphere.

The experience of nature, Thoreau believes, provides an antidote to both these problems.[89] Nature clearly demonstrates its overwhelming power and mystery, as if to put to rest our hubristic attempt to replace nature with our own clever technologies and industry. Nature provides the context in which we "witness our own limits transgressed, and some life pasturing freely where we never wander."[90] In nature, life is reduced to simple and essential elements, allowing us to live "near the bone where it is sweetest."[91] We learn, that is, to simplify our economic life, to abandon the ultimately self-defeating and impossible project of beating nature into submission. Yet, at the same time that nature humbles us, it can also inspire us. It teaches a beauty that transcends fads and conventions.[92] More importantly, it provides symbols to stimulate our minds and imaginations, within which we see the cycles, needs, hopes, potentials, and truths of our own lives. "I am thankful that this pond was made deep and pure for a symbol."[93] Nature can cut through our common sense, which Thoreau calls "the sense of men asleep, which they express by snoring."[94] In the metaphor of wakefulness that informs the entire book,[95] nature awakens us as from sleep or even death, sweeps away our lazy and confining habits of thought and belief, and provides our lives with fresh possibilities. Seen properly, the earth is, like us, alive.[96] Understanding this, we can find in nature our own cycles of moral renewal, such as when Thoreau writes of the spring thaw that "Walden was dead and is alive again,"[97] or that we, like the banks of the deep cut along the railroad, are "but a mass of thawing clay."[98] Nature renews our faith in the possibility of a more perfect world. It is a source of moral inspiration and faith, even while it counsels a greater acceptance of material necessity. The experience of nature can help us reverse the order of our current priorities regarding the material and the moral worlds.

Nature has a third important lesson for us. Thoreau writes, "In a pleasant spring morning all men's sins are forgiven. . . . Through our own recovered innocence we discern the innocence of our neighbors."[99] We may recover our own innocence in nature, but we also discover that this is something we share with others. Nature teaches a certain moral equality, or equal moral potential, among all men and women. "The impression made on a wise man is that of universal innocence."[100] At the same time that nature helps us to break with the traditions of our society, it helps to build deeper, more authentic connections with others, relationships based upon natural equality rather than social convention.[101]

We can see in all these lessons that the role of nature in *Walden* is essentially political: it is the means by which Thoreau proposes to break the chain of conventional wisdom that prevents us, in his view, from seriously doubting the necessity or the desirability of the status quo, or imagining an alternative. It is a tool for social criticism but a tool with a difference: it is universally available and must be reckoned as a necessary resource for all citizens of a democratic society. "Our village life would stagnate if it were not for the unexplored forests and meadows which surround it. We need the tonic of wildness."[102] The benefits of nature are obviously personal and private. But they are importantly public as well. A contemporary reviewer of *Walden*, in the *Churchman* magazine, was deeply offended by Thoreau's attack on the contemporary political economy:

> Mr. Thoreau is . . . at war with the political economy of the age. It is his doctrine that the fewer wants man has the better; while in reality civilization is the spur of many wants. To give a man a new want is to give him a new pleasure and conquer his habitual rust and idleness. The greater his needs and acquisitions, the greater his safety; since he may fall back from one advance post to another, as he is pressed by misfortune, and still keep the main citadel untouched.[103]

Thoreau is, indeed, at war with the political economy of the age, and his weapon in *Walden* is nature. Only with the aid of such a weapon will democratic citizens be able to maintain their moral and material independence against a political economy that endeavors to seduce them, as the *Churchman* reviewer so frankly admits, with the increasing, artificial, and never-ending desire for wealth.[104] Only with the aid of such a weapon will democratic citizens be able to cultivate an economy as a means to freedom instead of as an end in itself. Only then will citizens cultivate the independence required by their democratic responsibilities.

In addition to classical literature and nature, Thoreau offers in *Walden* one other general resource for helping us to "give up our prejudices," and this is the example of his own experience. As we have seen, this lesson is presented in the spirit of equality, since Thoreau believes his own discoveries are relevant to all in his audience and are not fruits of a rare genius or virtue beyond the reach of democratic citizens. *Walden* is never offered as a blueprint for others to follow; Thoreau is explicit in stating that each individual must invent the particulars of his or her own independence.[105] Nonetheless, the general principles and spirit of his experiment, Thoreau believes, can provide a guide and example for all who are interested in establishing and protecting their individual freedom. The intensity with which Thoreau seeks his independence may be unique, but he never claims that the search itself is beyond the grasp of others. As stated at the outset, Thoreau presents his example as that of a "representative man," relevant to all members of his political community.

The most famous elements of this lesson concern voluntary poverty and simplicity of lifestyle: "A man is rich in proportion to the number of things which he can afford to let alone";[106] "Give me the poverty that enjoys true wealth";[107] "Simplicity simplicity, simplicity! I say, let your affairs be as two or three, and not a hundred or a thousand."[108] Nature teaches a certain austerity, and Thoreau's own experience confirms the pleasures and rewards of such a life. Likewise, Thoreau attests to the usefulness of the other lessons of nature, such as those concerning humility, solitude,[109] and the cultivation of a present orientedness and spontaneity.[110] While all these truths are suggested to Thoreau through his interaction with nature, he, in turn, can provide through his own experience a direct access to them for the reader. In these cases his own example not only confirms the lessons of nature; it provides an alternative source from which the reader may learn.

There are, however, other less commonly recognized but equally important lessons to be gained from Thoreau's example. The first of these is found in the fact that Thoreau borrows an ax in order to begin work on his cabin. He comments that it is hard to begin an enterprise such as his move to Walden without borrowing from others, but that this should not worry us. It might, in fact, be the most "generous course" to follow, since it gives others an interest in our business.[111] Rather than hide the ways in which he depends on others while seeking his own independence, Thoreau draws them to our attention and praises the human relationships that serve as a springboard from which we launch our quest for independence. Thoreau borrows an ax, is given seed corn,[112] and frames his house with others less because he could not do the work alone than because it represents an opportunity to enjoy neighborly community: "No man was ever more honored in the character of his raisers than I."[113] The aid of others is partly responsible for his ability to declare his own independence by moving to the pond on the Fourth of July.[114] It is both impossible and undesirable to achieve our freedom alone, isolated from the help and goodwill of others. Thoreau's "individualism" is far from "rugged." Thoreau reminds us of our debts and dependencies, and assures us that these are not only necessary but positive goods. Freedom must never be confused with an absolute detachment or self-sufficiency.[115]

In light of this message, we might be confused by Thoreau's comment that he prefers a solitary dwelling to a communal one, and that "the man who goes alone can start today; but he who travels with another must wait till that other is ready, and it may be a long time before they get off."[116] These present no real problem for his argument, however, since Thoreau does not hold that we should pursue our life's tasks with others. Instead he argues that we should recognize and gratefully accept the aid given by others (and, by extension, we must in turn offer such aid) at crucial times. In addition, Thoreau implies in this passage that the reason cooperation, *"to get our living together,"* is so difficult is because we have not yet agreed about the nature of the desirable life.[117] In a society with a stronger shared moral commitment, a less solitary life than that promoted in *Walden* would be more practical and desirable. Be this as it may, we have already noted that Thoreau draws a significant distinction between a solitary and an isolated or hermitlike life. His focus in *Walden* is on establishing the conditions for an independent integrity rather than on the details of a future community that might emerge from a truly independent citizenry. It is clear that Thoreau has faith in the possibility of such a community. Remember that he advises us to sell our clothes and keep our thoughts, assuring us that, if we do, God will see that we "do not want society."[118] For now, however, the problem is to establish our freedom. Thoreau has not declared that freedom abolishes political community. All he has done is focused his attention and concern on what he takes to be a more immediate problem— encouraging the development of a morally free citizenry.[119]

More troublesome, perhaps, is Thoreau's claim that the good he does for others must be "for the most part wholly unintended."[120] This seems to allow Thoreau to live completely unconcerned with the lives of others, contrary to the spirit of neighborliness illustrated by his house-raising and the spirit of compassion we find in *Cape Cod*. It also appears contrary to Thoreau's criticism, mentioned earlier, of production aimed at profit rather than at creating functional and economical products. In the case of "philanthropy" he seems to accept the desirable but unintended consequences of self-interested behavior, although he rejects such an argument in the economic realm. As disturbing as these issues may be, however, they ignore the primary rhetorical purposes of the passage on philanthropy, which, like similar passages in *Cape Cod*, is intended to expose the cruelty of philanthropy as it is practiced in our society. Most charity is nothing more than an opportunity for the charitable to congratulate themselves at the expense of those receiving their attention.[121] Thoreau's point is not that we are free from obligations to others. Instead, it is that our current practices degrade the recipients of charity, robbing them of their independence and self-respect. Thoreau's overall advice is this: "Rescue the drowning man and tie your shoe-strings. Take your time, and set about some free labor."[122] Thoreau's interest is in how best to serve others, not to prove that we should ignore or deny the need to serve. His contention is that, outside of emergencies, we need above all a strong and independent sense of ourselves before we can be of great use to others. Thoreau's own experiment in independence at Walden is clearly an act aiming not only at his own good but at the benefit of his entire political community.[123] His views on charity do not indicate, any more than those comments on cooperative living, that Thoreau has changed his mind about the necessary and desirable communal elements of our quest for independence.[124]

The second major lesson from Thoreau's Walden experience is found in the chapter on "Higher Laws." Here Thoreau presents himself as a microcosm of a more general human development, from the "savage" to the "civilized." The chapter begins with the famous description of returning to his cabin late at night, catching a glimpse of a woodchuck, and feeling a "strange thrill of savage delight" that "strongly tempted" him to "seize and devour" the animal raw. This was not the only time such a thing happened to him. "Once or twice . . . while I lived at the pond, I found myself ranging the woods, like a half-starved hound, with a strange abandonment, seeking some kind of venison which I might devour, and no morsel could have been too savage for me."[125] Thoreau initially implies that these animal instincts represent one side of his personality, and that he values this element as much as he does the moral or spiritual component. "I found in myself, and still find, an instinct toward a higher, or, as it is named, spiritual life, as do most men, and another toward a primitive rank and savage one, and I reverence them both. I love the wild not less than the good."[126] This is a startling comment, since it suggests that wild nature stands in contrast with, rather than inclines toward, the moral world. Here Thoreau appears to be celebrating a complex moral dualism, suggesting that we best simply learn to live with both impulses regardless of how opposed or incompatible they may be.

As the chapter develops, however, the message changes significantly. Instead of presenting a human life torn in different directions, Thoreau now presents a story of human development, education, and progress. While it is true that even in civilization children savagely hunt and kill, "No humane being, past the thoughtless age of boyhood, will wantonly murder any creature, which holds its life by the same tenure that he does. The hare in its extremity cries like a child. I warn you, mothers, that my sympathies do not always make the usual phil-*anthropic* distinctions."[127] Thoreau's new contention is that his own moral development has been away from the "savageness" of his boyhood and toward a life that increasingly aspires to transcend all natural impulses and sensualism: "Is it not a reproach that man is a carnivorous animal?" "I believe that water is the only drink for a wise man." "The wonder is how they, how you and I, can live this slimy beastly life, eating and drinking."[128] Now our animal desires are portrayed as impurities to be expelled, impediments to a desirable life. "We are conscious of an animal in us, which awakens in proportion as our higher nature slumbers. It is reptile and sensual, and perhaps cannot be wholly expelled; like the worms which, even in life and health, occupy our bodies."[129] The "wild" that is celebrated at the beginning of the chapter is now a seed of sin, death, and decay. The conclusion is that "Nature is hard to be overcome, but she must be overcome. What avails it that you are a Christian, if you are not purer than the heathen, if you deny yourself no more, if you are not more religious?"[130]

It is true that nature is Thoreau's tool for distancing himself from the conventional world and thus gaining a needed moral independence. It is also true that nature presents its own dangers and seductions. Thoreau retreats to nature, only to find himself in danger of losing his moral life, of falling into an overwhelming animal sensualism. Thoreau's experience at Walden indicates that no matter how important the natural world is for us, and no matter how much we learn from it, we must never allow our love of nature to become an end in itself. We go to nature to shore up our moral independence, and we must be vigilant in pursuing this project. If we forget our moral purposes, nature may overwhelm us and erase our moral character altogether. "He is blessed who is assured that the animal is dying out in him day by day, and the divine being established."[131] For Thoreau, the higher laws require that we transcend the world of physical nature. As Robert Richardson writes, "In the end, *Walden* is not about submission to nature. . . . Nature teaches us to want to reach beyond nature."[132] Independence is not found by dissolving into the natural landscape but rather by respecting, enjoying, learning from, and finally rising above nature.

The final lesson from Thoreau's experience is simply that it was a success. *Walden* is a book about finding a career, a vocation, a calling and purpose in life that does not destroy our independence. The conventional options presented by society often appear confining and stifling, and Thoreau encourages us to avoid these preestablished paths: "I am not aware that any man has ever built on the spot which I occupy. Deliver me from a city built on the site of a more ancient city, whose materials are ruins, whose gardens cemeteries."[133] Building our lives on such a spot is frightening; having no strong and established precedent, it is necessarily a venture into the unknown. However, Thoreau's example gives reason to be optimistic. "I learned this, at least, by my experiment; that if one advances confidently in the direction of his dreams, and endeavors to live the life which he has imagined, he will meet with a success unexpected in common hours."[134] If Thoreau's experiment was a success, there is good reason for all of us to take courage in our own attempts to establish our lives on independent ground.

The economic man of Thoreau's generation is not only wrong in seeking his independence in the manner he does; he also has many reasons to believe in the possibility of a truer independence, and a wealth of resources for cultivating independence are at his disposal. America is indeed a land of opportunity for those who know how to seek it.

THOREAU'S VISION of a new and desirable America is not simply that we should return to the preindustrial agrarian production of independent yeomen farmers, although he has much to say in favor of such an economy.[135] Thoreau actually admires the energy, drive, ingenuity, and industry of the Yankee farmer, and he does not wish to replace these virtues with an economic fatalism or quietude. Thoreau even speaks well of the "enterprise and bravery" of commerce, how it is "unexpectedly confident and serene, alert, adventurous, and unwearied." The railroad itself has the virtue of making the world a smaller place, of making Thoreau a "citizen of the world."[136] The problem with the current economy is that it is out of control, is no longer the servant of our needs but instead the master that drives us. "With a little more wit we might use these materials so as to become richer than the richest now are, and make our civilization a blessing."[137] This will not happen, however, until we understand that freedom and wealth are different values, and focus our energy and industry on the cultivation of the former. Ambition, alone, is not a vice for Thoreau; what could possibly be more ambitious than Thoreau's own experiment at Walden?[138] Ambition focused on the wrong object is the source of our confusion. Thoreau's vision of a new America is anticapitalist but profoundly Yankee.[139]

Most of the elements of this America are clear from what has already been said about Thoreau's analysis of the nature of our problems and the ways in which we might begin to "give up our prejudices," thus enabling a meaningful reform: a new America would be economically simpler but morally industrious;[140] it would copy the wild apple and Thoreau's bean field, combining the "wisdom" of civilization with the "hardiness" and independence of nature;[141] finally, it would link personal independence with justice and political community.[142]

In a remarkable passage from the chapter "House-Warming," Thoreau contrasts his tiny cabin with an ideal house he has imagined: "I sometimes dream of a larger and more populous house, standing in a golden age, of enduring materials, and without ginger-bread work, which shall still consist of only one room, a vast, rude, substantial, primitive hall, without ceiling or plastering, with bare rafters and purlins supporting a sort of lower heaven over one's head." The description continues for a page or so. It is a huge house, allowing some to live "in the fire-place," some "in the recess of a window," some "on the settles," and some "at one end of the hall" or the other, some even "aloft on rafters with the spiders, if they choose." The traveler is always welcome, everything is open and visible, and nothing is hidden. The inhabitants share equally in everything, and the guests are excluded from nothing. Their house is as "open and manifest as a bird's nest," and this allows for an equally open and manifest communion among those who live there.[143] This house, of course, is just a "dream" of a "golden age." But the dream does suggest the hopes that Thoreau has for free and independent men and women. The project of *Walden* is to take the first step, a step well prior to the actual construction of such a house but without which such a house is nothing more than an unrealizable fantasy.[144] Until we are no longer confused about the nature and sources of our independence, our political community will be incomplete, inhibited, and corrupt.

CHAPTER 6

Resistance

I wish my neighbors were wilder.
—Thoreau, *Journal*

THOREAU'S WRITINGS fall into two distinct but related political projects. The vast bulk of his literary output is best thought of as relating to his chosen vocation as a social critic, as America's "bachelor uncle," who uses his pen in an effort to awaken his fellow citizens to possibilities greater and more morally satisfying than the infinite expansion of their commercial and industrial wealth. This is the Thoreau who explores the foundations of our political community, some of the ideal-typical Americans we find in this community, and the dangers these characters present as well as the potentials they inspire. This is the Thoreau who constantly evaluates not only our private but our collective moral options, and insists that we honestly face the relationship between the nature of our moral commitments and the type of individuals and society we are becoming.

There is another set of political writings that are more topical and polemical, focusing mainly on the crime of slavery. Although much more commonly read and discussed by those interested in Thoreau's political views, these texts are quite short and few in number: most significantly, they include "Civil Disobedience," "Slavery in Massachusetts," and "A Plea for Captain John Brown." Angry and powerful, these essays were born of the force of three specific events: Thoreau's arrest for nonpayment of taxes, the Anthony Burns affair, and John Brown's attack on Harpers Ferry.

The relationship between these two sets of political writings is complex.

99

On the one hand, the polemical political writings constitute a natural completion of the more general political writings that make up the bulk of Thoreau's work. If Thoreau's overall political intention culminates in *Walden* with the attempt to teach a particular understanding of the promise of American freedom, "Civil Disobedience," "Slavery in Massachusetts," and "A Plea for Captain John Brown" are exhortations concerning the obligations of free individuals confronting significant injustice. Political resistance, as Thoreau says in "Civil Disobedience," is the necessary fate for independent individuals facing political evil: "A very few, as heroes, patriots, martyrs, reformers in the great sense, and men, serve the State with their consciences also, and so necessarily resist it for the most part; and they are commonly treated by it as enemies."[1] These three essays can be thought of as specific applications of Thoreau's more general social criticism, the employment of the principles he prods and probes and promotes in his other writings, to particular political events. Given the real character of the political world, free and independent individuals necessarily find themselves resisting the state from time to time and in various ways. Developing our independence will necessarily make us "bad subjects," as Thoreau hopes he is himself.[2]

On the other hand, these polemical essays all express a noticeable impatience, an irritation about the intrusion of these political events into Thoreau's routine and concerns. In "Civil Disobedience" Thoreau concludes his criticisms of the American government by claiming that "the government does not concern me much, and I shall bestow the fewest possible thoughts on it. It is not many moments that I live under a government, even in this world."[3] In "Slavery in Massachusetts" he complains, "The remembrance of my country spoils my walk,"[4] and in "A Plea for Captain John Brown" Thoreau almost defensively explains why he has not lived the life represented by Brown: "At any rate, I do not think it is quite sane for one to spend his whole life in talking or writing about this matter, unless he is continuously inspired, and I have not done so. A man may have other affairs to attend to."[5] Thoreau is not expressing a desire to withdraw from social criticism and public concern. Instead, he is angry about being distracted from the broader social criticism he sees as his life's work. In this sense, these essays are less important for those who want to understand Thoreau's overriding political project than they first appear. They are applications, yes, calls to resistance, but they are also interruptions. We saw in chapter 5 that in *Walden* Thoreau tells us to "rescue the drowning man and tie your shoe-strings. Take your time, and set about some free labor."[6] In these essays Thoreau is doing his part, as he understands it, to respond to a political emergency and help "rescue the drowning." These few essays do not, however, represent the "free labor" Thoreau aspires to. They are too limited in scope and purpose to achieve that end.

When we read these texts it is important to keep these complexities in mind. "A Plea for Captain John Brown" grows naturally from the arguments of "Civil Disobedience" and "Slavery in Massachusetts," just as the positions taken in all three essays are consistent with the social criticism found in the rest of Thoreau's writings. In this sense John Brown represents a fifth American type, an individual who achieves the level of independence needed to nurture an active resistance to political evil. Such resistance is not commonly found among our citizenry, but Thoreau believes it is demanded by the facts of our political life. Regardless of how true this claim is, or how well Thoreau supports it, we should not expect to find in these essays the keys to understanding Thoreau's greater political project and vision. Rather, the reverse is much closer to the truth: it is the context of the broader political project found in his major works—*A Week, The Maine Woods, Cape Cod,* and *Walden*—that gives these essays their full meaning.

THE POWER of these three essays is rhetorical, not philosophical, and this is, from Thoreau's perspective, as it must be.[7] The issue at stake in each case is slavery, and Thoreau rightly refuses to recognize any claim that there is a moral debate to be had on this issue. From any perspective that is even remotely respectful of the American commitment to human liberty, slavery is nothing short of an abomination. By being a slave society, we have distorted the moral character of our nation so dramatically as to make the professed principles of our founding almost irrelevant to contemporary political practices. Thoreau writes in "Slavery in Massachusetts": "They who have been bred in the school of politics fail now and always to face the facts. Their measures are half measures and make-shifts, merely. They put off the day of settlement indefinitely, and meanwhile, the debt accumulates."[8] This debt is the strain put upon the justice of our political community, and any attempt to compromise between the competing claims of slavery and liberty is itself a fundamental threat to the life of any respectable America.

Slavery, in short, is a morally easy, if politically difficult, issue: there is nothing whatsoever to be said in its favor. It is the most obvious of crimes, and simply must end if the nation is to have an opportunity to live up to the standards it claims for itself. "This people must cease to hold slaves, and to make war on Mexico, though it cost them their existence as a people."[9] Men and women of good will may honestly believe that a market economy will lead to a flourishing of the American dream of individual freedom, and this is why Thoreau devotes so much of his career to convincing them they are mistaken. In contrast, only morally corrupted or cynical people, people whose moral sensibilities have become seriously stunted or distorted, can even begin to entertain a claim about the moral acceptability of slavery. To deal with such individuals, it is not useful to provide a calm example or a detailed argument. Rather, the only chance of influencing them is to shock them out of their moral lethargy through strong, even exaggerated, political rhetoric. And it is precisely this type of rhetoric these essays provide.

Consider "Civil Disobedience." Thoreau opens the essay, in effect, by flattering his audience. He famously begins by accepting the motto "That government is best which governs least," then quickly taking the point one step further, saying, "That government is best which governs not at all."[10] The passage builds to a swift climax in the second paragraph, where Thoreau suggests it is his fellow citizens, independent from any political institutions, who represent the real vigor and virtue of American society: "This government never of itself furthered any enterprise, but by the alacrity with which it got out of its way. *It* does not keep the country free. *It* does not settle the West. *It* does not educate. The character inherent in the American people has done all that has been accomplished; and it would have done somewhat more, if the government had not sometimes got in its way."[11] Thoreau here appears to hold a classic anarchist view, condemning all political organization and praising civil society. Governments are bad, but the people are good. Ideally we would dissolve our political institutions, and American society could then go about its business unfettered.

Given these first two paragraphs, it is startling to read the third, which disclaims the anarchist conclusion seemingly implied by Thoreau's comments thus far: "But, to speak practically and as a citizen, unlike those who call themselves no-government men, I ask for, not at once no government, but *at once* a better government."[12] Thoreau obviously understands the distinction between the anarchist and the citizen, one who rejects government altogether and one who desires a just government, and he unambiguously embraces the role of the citizen.[13] He even implies that the alternative is impractical, a politically ineffectual self-indulgence.

Why is it that Thoreau begins the essay as he does, drawing so much distance between government and civil society, between politics and individual life, only to back away from what appears to be the logical conclusion of his views? We know, because he tells us, that it is not in order to promote anarchism. Instead, this opening serves two rhetorical purposes. First, as the essay develops, Thoreau insists upon the moral independence of American citizens. In order to make this point effectively, he must disentangle the moral responsibilities of government and citizens. By distinguishing between the sphere of government and the sphere of free individual action as radically as he does at the outset, he strengthens the position from which he will make claims about the moral resources available to citizens for resisting unjust government. Thoreau is challenging all of us to assert our moral independence, as when he writes: "For my own part, I should not like to think that I ever rely on the protection of the State. You must live within yourself, and depend upon yourself."[14] Second, by flattering his audience in the opening paragraphs, he sets them up for criticism in what follows. If they are so virtuous and free, why are they so craven before the current government? The flattery supplies the standards by which Thoreau will measure and criticize the American citizenry. It is a rhetorical weapon used to seduce the audience into accepting the standards Thoreau will then wield against it.

And this is just what happens. Thoreau immediately suggests that the reason the government is able to pursue unjust and immoral policies is because the citizenry has failed to live up to its moral responsibilities. "Must the citizen ever for a moment, or in the least degree, resign his conscience to the legislator? Why has every man a conscience, then? I think that we should be men first, and subjects afterward. It is not desirable to cultivate a respect for the law, so much as for the right."[15] To the degree that we behave as subjects, rather than citizens, we are degraded and robbed not only of our independence but of our very humanity. "The mass of men serve the State thus, not as men mainly, but as machines, with their bodies. . . . Such command no more respect than men of straw, or a lump of dirt. They have the same sort of worth only as horses and dogs."[16] Thoreau's insults are scathing, merciless, and obviously designed to provoke. "Oh for a man who is a *man,* and, as my neighbor says, has a bone in his back which you cannot pass your hand through!"[17] We fancy ourselves brave and free but behave like cowards and slaves.

The first task of Thoreau's political rhetoric in "Civil Disobedience," then, is to assert the freedom of the American citizen and our failure to exercise and even recognize this freedom in practice. The second task is simply to demand that we squarely face the true character of the government and the institutions it protects. Even if we are uncertain about the justice of our institutions, it is terribly difficult to develop the moral confidence required to defy the status quo, since the status quo always carries with it a presumption of legitimacy and respectability. It is just this moral self-confidence that Thoreau attempts to encourage when he claims, for example, that "when a sixth of the population of a nation which has undertaken to be the refuge of liberty are slaves, and a whole country is unjustly overrun and conquered by a foreign army, and subjected to military law, I think that it is not too soon for honest men to rebel and revolutionize."[18] Thoreau's intention here is to provide us with a necessary slap in the face, the strong language that will bring us to our senses and make us wake up to the reality of the political evil our government is promoting. This is not only a matter of persuading us that slavery and imperialism are wrong. It is a matter of insisting that we are the slaveholders and the imperialists. When we do nothing, or assume it is our civic duty to respect the laws that produce these horrors, we forfeit our moral integrity. "Those who, while they disapprove of the character and measures of a government, yield to it their allegiance and support, are undoubtedly its most conscientious supporters, and so frequently the most serious obstacles to reform."[19] When we are honest about the nature of slavery and imperialism, and honest about our obligations as free and independent citizens, we will necessarily resist these institutions and view the government as illegitimate to the degree that it is associated with them. Thoreau is calling us to our civic responsibilities, which in this case requires political resistance to injustice, in the name of the independence we claim to hold dear.

Thoreau's tone at the end of the essay is much more conciliatory toward his audience, almost flattering as it was at the outset. Again he expresses faith in the potential of a free American citizenry and encourages us to have faith in our independence. We citizens must trust our own moral judgments and assert our rightful control over the political leadership. "If we were left solely to the wordy wit of legislators in Congress for our guidance, uncorrected by the seasonable experience and the effectual complaints of the people, America would not long retain her rank among the nations."[20] The rhetorical strategy is complete, opening with praise for our accomplishments, then vigorously scolding us for our failures, and finally assuring us of our ability to regain our integrity. In this capacity he reminds us that "to be strictly just," government "must have the sanction and consent of the governed."[21] The free individual is obliged to exercise that consent, to unceasingly insist that the actions of government conform to the moral standards we agree to.

One final point is important to recognize about Thoreau's approach in "Civil Disobedience." We must remember that Thoreau desires to speak "practically and as a citizen." The resistance he is promoting, and the moral authority he challenges us to assert, is demanded by the existence of unjust laws, radical political evils.[22] Thoreau is by no means advocating a cantankerous flouting of our independence in the face of all political authority. "I do not wish to quarrel with any man or nation. I do not wish to split hairs, to make fine distinctions, or set myself up as better than my neighbors. I seek rather, I may say, even an excuse for conforming to the laws of the land. I am but too ready to conform to them."[23] The problem facing the nation is not that Americans are resistent to governance, too independent to build a functional political community. In fact, the problem is exactly the opposite. The American citizenry has proven itself remarkably compliant and complacent, too governable by far. Jane Bennett observes that "Thoreau was less concerned to articulate the conditions under which disobedience would be legitimate than he was to explore those under which men could render themselves capable of disobedience."[24] His intention is to spark some meaningful political resistance to slavery and the war with Mexico. It is not to make an abstract philosophical argument about the nature of citizenship in general. Thoreau believes America is facing a crisis, partly because of the moral timidness and uncertainty of the citizenry, and it is this immediate problem that receives his attention in this essay.

"Slavery in Massachusetts," Thoreau's most powerful political essay, follows a rhetorical strategy similar to that found in "Civil Disobedience." Thoreau's intention is to force his audience to recognize two significant facts: the servility of the Massachusetts citizenry, and the full character of the evil being promoted by the state. To understand the extent of the latter, Thoreau reminds his readers that by returning Anthony Burns to bondage, the government of Massachusetts becomes directly responsible for promoting slavery. "The whole military force of the State is at the service of a Mr. Suttle, a slaveholder from Virginia, to enable him to catch a man whom he calls his property; but not a soldier is offered to save a citizen of Massachusetts from being kidnapped!"[25] American citizens do not appear to fully grasp the magnitude of the evil of slavery.

Much has been said about American slavery, but I think that we do not even yet realize what slavery is. If I were seriously to propose to Congress to make mankind into sausages, I have no doubt that most of the members would smile at my proposition, and if any believed me to be in earnest, they would think that I proposed something much worse than Congress had ever done. But if any of them will tell me that to make a man into a sausage would be much worse,—would be any worse, than to make him into a slave,—than it was to enact the Fugitive Slave Law, I will accuse him of foolishness, of intellectual incapacity, of making a distinction without a difference. The one is just as sensible a proposition as the other.[26]

Thoreau's satire reflects the frustration he experiences when we discuss the laws and public policy of slavery in the same manner that we discuss any other public business. By reducing slavery to a mundane political issue, we blind ourselves to the moral outrage being committed. In effect, we become incapable of distinguishing political atrocities from the acceptable give-and-take of public life.

The reason for this moral blindness, Thoreau suggests, is that we are much too willing to delegate our moral responsibilities to our political representatives. It is inconceivable to Thoreau that we should allow Burns's fate to be placed in the hands of a Massachusetts judiciary that has proven itself (as in the Simms case three years earlier) more concerned with upholding the Fugitive Slave Law than with the justice of the matter. "Does anyone think that Justice or God awaits Mr. Loring's [the judge's] decision? For him to sit there deciding still, when this question is already decided from eternity to eternity, and the unlettered slave himself, and the multitude around, have long since heard and assented to the decision, is simply to make himself ridiculous."[27] Only by suspending our habitual inclination to think of the state as legitimate and our political leadership as virtuous will the full character of the Fugitive Slave Law become clear. "It was born and bred, and has its life only in the dust and mire, on a level with the feet, and he who walks with freedom, and does not with Hindoo mercy avoid treading on every venomous reptile, will inevitably tread on it, and so trample it under foot,—and Webster, its maker, with it, like the dirt-bug and its ball."[28] In one of the most powerful sentences in all of his writings, Thoreau says, "If there is any hell more unprincipled than our rulers, and we, the ruled, I feel curious to see it."[29]

Thoreau holds very little hope that the government can, of itself, come to its moral senses. "The law will never make men free; it is men who have got to make the law free."[30] The citizens alone can force the government and its laws to conform to the dictates of principle. Thoreau holds out the most hope for the character of rural America, which is less corrupted by the political sophistication of the urban centers. "When, in some obscure country town, the farmers come together to a special town meeting, to express their opinion on some subject which is vexing the land, that, I think, is the true Congress, and the most respectable one that is ever assembled in the United States."[31] But this comment is more a call for Americans to assert their independence from corrupt political institutions than a claim about the political health of democracy in the American hinterland. In fact, all Americans appear much too willing to assume the perspective of the government at the expense of our moral sensibilities. "We are not a religious people, but we are a nation of politicians."[32] Again, "The majority of the men of the North, and of the South, and East, and West, are not men of principle."[33] Over and over, Thoreau's demand is that we assume, above all else, the responsibility for making our own moral judgments according to principles that are independent of narrow political calculation. "I would remind my countrymen, that they are to be men first, and Americans only at a late and convenient hour."[34] As in "Civil Disobedience," the rhetorical task is to challenge American citizens to exercise the independence of judgment we brag of but so rarely practice.

In "A Plea for Captain John Brown" Thoreau has found his patriot, a man "of rare common sense and directness of speech, as of action; a transcendentalist above all, a man of ideas and principles."[35] Brown is the man of courage and conviction that Thoreau promotes in "Civil Disobedience" and "Slavery in Massachusetts" but had until now been unable to find in the society around him. For Thoreau, Brown becomes the model of the free American, a symbol of our national promise:

> He was a superior man. He did not value his bodily life in comparison with ideal things. He did not recognize unjust human laws, but resisted them as he was bid. For once we are lifted out of the trivialness and dust of politics into the region of truth and manhood. No man in America has ever stood up so persistently and effectively for the dignity of human nature, knowing himself for a man, and the equal of any and all governments. In that sense he was the most American of us all.[36]

Brown is, in fact, more "American," more representative of the possibilities of American liberty, than even the founders of the nation. He fought for a more universal freedom than the revolutionaries, and had the courage to confront his own nation for that freedom's sake. "He was like the best of those who stood at Concord Bridge once, on Lexington Common, and on Bunker Hill, only he was firmer and higher principled than any that I have chanced to hear of as there. . . . They could bravely face their country's foes, but he had the courage to face his country herself, when she was in the wrong."[37] Thoreau writes that Brown is actually "too fair a specimen of a man to represent the like of us,"[38] but this insult is intended to spur us to live up to Brown's standards, not fatalistically accept our moral cowardice. Brown is the greatest American, whose actions constitute "the best news that America has ever heard."[39] John Brown and his men give hope that America has not yet entirely extinguished, through our corrupt institutions and unjust practices, the principles upon which it claims to (and potentially will) be built.

Thoreau's primary target in this essay is those who contend that Brown is insane, foolish, criminal, or desperate. People who make these claims understand neither the enormity of the injustice of slavery nor the power of principled resistance to unjust power. Brown's warfare in Kansas, Thoreau contends, was the primary reason that "Kansas was made free."[40] Even more importantly, at Harpers Ferry Brown and his men taught us "how to die," and thereby "have at the same time taught us how to live."[41] The reason that unjust institutions exist in the United States is not because we have utterly perverse political values or an unredeemably immoral political inheritance from which to draw our civic principles. On the contrary, although the nation's commitment to liberty has been grotesquely distorted by slavery, the ideal continues to inspire.[42] Only when we remember to live according to this ideal, however, will we recognize slavery as the horror and hypocrisy it is. Brown and his followers are examples of free and principled men, and finding inspiration in these examples can give us the courage of our convictions.[43] Their lives and deaths thus represent a necessary first step in the abolition of slavery, and those who claim that Brown threw his life away to no effect simply do not understand the nature or power of moral action.[44] Thoreau's rhetoric reaches quite extraordinary heights in his praise of Brown's character, claiming that he is "superior to nature" and "has a spark of divinity in him."[45] Far from being an insane or criminal or foolish man, Brown is actually Christlike: "Some eighteen hundred years ago Christ was crucified; this morning, perchance, Captain Brown was hung. These are the two ends of a chain which is not without its links. He is not Old Brown any longer; he is an Angel of light."[46]

Like "Civil Disobedience" and "Slavery in Massachusetts," the "Plea for Captain John Brown" tries to convey the degree to which our daily moral evaluations are warped. Those who argue, for example, that opponents of slavery do best to pursue moral suasion and that violent methods like Brown's are unjustified are guilty of misunderstanding the situation.

> The slave-ship is on her way, crowded with its dying victims; new cargoes are being added in mid ocean; a small crew of slaveholders, countenanced by a large body of passengers, is smothering four millions under the hatches, and yet the politician asserts that the only proper way by which deliverance is to be obtained, is by "the quiet diffusion of the sentiments of humanity," without any "outbreak." As if the sentiments of humanity were ever found unaccompanied by its deeds, and you could disperse them, all finished to order, the pure article, as easily as water with a watering-pot, and so lay the dust. What is that that I hear cast overboard? The bodies of the dead that have found deliverance. That is the way we are "diffusing" humanity, and its sentiments with it.[47]

Thoreau refuses to admit any image of slavery other than one that captures its full murderousness. As in his other polemical essays, he is constantly struggling against the tendency of white Americans to think of slavery in more benign terms, as a bad and unpleasant institution, perhaps, but not one that requires a vigorous response. Slavery, however, is not merely unfortunate; it is a case of radical evil with which there can be no principled compromise.[48]

By using its soldiers to suppress the insurrection at Harpers Ferry, the government clarified its own role in protecting and promoting slavery.[49] As affairs now stand in America, citizens must resort to private actions in order to promote America's highest civic values. "The only *free* road, the Underground Railroad, is owned and managed by the Vigilant Committee."[50] When we have come to this, the government has lost its legitimacy, its moral authority. "If private men are obliged to perform the offices of government, to protect the weak and dispense justice, then the government becomes only a hired man, or clerk, to perform menial or indifferent services."[51] When the government is implicated in the crime, it is obvious that citizens must assume the responsibility for establishing justice.

Thoreau makes no inflated claims about the virtues of violence, but he does claim that violence against the slaveholder is a fully justified response to the infinitely greater violence of slavery: "I do not wish to kill nor to be killed, but I can foresee circumstances in which both these things would be by me unavoidable. We preserve the so-called 'peace' of our community by deeds of petty violence every day."[52] It is only in the context of an enormous political evil that violence becomes justified, and the burden of Thoreau's rhetorical case, here and elsewhere, is precisely that slavery constitutes such an evil. Once we are convinced, or reminded, of the brute realities of slavery, resistance, even violent resistance, becomes a fully justified and perhaps even required course of action. "It was his [Brown's] peculiar doctrine that a man has a perfect right to interfere by force with the slaveholder, in order to rescue the slave. I agree with him. They who are continually shocked by slavery have some right to be shocked by the violent death of the slaveholder, but no others. Such will be more shocked by his life than by his death."[53] Thoreau's position is not an attack on political power in general; rather, it is a demand that citizens assume the responsibility to resist unjust political power.

If we find Thoreau's rhetoric about Brown inflated, possibly even irresponsible, it is interesting to compare "A Plea" with the John Brown speeches and writings of African Americans. "A Plea for Captain John Brown" was delivered as a lecture in Boston at a meeting in which Thoreau was asked to stand in for Frederick Douglass, who had fled the country under suspicion that he was implicated in the attack on Harpers Ferry. The similarities between Thoreau's defense of Brown and the defense offered by Douglass in an editorial from the same period are obvious. Like Thoreau, Douglass insists that slavery is a system of brute force that must be "met with its own weapons."[54] Like Thoreau, Douglass's primary concern is to defend Brown's acts from those who discredit them as insane or irrational or desperate.[55] Like Thoreau, Douglass holds that our lack of sympathy for Brown's moral principles is evidence of our own moral sloth and deterioration.[56] And, like Thoreau, Douglass holds that what is compelling about Brown is that he is an example of a just man who found the strength to resist injustice, a rare case of a man acknowledging and living up to the moral obligations facing every citizen: "Posterity will owe everlasting thanks to John Brown for lifting up once more to the gaze of a nation grown fat and flabby on the garbage of lust and oppression, a true standard of heroic philanthropy, and each coming generation will pay its installment of the debt."[57]

The similarities between Thoreau and Douglass are not the end of the story. During the crisis of Harpers Ferry and Brown's execution, many black leaders spoke in a voice remarkably similar to Thoreau's. Charles H. Langston, in a letter to the *Cleveland Plain Dealer*, writes that Brown's "aims and ends were lofty, noble, generous, benevolent, humane, and God like." Langston suggests, as does Thoreau, that Brown reflects the best traditions of both Christianity and the American Revolution, and that Brown's abolitionism requires only that we live up to the principles for which our nation is supposed to stand.[58] Black citizens of the Pittsburgh area declared John Brown a "hero, patriot, and Christian."[59] The Reverend J. S. Martin, speaking in Boston, uses language strikingly similar to Thoreau's when he says, "I say, my friends, that no man ever died in this country as John Brown has died to-day."[60] "A Plea for Captain John Brown" may have contained a rhetoric rare and extreme within white society, but the essay is remarkably in tune with the public responses of African Americans at the time of Harpers Ferry.[61]

This similarity continues during the post–Civil War period and down to the present. Although African Americans obviously speak in many voices about the Brown legacy, it is not at all unusual to find assessments of him very much like those of the prewar period. More than twenty years after Harpers Ferry, Frederick Douglass's comments about Brown become even more extravagant, even more like Thoreau's, such as when Douglass compares Brown to Socrates and Christ, credits him with beginning "the war that ended American slavery and made this a free Republic,"[62] and calls Brown "*the* man of the nineteenth century."[63] Historian George Washington Williams, in 1880, ranked Brown among "the world's greatest heroes."[64] Speaking at the John Brown Day at Harpers Ferry in 1906, Reverdy C. Ransom claimed that Brown was the modern most akin to the ancient Hebrew prophets, and he equated Brown with the best in America's own Puritan inheritance: "He had all of the moral uprightness and strict religious character of the Puritan, as well as his love of liberty and hatred of oppression and tyranny."[65] In his admiring biography of Brown, published in 1909, W. E. B. Du Bois called Brown "the man who of all Americans has perhaps come nearest to touching the real souls of black folk."[66] Half a century later, Langston Hughes wrote that "John Brown's name is one of the great martyr names of all history and the men who fought with him rank high on the scrolls of freedom."[67] And in 1964 Lerone Bennett Jr., senior editor of *Ebony* magazine, revived transcendental language to describe Brown: "He was of no color, John Brown, of no race or age. He was pure passion, pure transcendence. He was an elemental force like the wind, rain and fire. . . . [He] lived and breathed justice."[68]

Benjamin Quarles, who has documented African American views of John Brown, writes that there is a common core of concern throughout these writings: "On one thing about Brown all blacks seem to have been in agreement—their single-minded negative reaction to the charge that he was mentally unbalanced."[69] The claim that Brown was crazy, so common among white commentators and historians, is insulting and beside the point from this perspective.[70] As historian and Brown biographer Stephen Oates writes:

> To label Brown as an insane man . . . is to disregard or minimize the more favorable traits of his personality, especially his sympathy for the suffering of black people in the United States. And it is to ignore the piercing insight he had into what his raid might do to sectional tensions that already existed. Nor can John Brown be removed from the context of the violent, irrational, and paradoxical times in which he lived. . . . It was not only his angry, messianic mind, but the racist, slave society in which he lived—one that professed "under God" to provide liberty and justice for all—that helped bring John Brown to Harpers Ferry.[71]

To explain Brown's acts as the expressions of mental illness is to trivialize the enormity of the crime of slavery and the clarity with which Brown recognized the nature of that crime. And this, as we have seen, is precisely the point Thoreau is so concerned to drive home in "A Plea for Captain John Brown." What is most impressive about this essay is not how inflammatory the rhetoric has become, or how it expresses some recognizable imbalance or perversity on Thoreau's part.[72] Rather, it is the degree to which Thoreau is one of so few white Americans who could believe that the significance of John Brown lay far beyond matters of personal psychology or the tactical wisdom of the attack on Harpers Ferry, and the rhetorical ferocity with which he drives this point home. As in "Civil Disobedience" and "Slavery in Massachusetts," the language is purposefully exaggerated in order to shock an audience that suffers, Thoreau believes, from moral blindness and complacency.

IN ADDITION to the rhetorical similarity between these essays, it is important to note certain key substantive continuities in Thoreau's responses to these three political events. First, Thoreau is consistent throughout in his views concerning the methods of resistance to unjust institutions. In "Civil Disobedience" Thoreau not only demands that we resist unjust laws; he suggests that such resistance can rightly take the form of violent rebellion if the injustice of the laws is itself of a violent and dehumanizing nature: "When the subject has refused allegiance, and the officer has resigned his office, then the revolution is accomplished. But even suppose blood should flow. Is there not a sort of blood shed when the conscience is wounded? Through this wound a man's real manhood and immortality flow out, and he bleeds to an everlasting death. I see this blood flowing now."[73] In "Slavery in Massachusetts" Thoreau is equally unyielding in his insistence that we renounce all political allegiance to institutions involved in enforcing the Fugitive Slave Law: "Let each inhabitant of the State dissolve his union with her, as long as she delays to do her duty."[74] While he does not explicitly endorse violent rebellion in this essay, there is no reason to believe that he has altered his views in the five years since the publication of "Civil Disobedience." His anger is itself fierce and violent, most famously when he says that his "thoughts are murder to the State, and involuntarily go plotting against her."[75] Thoreau reminds us that this "is not an era of repose," that we have "used up all our inherited freedom," and that "if we would save our lives, we must fight for them."[76] He never suggests that this fight for our freedom must be limited to nonviolent methods. Thoreau was completely supportive of the mobs that gathered to try to rescue, by force, Anthony Burns from the government, and nothing he says in the essay indicates a moral squeamishness about the violent resistance to injustice.[77] There is nothing in either "Slavery in Massachusetts" or "Civil Disobedience," in other words, that should make us surprised by Thoreau's support for John Brown and his methods, such as when he says that at Harpers Ferry, "I think that for once the Sharp's rifles and the revolvers were employed in a righteous cause. The tools were in the hands of one who could use them."[78] Thoreau never exaggerates the desirability of violent resistance, but neither does he consider it out of bounds as a response to significant political evils.[79]

Second, Thoreau's criticisms of government in these essays are criticisms of *unjust* government, and these always imply that just government is both possible and desirable. We saw previously that Thoreau's task in "Civil Disobedience" is to speak as a citizen who demands, "*at once* a better government." In "Slavery in Massachusetts" Thoreau says that if he were to find "a free State, and a court truly of justice," he would "fight for them, if need be."[80] Thoreau even provides a standard by which we can recognize such a state: "The effect of a good government is to make life more valuable,—of a bad one, to make it less valuable."[81] Thoreau's defense of John Brown, too, suggests a desire for a better, just political order, not simply the destruction of our flawed polity. Brown is praised as "an old-fashioned man in his respect for the Constitution, and his faith in the permanence of this Union."[82] The clear implication is that Thoreau holds the general principles of the Constitution to be perfectly adequate for informing our understanding of the nature of just government; his defense of Brown is, in fact, a sort of defense of that government.[83] As in "Slavery in Massachusetts," Thoreau provides a standard for evaluating the legitimacy of a state: "The only government that I recognize,—and it matters not how few are at the head of it, or how small its army,—is that power that establishes justice in the land, never that which establishes injustice."[84] We should not be misled by the primary focus of these essays to think that Thoreau held a simple hostility to government in general. In "Life without Principle," Thoreau writes:

> Government and legislation! these I thought were respectable professions. We have heard of heaven-born Numas, Lycurguses, and Solons, in the history of the world, whose names at least may stand for ideal legislators; but think of legislating to *regulate* the breeding of slaves, or the exportation of tobacco! What have divine legislators to do with the exportation or the importation of tobacco? what humane ones with the breeding of slaves? Suppose you were to submit the question to any son of God,—and has He no children in the nineteenth century? is it a family which is extinct?—in what condition would you get it again? What shall a State like Virginia say for itself at the last day, in which these have been the principal, the staple productions? What ground is there for patriotism in such a state? I derive my facts from statistical tables which the States themselves have published.[85]

Thoreau's interest in these polemical works is to force us to recognize the injustice of our politics and to promote an appropriate political resistance and rebelliousness in response. This by no means indicates that Thoreau finds all political power threatening or illegitimate. On the contrary, his defense of political resistance is consistently informed by an understanding of and commitment to a just political order, an order that does not insult "the names at least" of the likes of Numa, Lycurgus, and Solon.[86]

Third, despite Thoreau's commitment to promoting a just political order, there is a tension in these writings between the duties of citizenship and the liberty of the individual. In "Civil Disobedience" Thoreau argues that a just political order is one in which individuals are allowed to simply withdraw from political life if they so choose. "I please myself with imagining a State . . . which . . . would not think it inconsistent with its own repose, if a few were to live aloof from it, not meddling with it, nor embraced by it, who fulfilled all the duties of neighbors and fellow-men."[87] Thoreau believes these individuals will be few in number, and that in order to earn the toleration they desire they must fulfill their obligations as "neighbors and fellow-men." A free society is one in which some individuals, perhaps men and women with philosophical dispositions not unlike his own, will always appear aloof and detached from conventional civic affairs. It is interesting to recognize that in Thoreau's case, this appearance is not the reality; as I have argued throughout this book, Thoreau is a committed social critic, but this role necessarily places him in a position one step removed from the everyday bustle of politics and society. Be this as it may, it is clear that the fruit of freedom, in Thoreau's view, will sometimes include individuals who assume, despite being good neighbors, little direct role as citizens in public life.

The current political order is terribly unjust to the degree it is implicated in the crime of slavery. But this is also an order that has left Thoreau pretty much unmolested in his role as a social critic. In this political context Thoreau seems ambivalent about the civic role of individuals like himself. After praising John Brown, for example, Thoreau appears defensive about his own role in current political events; we saw earlier that Thoreau declares that he does not devote all his time to "talking or writing about this matter" since he has "other affairs to attend to." Thoreau's "other affairs," as we have seen, include the overwhelmingly ambitious and intensely political project of helping to shape his nation's moral character. Thoreau's defensiveness concerns the degree to which he is obliged, or perhaps shamed by the example of John Brown, to throw himself headlong into the particular battles of contemporary politics. The question here concerns Thoreau's obligation to suspend his role as a critic and assume instead the role of an activist. Thoreau recognizes the distinction between these two activities—and how the social distance required by the former negates the political engagement of the latter and vice versa. Although Thoreau does not resolve this tension in these essays, nor can he, given the immediate tasks at hand, the essays themselves are contributions to the "activist" side of this divide. Thoreau was moved by events to temporarily assume an activist role, but this was neither a role he relished nor one for which he felt particularly suited; it is impossible to ignore the bitterness with which Thoreau complains about how the behavior of the government in the Burns affair "spoils" his walk. But Thoreau's willingness to occasionally assume this role suggests his ambivalence about the immediate civic obligations facing those few free and philosophical individuals like himself, at least in our currently imperfect political community.

A fourth substantive element of note in these essays is Thoreau's understanding of the relationship between nature and politics. In "Civil Disobedience" Thoreau tells us that immediately after his release from jail he withdrew to the countryside to head a huckleberry party, "and then the State was nowhere to be seen."[88] Likewise, in "Slavery in Massachusetts" Thoreau follows his comment about his thoughts being murder to the State with an account of his joy at discovering a white water lily. In both cases nature provides Thoreau with a retreat and a refuge from the political corruption he loathes. But this is only the beginning of nature's offering to Thoreau. It is his home in the countryside at Walden Pond that provides the environment in which Thoreau can respond to his arrest by writing "Civil Disobedience." Nature, that is, provides the resources that allow Thoreau not only the distance from which to be a social critic but the space to be a sort of political activist as well. In "Slavery in Massachusetts" the symbol of the water lily not only provides Thoreau with a device for criticizing the Fugitive Slave Law; it also provides him with a reason for optimism in the face of this terrible political situation:

> But it chanced the other day that I scented a white water-lily, and a season I had waited for had arrived. It is the emblem of purity. It bursts up so pure and fair to the eye, and so sweet to the scent, as if to show us what purity and sweetness reside in, and can be extracted from, the slime and muck of earth. . . . I shall not so soon despair of the world for it, notwithstanding slavery, and the cowardice and want of principle of Northern men. . . . It reminds me that Nature has been partner to no Missouri Compromise. . . . So behave that the odor of your actions may enhance the general sweetness of the atmosphere, that when we behold or scent a flower, we may not be reminded how inconsistent your deeds are with it. . . . The foul slime stands for the sloth and vice of man, the decay of humanity; the fragrant flower that springs from it, for the purity and courage which are immortal.[89]

Nature first allows Thoreau to remove himself from political life, but it then provides him with the means and the desire to reengage the political world, just as the water lily's beauty contrasts with the ugliness of slavery while also symbolizing the possibility of a just political order growing out of the "slime and muck" of our contemporary politics.[90] Nature is not an end in itself but rather a resource at Thoreau's disposal, a tool to be used in the task of exposing injustice and promoting justice. In fact, justice represents a transcendence of nature, just as John Brown "shows himself superior to nature" and thus has a "spark of divinity in him." It is a just polity, not the natural world, that is Thoreau's primary concern.[91]

In none of these substantive matters, from the appropriate resistance to unjust laws to the role of nature in aiding this resistance, has Thoreau broken new ground or strayed from the perspective found in his more general social criticism. Slavery represents the most obvious, the most corrupting, and the most terrible of contemporary injustices in America, and Thoreau's response to it is both consistent and harmonious with his broader political perspectives. But we should not expect, nor do we find, that this response requires a significant theoretical effort on Thoreau's part. Slavery calls us to resistance, and the individual who resists, like John Brown, provides us with a model of a free and righteous man. But even if, or when, America abolishes slavery, there will still be significant battles to be fought over the character of the American political community, battles in which the truth will be less obvious to and compatible with our common sense. For Thoreau, slavery is a brute political fact that will either destroy or be destroyed by America. The response to slavery requires the courage of our convictions; our conventional convictions, that is, are perfectly sufficient to guide us here. Thoreau's polemical political essays are calls to political resistance, and are thus important as activist documents. But Thoreau never claims, nor should we believe, that these texts are the proper starting points for understanding his overall political project. They are the relatively minor fruit of that project, and not its source.

If we place these three essays at the center of Thoreau's political thought, we are forced to think of him primarily as an activist. And as a political activist, Thoreau does not appear to have the courage of his own convictions. He talks a good fight from time to time, but on the whole his concentration lies elsewhere. This leads Barry Kritzberg to write disparagingly of Thoreau's short attention span for current events:

> Thoreau was momentarily distracted by various incidents connected with the anti-slavery movement, but—after each occasion—he returned to his self-appointed tasks. His fundamental principles, ethereal and transcendental as they were, suffered little modification from these disturbing episodes. He would sometimes deliver jeremiads on the evils of his times, only to draw back and do nothing more, insisting that he had other, more important affairs to attend to.[92]

If we insist on evaluating Thoreau primarily as an activist, denying that any deeper political project is represented by Thoreau's "self-appointed tasks," we must admit that he is a rather poor and erratic specimen of this political type.

If, however, we understand that these essays grow out of particular political "emergencies" that Thoreau believed, in good conscience, he must respond to, and that the core of his political thought lies elsewhere, we will be able to appreciate Thoreau's integrity as a social critic. While the critic is sometimes forced to employ an activist rhetoric or engage in other acts of political resistance, there is a necessary tension between these roles, and the critic on the whole does well to jealously protect his or her independence. There are times when we all must find the courage to resist radical political evil, and Thoreau rightly reminds us of this in no uncertain terms. But Thoreau's primary political concern, as America's "bachelor uncle," is consistently focused on the character of the America that will emerge after the issue of slavery is resolved, after our social and political life is no longer distorted by such an obvious contradiction between our ideals and our institutions. This is why in "Life without Principle" the target of Thoreau's rage is not slavery but, instead, the California gold rush. The "rush to California" reflects "the greatest disgrace on mankind" because it represents an insidious and largely unrecognized moral sickness.[93] Slavery is a flat-out contradiction with the fundamental principles of our society. The gold rush represents the rotting of those principles from within, the perversion and self-destruction of freedom rather than its defeat at the hands of an obvious foe. The America that can grow once the most obvious insults to its principles are removed is what demanded Thoreau's unremitting attention throughout his career. The polemical political essays are rhetorically powerful calls to duty in times of extremity, but we must not confuse these calls with Thoreau's deeper analysis of the possibilities and problems for American democratic values. To do so would be to blind ourselves to Thoreau's importance as one of America's most acute and committed social critics.

CHAPTER 7

Conclusion

*Herein is the tragedy; that men doing outrage to their proper natures, even those
called wise and good, lend themselves to perform the office of inferior and
brutal ones. Hence come war and slavery in; and what else may not come in by
this opening?*

     —Thoreau, *A Week on the Concord and Merrimack Rivers*

The mass of men are very easily imposed on.

     —Thoreau, *Faith in a Seed*

THOREAU ASKS, in "Civil Disobedience," "How does it become a man to
behave toward this American government to-day?"[1] If we expand the
question to include not only the government but the political community
as a whole, this can be understood as the question that informs the vast
bulk of Thoreau's political thought. I have argued that Thoreau is important primarily as a critic, one who employs all his resources as a writer to
persuade us to ask his question, to resist our inclination to simply and
habitually accept the legitimacy of the social and political world in which
we live. Thoreau does not develop a detailed theory of political legitimacy,
but he does offer a powerful commentary on the topic. His project is too
democratic to simply present us with a completed evaluation of our political life. Instead we are provided with a constant reminder that we, as
democratic citizens, are responsible for independently evaluating the behavior of our government and political community, especially in the face
of significant injustice or tyranny. We can think of Thoreau as the first and

the greatest American writer to attack the complacency of the emerging American middle class. But he also speaks across class lines to all American citizens, or at least to that vast majority who do not naturally enjoy "strong and valiant natures"[2] and have to struggle to exercise a democratic independence.

Thoreau's question is neither unique or new, but even though it is as old as the tradition of political philosophy, it has taken on a special urgency in the modern world. Hannah Arendt opens her masterwork, *The Human Condition,* with the following comment:

> What I propose in the following is a reconsideration of the human condition from the vantage point of our newest experiences and our most recent fears. This, obviously, is a matter of thought, and thoughtlessness—the heedless recklessness or hopeless confusion or complacent repetition of "truths" which have become trivial and empty—seems to me among the outstanding characteristics of our time. What I propose, therefore, is very simple: it is nothing more than to think what we are doing.[3]

While Arendt's concerns grow out of the experience of twentieth-century totalitarianism, and Thoreau's from the experience of nineteenth-century slavery and imperialism, they share a deep anxiety about the apparent unwillingness or inability of modern citizens to recognize and denounce political evil. Like Thoreau, Arendt concludes that we are threatened by our political passivity:

> The trouble with modern theories of behaviorism is not that they are wrong but that they could become true, that they actually are the best possible conceptualization of certain obvious trends in modern society. It is quite conceivable that the modern age—which began with such an unprecedented and promising outburst of human activity—may end in the deadliest, most sterile passivity history has ever known.[4]

The danger here is less a passivity of participation than a passivity of judgment. Robert Coles writes that Christopher Lasch repeatedly asked,

> "Where is our conscience, these days?" By that he meant the tough, muscular, tenacious kind of conscience that won't bend and weave and bob and yield to trends and fads and fashions, but says *right* or *wrong,* and backs up what is proclaimed with those great instruments of our humanity—anxiety, fear, guilt, which are not to be reflexively banished to the clinic, but, yes, from time to time,

greeted with relief and gratitude, evidence that we are worrying about matters real and ever so important: how we should, we *ought* to behave.[5]

It is obvious that democratic citizens ought to think and judge, but it is equally obvious that we often fail to fulfill these obligations. As Lasch's and Arendt's worries suggest, Thoreau's project is at least as important today as it was in the middle of the nineteenth century.[6]

If Thoreau's question is not terribly original, his discussion of the issues it raises is complex and important. First, the judgment Thoreau is concerned about is not to be confused with "good citizenship" or active political participation (Thoreau himself refrained from voting) or a constant political engagement. On the contrary, Thoreau encourages us to build well-insulated private lives. Only then will we have the resources to resist the type of tyrannical political enthusiasms he lampoons in *Walden* by saying that the music from the town militia makes him want to "spit a Mexican with a good relish."[7] Thoreau's cabin at Walden Pond symbolizes the distance required by a citizen if he or she will be able to recognize that muster for what it is: a "disease," in Thoreau's words, a festival celebrating and promoting an unjustifiable imperialism.[8] The greatest political danger, in Thoreau's view, is not that we will become politically uninvolved but that we are politically thoughtless and chauvinistic. As we saw in chapter 6, he wants to remind us that we "are to be men first, and Americans only at a late and convenient hour."[9] Robert Wiebe has recently argued that the first step toward building a more democratic politics in America is the promotion of a "healthy disrespect" toward the political status quo.[10] Thoreau is promoting just such a political irreverence or disrespect. As he suggests in "Civil Disobedience," we need to learn to serve the state "as men mainly."[11] Such is not a denial of our citizenship but a claim about the character of a free citizenry in a large, modern, impersonal state. Free citizens must always be wary and skeptical of centralized power. Only then can they recognize the devil in politics when they see him.

Second, Thoreau claims there is a necessary connection between political independence and social independence. Put negatively, our political injustices are related to the injustices in our society. In *Walden*, for example, we have seen that Thoreau explicitly equates the growth of luxury and economic inequality in American society with the slavery and warfare enforced by the state.[12] Our political pathologies, in fact, often grow out of and reflect the pathologies of our social lives, and must be addressed in a similar manner.

The nation itself, with all its so called internal improvements, which, by the way, are all external and superficial, is just such an unwieldy and overgrown establishment, cluttered with furniture and tripped up by its own traps, ruined by luxury and heedless expense, by want of calculation and a worthy aim, as the million households in the land; and the only cure for it as for them is a rigid economy, a stern and more than Spartan simplicity of life and elevation of purpose.[13]

Put positively, an independent moral and political life can only grow out of a restrained and relatively independent economic life. This independence does not literally require economic self-sufficiency (remember that Thoreau purchased rice with money earned by selling his bean crop). But it does require an Aristotelian commitment to freeing people to pursue humane activities beyond the economy itself, as well as a resistance to the seductions of the capitalist market and its promises of ever-expanding wealth and pleasures.

Thoreau's claim is simply that the justice and restraint of our economic life are deeply implicated in the justice and restraint of our political life. Again, this message is not unique to Thoreau. But he makes the point as powerfully as anyone in the American tradition. It is also, incidentally, a message we frequently forget or ignore. The result, in Thoreau's time as in our own, is the deterioration of both our public and private lives. "Every man is the lord of a realm beside which the earthly empire of the Czar is but a petty state, a hummock left by the ice. Yet some can be patriotic who have no *self*-respect, and sacrifice the greater to the less. They love the soil which makes their graves, but have no sympathy with the spirit which may still animate their clay. Patriotism is a maggot in their heads."[14] A well-ordered polity and a respectable patriotism can only be built upon an equally well-ordered and respectable economic life. Neither appears likely, since our commitment to capitalism has made us so preoccupied with "improving our houses" that we have forgotten that the point of economic abundance is to allow for the improvement of "the men who are to inhabit them."[15] Or, as Thoreau says, "We now no longer camp as for a night, but have settled down on earth and forgotten heaven."[16] Our overwhelming materialism and consumerism are bound to distort our political values, behavior, and institutions.

A third point, however, is that for Thoreau there is nothing necessary or inevitable about our choosing to live one way or another. It is certainly true that the contemporary political economy is a powerful force, and one that threatens to overwhelm us. But just as Thoreau rejects the modern dogma of progress,[17] so he rejects a fatalism or a self-indulgent pessimism. As we saw in chapter 5, *Walden* concludes with the hopeful lesson that "if one advances confidently in the direction of his dreams, and endeavors to live the life which he has imagined, he will meet with a success unexpected in common hours."[18] The promise here, importantly, is not for the creation of a utopian or perfect world but for a more humble (and more plausible) "unexpected" level of success. What Thoreau holds out is hope in our ability to shape our own lives, even while acknowledging our social and political constraints. The entrepreneur, rather than the pilgrim or the pioneer, has emerged as our most prominent symbol and social type, but Thoreau is cautiously hopeful about harnessing this entrepreneurial spirit for the sake of more humane and satisfying objects than capitalism cultivates. The tool at our disposal to help us nurture this free life is nature, the experience of which Thoreau hopes will make us wilder, more autonomous and self-directing.[19] Thoreau's writings always testify to his hope for the future America, even if he understands quite clearly the power of the forces working against the type of independent individualism he defends.

Fourth, and perhaps most importantly, the individualism Thoreau is promoting in no way precludes a commitment to citizenship or a just political order. This is certainly the most misunderstood element of Thoreau's political thought. Because his main focus is on fostering resistance to unjust political power, most interpreters assume he objects to political power in general. As I hope has become clear in the previous chapters, however, this interpretation is simply not justified by a close reading of Thoreau's texts. Just because his attention is primarily directed toward resistance to contemporary political evils, we must not conclude that Thoreau believes all politics to be evil. And just because he sometimes despaired of American civic life, we must not conclude that he was an anarchist.[20] There is ample evidence to the contrary, suggesting that Thoreau looked forward to a time when responsible democratic citizens could establish a legitimate political order. For the sake of this higher citizenship, however, we often have to learn to be "not too good" as citizens in the present state of affairs, at least from the perspective of the modern liberal state.[21]

IT IS EASY ENOUGH to understand why conservatives find Thoreau's individualism and rebelliousness distasteful. From their perspective, Thoreau's insistence that citizens judge the state is a threat to all established public authority. C. Carroll Hollis, for example, believes that "when Thoreau considers the obligation of the citizen to obey the law, he not only rejects that obligation in the light of his extreme individualism but ultimately denies authority itself."[22] Thoreau's understanding of individual responsibility appears anarchic, even antisocial. This view of Thoreau, however, is both an exaggeration and based upon a misunderstanding. It is an exaggeration since, as we have seen, Thoreau's objection is to unjust, abusive, and illegitimate authority and not to authority per se. His disrespect is reserved for those elements of the polity that deserve disrespect, and, frankly, Thoreau identified the shameful elements of our social and political life about as accurately as anyone can ask for. The conservative's dislike of Thoreau is based upon a misunderstanding since Thoreau shares with the conservative a view that political power and authority can and should be deployed for the purpose of promoting good human lives. Far from desiring the dissolution of all authority, Thoreau, as we have seen, demands only that authority be exerted for the promotion of desirable ends. Conservatives share more with Thoreau than they suspect.

If conservatives worry about Thoreau's individualism, liberals worry about the style of moral evaluation in his polemical political writings. We have seen that some, like Heinze Eulau, believe Thoreau's individualism is built upon a moral anarchism and subjectivism.[23] Others, like Laraine Fergenson, believe the opposite—that Thoreau appeals to a moral foundationalism inappropriate in a diverse liberal society: "When one traces the doctrine of higher law to its absolutist and religious base, its problems in today's climate of secularism and moral relativism become apparent: it lends itself to misappropriation and self-delusion."[24] Both sets of concerns share a belief that Thoreau's arguments are antidemocratic and reveal a dangerous moral authoritarianism, self-righteousness, and intolerance.[25]

I have explained throughout this book why I believe this is an inaccurate understanding of Thoreau's project, why Thoreau is a friend rather than an enemy of democratic citizenship, how his language and self-criticisms reflect democratic sensibilities, how he encourages the development of the independence required of a strong and sensible democratic citizenry. What is important to note here is that these critics are not only put off by the substance of Thoreau's views; they also object to what they believe is his refusal to engage in "reasonable" public debate. It is certainly true that Thoreau is not a "philosopher" in any academic or technical sense. Thoreau, in fact, greatly distrusted moral philosophers of this type and contrasted his own ambitions with theirs: "The naturalist pursues his study with love, but the moralist persecutes his with hate."[26] Thoreau's philosophical project differs from these "moralists" in two ways. First, he does not believe, any more than Plato does, that pure and dispassionate "reason" is sufficient for changing anyone's mind, undermining their prejudices, or jolting them out of their complacency. On the contrary, he suspects that such reason often masks and rationalizes cruelty, self-interest, and preconceptions.[27] Second, and as a result of his distrust of a narrow conception of reason, Thoreau's philosophical tools are literary rather than technical, designed not so much to "convince" us as to "wake us up."[28] Some critics have wrongly concluded from this that Thoreau can only be properly understood on narrowly literary grounds, that he simply has no interest in philosophy or ability in moral argument.[29] But this misunderstands what I have earlier pointed to as Thoreau's great ambition. Thoreau employs his literary skills for the purpose of showing, shocking, shaming, seducing, and inspiring us. His ambition is philosophical in a broad and old-fashioned sense; he wants to speak directly not only to our reason but to our spirit and desire as well, to the whole of our lives.[30] He is evocative rather than analytical, and this is a sign of his philosophical hubris rather than his philosophical failure.

Modern liberals are therefore right to see Thoreau's method as different from their own. They are wrong, however, to presume that this demonstrates either an irrationalism or a hostility toward democracy.[31] Thoreau's rhetorical skill is employed to energize and uplift us, and at times to discredit us before our own professed ideals. His success or failure depends entirely on his own literary skill and the accuracy with which he understands our individual and common values. In this sense the project's presuppositions are both politically and intellectually democratic.[32] In addition, Thoreau is suggesting that, at critical moments, those who counsel calm and dispassionate reason are guilty of complicity with political evil. How are we to speak to those for whom slavery is a narrowly political problem, a big problem but a merely political problem nonetheless? To simply frame the question in policy terms, as the political process always encourages us to do, is morally outrageous and appalling; it fails to acknowledge that a heinous crime is being committed, and thus shares guilt for the perpetuation of the crime. Thoreau's literary skills are directed toward producing a moral recognition and awakening to such crimes that a narrower form of public reason can never achieve. We must remember that these skills are never used for trivial ends or purposes; Thoreau is clear that the type of resistance he encourages is justifiable only in relation to extreme evils and events.[33] In the face of such evils and events, however, Thoreau offers a moral inspiration his liberal critics can never approach.

Finally, there is the criticism of Thoreau by radicals. Like conservatives, radicals dislike Thoreau's individualism, but their disapproval is for exactly the opposite reason: rather than being a threat to the authority of the state (as conservatives fear), radicals suspect that it actually ends up protecting the state by diffusing and depoliticizing radical discontent. This is Leo Marx's criticism of *Walden:* "What politically minded admirers of *Walden* tend to ignore, I think, is the effect of the book's action as a whole in dissipating the radical social awareness it generates at the outset. Considered as a single structure of feeling, Thoreau's masterwork may be described as superbly effective in transmuting incipiently radical impulses into a celebration of what Emerson called 'the infinitude of the private man.' "[34] Truman Nelson makes the same point about Thoreau's polemical political works: "Here is Thoreau's fatal contradiction full blown. In one vein he wants to arouse, he wants to lead, he wants to help settle the great struggle of his time, by force if necessary, and in the other he proclaims himself an avowed recluse, unable to share a common opinion with anyone."[35] Quite simply, Thoreau is not a good movement man. He is too detached and independent to be an effective or useful or inspiring radical. There may be elements of good radical analysis in his work, such as his criticism of capitalism or his defense of John Brown, but the overall effect is depoliticization rather than mobilization.

The novelist Milan Kundera has written that modern political activity is organized around certain symbols, slogans, and images he calls "kitsch." Kitsch, he believes, is "the aesthetic ideal of all politicians and all political parties and movements."[36] The kitsch of the Left is solidarity, the "Grand March" of the oppressed against all forms of tyranny.

> The fantasy of the Grand March . . . is the political kitsch joining leftists of all times and tendencies. The Grand March is the splendid march on the road to brotherhood, equality, justice, happiness; it goes on and on, obstacles notwithstanding, for obstacles there must be if the march is to be the Grand March. . . . What makes a leftist a leftist is not this or that theory but his ability to integrate any theory into the kitsch called the Grand March.[37]

Thoreau, like Kundera, is deeply distrustful of mass politics, suspecting that it replaces judgment with less admirable impulses.[38] And it is clearly true that Marx and Nelson value the unity forged by political struggle in a

126

way that never attracted Thoreau. They are right to believe that this excludes him from a conventional type of radical politics.

The skepticism about radical political movements that Thoreau shares with Kundera, however, does not mean he is hostile to human solidarity. His claim about radical movements is the same as his claim about all forms of community: they are admirable and desirable only to the degree that they respect and cultivate the moral integrity of their membership. Put another way, Thoreau desires a radicalism beyond slogans and ideologies, beyond the kitsch Kundera exposes. In light of the experience of the twentieth century, Thoreau's skepticism about radical movements certainly looks, at the very least, prudent and perhaps quite farsighted. The real possibilities for a radicalism built by independent democratic citizens, rather than the slogans of mass ideological politics, are as of yet not fully known, and we may have reason to be pessimistic about the likelihood of such developments. But anything less may be a cure worse than the disease, a potential subversion of any democratic community worthy of our respect. The real problem with Thoreau's radicalism is not that it is privatizing but that it is demanding. It requires an old-fashioned Protestant vigilance on the part of every individual, a responsibility that can never be abdicated to, or assumed by, a larger political group or movement.

In contrast to conventional criticisms from the Left, Right, and center, I believe the true weakness of Thoreau's views is neither his individualism nor the literary and philosophical tools he utilizes as a social and political critic. Rather, it is his naturalism, his belief that the American landscape can provide an alternative source of inspiration, can teach a way of life that encourages the moral independence required by democratic citizens. Thoreau expects two significant moral services from nature: first, that it stimulate our sense of freedom and autonomy and, second, that it humble and discipline our human arrogance. In its first incarnation nature provides the environment that liberates us from convention and common sense, that allows us the space to cultivate an independent sense of ourselves, our needs, our views, and our desires. In the second, we have seen, it allows us to "witness our own limits transgressed,"[39] teaching us a proper humility by constantly reminding us of our own limited powers. For Thoreau, nature first teaches us our independence, then controls and moderates this independence within proper boundaries.

There is no reason for us to believe, however, that our experience of nature will necessarily function in the way Thoreau hopes it will. While contact with and awareness of nature may produce a sense of independence, they are equally likely to exacerbate feelings of personal incompetence and absolute dependency on the artifacts of human society. The more intensely we experience nature, the more we may recognize our own vulnerability, thus producing a lesser rather than a greater sense of our autonomy. And although we may be moved by nature to feel a sense of awe and respect, it is equally common for nature to inspire in Americans a very different response. The farmer is inspired to subdue and pacify and domesticate nature through the sweat of the brow; well-equipped young hiking and climbing enthusiasts are inspired by the mountains as the terrain for their athletic achievement; even the poet is inspired by nature to reach for self-aggrandizing knowledge, such as when Thoreau writes:

> Ive searched my faculties around
> To learn why life to me was lent
> I will attend his faintest sound
> And then declare to men what God hath meant[40]

Furthermore, we can see from the arrogance of Thoreau's own poem that the moral autonomy he seeks is not always or necessarily compatible with the sense of reverence and humility he also desires. Nature's lessons are more ambiguous and difficult than Thoreau wants to admit.

Nature, therefore, may not be as useful or reliable as a source of moral inspiration for American citizens as Thoreau hopes. If this is true, Thoreau is left with a less effective vehicle for conversion of the American soul than he suspects. While he obviously understands the need to tutor his audience in the proper manner of experiencing and appreciating nature, thereby implicitly acknowledging the possibility of alternative responses toward the natural world, Thoreau does not always appear to be fully aware of the degree to which he, too, gets tangled in these differing and not always appropriate or compatible attitudes toward "the wild." Which is simply to say that even if Thoreau is right about our need to redefine our own freedom, and to develop a sharp and vigilant eye for political outrage, he has not completely solved the problem of providing us with a foolproof tool or method for achieving these goals. But could we really expect otherwise?

IT IS IMPORTANT to be clear about what Thoreau does and does not have to offer as a social critic and political thinker. He is obviously not a conventional political theorist, addressing a full range of issues, from justice to the nature of the state to problems of political obligation, for example, that traditionally occupy such theorists. Nor is there in Thoreau's work a fully developed portrait of a desirable democratic political order, although he gives many more hints about this than is usually recognized. What Thoreau does give us is a powerful analysis of the options, opportunities, and dangers before the American political community. Reflecting this analysis, and Thoreau's investigation of the American commitment to freedom that grows out of it, is Thoreau's insistence that independent citizens are obliged to recognize and resist the evils perpetuated by their own polity. No writer has more powerfully portrayed the American betrayal of its own commitment to individual liberty, or more lovingly described the possibilities for achieving freedom's promise. And no American writer has been more vigorous in his demand that we call the devil by his proper name and refuse to grant him political legitimacy. Thoreau never underestimated the difficulty of either project. The free life is the fruit of only the sternest discipline, and the recognition of political evil is possible only when we manage to awaken from our moral lethargy. But America's "bachelor uncle" hoped against the odds that American citizens would eventually rise to both tasks, that "our children's children . . . may perchance be really free." While Thoreau does not address all the problems and challenges we face in political life, those he does address continue to be of the greatest moment, and his discussion of them continues to resonate with an urgent force.

NOTES

Chapter 1. Introduction

1. Nancy L. Rosenblum, "Thoreau's Militant Conscience," *Political Theory* 9 (February 1981): 91.

2. Philip Abbott, *States of Perfect Freedom* (Amherst: University of Massachusetts Press, 1987), p. 62. Abbott is referring to *A Week on the Concord and Merrimack Rivers, Walden,* and *Cape Cod.*

3. "It should be noted . . . that the combination of political radicalism and self-absorption is a common trait in American culture." Ibid.

4. Richard J. Ellis, *American Political Cultures* (New York: Oxford University Press, 1993), p. 141.

5. "During my early college days I read Thoreau's essay on civil disobedience for the first time. Fascinated by the idea of refusing to cooperate with an evil system, I was so deeply moved that I re-read the work several times. I became convinced then that non-cooperation with evil is as much a moral obligation as is cooperation with good. No other person has been more eloquent and passionate in getting this idea across than Henry David Thoreau. As a result of his writings and personal witness we are the heirs of a legacy of creative protest." Martin Luther King Jr., "A Legacy of Creative Protest," in *Thoreau in Our Season,* ed. John H. Hicks (Amherst: University of Massachusetts Press, 1967), p. 13.

6. For one of the most thoughtful examples of this claim, see Laraine Fergenson, "Thoreau, Daniel Berrigan, and the Problem of Transcendental Politics," *Soundings* 65, (Spring 1982): 103–22.

7. James Russell Lowell, "Thoreau," in *Thoreau: A Century of Criticism,* ed. Walter Harding (Dallas: Southern Methodist University Press, 1954), p. 48.

8. George Hochfield, "Anti-Thoreau," *Sewanee Review* 96 (Summer 1988): 435.

9. C. Roland Wagner, "Lucky Fox at Walden," in *Thoreau in Our Season*, ed. John H. Hicks (Amherst: University of Massachusetts Press, 1967), p. 130.

10. Vincent Buranelli, "The Case against Thoreau," *Ethics* 67 (1957): 259.

11. Quoted in Leonard N. Neufeldt, "Emerson, Thoreau, and Daniel Webster," *ESQ* 26 (1980): 34.

12. Quoted in Walter Harding, ed., *Thoreau, Man of Concord* (New York: Holt, Rinehart and Winston, 1960), p. 159.

13. Joyce Carol Oates, "The Mysterious Mr. Thoreau," *New York Times Book Review*, 1 May 1988, p. 31.

14. Robert Louis Stevenson, *Familiar Studies of Men and Books* (London: Chatto and Windus, 1924), p. 133.

15. Hochfield, "Anti-Thoreau," p. 434.

16. Heinz Eulau, "Wayside Challenger: Some Remarks on the Politics of Henry David Thoreau," in *Thoreau: A Collection of Critical Essays*, ed. Sherman Paul, (Englewood Cliffs, N.J.: Prentice-Hall, 1962), p. 125.

17. In Joel Myerson, ed., *Critical Essays on Henry David Thoreau's Walden* (Boston: G. K. Hall, 1988), p. 35.

18. John Patrick Diggins, "Thoreau, Marx, and the 'Riddle' of Alienation," *Social Research* 39 (Winter 1972): 581.

19. "That a man so withdrawn is equipped to be a qualified social critic may certainly be questioned." Hubert H. Hoeltje, "Misconceptions in Current Thoreau Criticism," *Philological Quarterly* 47 (October 1968): 567, 565.

20. Lowell, "Thoreau," p. 48.

21. Quoted in Harding, *Thoreau, Man of Concord*, p. 116. Lowell and Whitman are, I believe, way off the mark here. Canby is much closer to the truth when he writes that Thoreau "had a sympathy for everyday human nature which the Transcendentalists lacked." Henry Seidel Canby, *Thoreau* (Boston: Houghton Mifflin, 1939), p. 173.

22. Taylor Stoehr, *Nay-Saying in Concord* (Hamden, Conn.: Archon Books, 1979), p. 109; Canby, *Thoreau*, p. 18.

23. As Robert Richardson writes, despite Thoreau's criticism of reformers, he "shared, from an early age, the general hunger of the times for reform, renewal, and regeneration." Robert D. Richardson, *Henry Thoreau* (Berkeley and Los Angeles: University of California Press, 1986), p. 104.

24. See Mary Elkins Moller, *Thoreau in the Human Community* (Amherst: University of Massachusetts Press, 1980).

25. Vernon L. Parrington, *Main Currents in American Thought*, vol. 2 (New York: Harcourt, Brace, 1927), p. 401.

26. Emma Goldman, *Anarchism and Other Essays* (Port Washington, N.Y.: Kennikat Press, 1969), p. 62.

27. Henry Miller, "Preface to Three Essays by Henry David Thoreau," in Harding, *Thoreau: A Century of Criticism*, p. 162.

28. Jane Bennett, *Thoreau's Nature* (Thousand Oaks, Calif.: Sage, 1994), pp. 21, xxiv, 86, 82.

29. Abbott, *States of Perfect Freedom*, pp. 61–62.

30. And impairs his ability to participate in political life as well. See Leo Stoller, *After Walden* (Stanford, Calif.: Stanford University Press, 1957), p. 153.

31. *Graham's Magazine* 45 (September 1854), quoted in Myerson, *Critical Essays*, p. 22. Perry Miller puts the point this way: "In all literature of the world, here is the case of a sensible man who found nobody so interesting to talk with as himself." Perry Miller, *Consciousness in Concord* (Boston: Houghton Mifflin, 1958), p. 5.

32. Francis B. Dedmond, "Thoreau and the Ethical Concept of Government," *The Personalist* 36 (1955): 46.

33. Ellis, *American Political Cultures*, p. 148.

34. Eulau, "Wayside Challenger," p. 126.

35. Rosenblum, "Thoreau's Militant Conscience," p. 106.

36. Ibid., p. 100.

37. Nancy L. Rosenblum, *Another Liberalism* (Cambridge, Mass.: Harvard University Press, 1987), p. 114. Emerson once wrote that Thoreau "did not feel himself except in opposition." Quoted in Sherman Paul, *The Shores of America* (Urbana: University of Illinois Press, 1958), p. 33.

38. Rosenblum, *Another Liberalism*, p. 114. Wilson Carey McWilliams has pointed out, in private correspondence, the apparent anachronism of Rosenblum's claim here. To the degree that there is common ground between Nietzsche and Thoreau, it would have had to have been established from the opposite direction than that implied by Rosenblum's comment, with Nietzsche being influenced by New England transcendentalism rather than vice versa.

39. Instead, he calls him a "demented moralist who condones enthusiastically the most hideous crimes as long as they flow from his postulates." Buranelli, "The Case against Thoreau," p. 263.

40. Ibid., p. 267.

41. Ibid., p. 266.

42. In slightly less hysterical versions of this argument, Frederick Sanders claims, "There is an authoritarian, even dictatorial, quality about him that shows itself in the condescending impatience with which he regards people who do not share his rigorous ideals," and Heinz Eulau contends that "Thoreau's politics suggests that it is a small step, indeed, from insistence on the principle of morality to insistence on the principle of expediency." Frederick K. Sanders, "Mr. Thoreau's Timebomb," *National Review* 4 (June 1968): 544; Eulau, "Wayside Challenger," p. 130.

43. Fergenson, "Thoreau, Daniel Berrigan, and the Problem of Transcendental Politics," p. 115.

44. Buranelli, "The Case against Thoreau," p. 260. Irving Howe writes that "Thoreau seems to have clung to a rigid theoretical individualism—a posture—long after he came to live by more generous and complex values. Only seldom was

his thought a match for his perceptions." Irving Howe, *The American Newness* (Cambridge, Mass.: Harvard University Press, 1986), p. 36.

45. See, for example, Truman Nelson, "Thoreau and the Paralysis of Individualism," *Ramparts* 4 (March 1966): 17–26.

46. Thoreau once wrote to a friend, "I trust that you realize what an exaggerator I am,—that I lay myself out to exaggerate whenever I have an opportunity,—pile Pelion upon Ossa, to reach heaven so." Exaggeration was obviously a cultivated habit, and Thoreau thought of it as a virtue. In the first volume of his *Journal* he writes, "We live by exaggeration," and in his early essay on Carlyle he exclaims, "Exaggeration! was ever any virtue attributed to a man without exaggeration? was ever any vice, without infinite exaggeration?" Henry David Thoreau, *The Correspondence of Henry David Thoreau,* ed. Walter Harding and Carl Bode (New York: New York University Press, 1958), p. 304 (10 April 1853); Henry D. Thoreau, *The Journal of Henry D. Thoreau,* vol. 1, ed. Bradford Torrey and Francis H. Allen (Boston: Houghton Mifflin, 1949), p. 412; Henry David Thoreau, *Early Essays and Miscellanies,* ed. Joseph J. Moldenhauer and Edwin Moser (Princeton, N.J.: Princeton University Press, 1975), p. 264.

47. Eulau, "Wayside Challenger," p. 126.

48. Perhaps this is one of the reasons Stanley Hyman insists (wrongly, I think) that any new book on Thoreau must "recognize that he was primarily a writer, not a naturalist, reformer, or whatever." Stanley Edgar Hyman, "Henry Thoreau Once More," *Massachusetts Review* 4 (1962): 169.

49. See, for example, Wilson Carey McWilliams, *The Idea of Fraternity in America* (Berkeley and Los Angeles: University of California Press, 1973), pp. 294–97; Paul, *The Shores of America,* pp. 75, 244, 322; John C. Broderick, "Thoreau's Proposals for Legislation," *American Quarterly* 7, (1955): 285–90.

It is also important to note that in American literary studies Thoreau has always enjoyed a much wider and more positive reputation than he has among students of American political thought. Lawrence Buell claims, in fact, that "Thoreau has become the closest approximation to a folk hero that American literary studies has ever seen." Lawrence Buell, "The Thoreauvian Pilgrimage: The Structure of an American Cult," *American Literature* 61 (May 1989): 175.

50. *Journal,* 2: 267–68.

51. Ibid., p. 83.

52. For this reason, Michael Walzer is very distrustful of detached critics. He nonetheless admits that democratic criticism requires both a connection with and distance from the demos, much as Socrates' (and, I would add, Thoreau's) example suggests. See Michael Walzer, *The Company of Critics* (New York: Basic Books, 1988), pp. 12–14 and passim.

53. Miller, *Consciousness in Concord,* p. 211.

54. *Journal,* 2: 314–15.

55. Ibid., p. 333.

56. Ibid., p. 421.

57. Ibid., 9: 45, 337.

58. Ibid., p. 432.

59. *Correspondence,* p. 283. See, too, *Journal,* 2: 406.

60. *Journal,* 2: 392.

61. Ibid., p. 393.

62. I assume that this passage, on one obvious level, has something to do with Thoreau's sexuality and the various terrors it raises for him. I have, however, no expertise in such psychoanalysis, and these issues are at any rate irrelevant to my purposes.

63. See *Correspondence,* p. 216; *Walden,* in Henry David Thoreau, *A Week on the Concord and Merrimack Rivers; Walden, or, Life in the Woods; The Maine Woods; Cape Cod* (New York: Library of America, 1985), p. 361.

64. *Journal,* 3: 71.

65. "Life without Principle," in Henry D. Thoreau, *Reform Papers,* ed. Wendell Glick (Princeton, N.J.: Princeton University Press, 1973), p. 174. Steven Fink argues, "Early and repeated [publication] failures had driven Thoreau to regard posterity as his ultimate audience even as he did his best to win over the popular audience of his day." Steven Fink, *Prophet in the Marketplace* (Princeton, N.J.: Princeton University Press, 1992), p. 285.

66. "Eccentric" is perhaps the word most frequently used to describe Thoreau by contemporary reviewers of *Walden.* See Bradley P. Dean and Gary Scharnhorst, "The Contemporary Reception of *Walden,*" in *Studies in the American Renaissance, 1990,* ed. Joel Myerson (Charlottesville: University Press of Virginia, 1990), pp. 293–328.

67. In *Walden* Thoreau comments about his visitors at the pond: "Finally, there were the self-styled reformers, the greatest bores of all." *Walden,* p. 445. Thoreau was, nonetheless, more active in reform politics than he reveals in his writings.

Taylor Stoehr observes, "Ironically enough, Thoreau's efforts to 'keep himself unstained and aloof' ultimately resulted in a much more intimate contact with his posterity, and a much more lasting political influence than either Alcott or Emerson achieved." Stoehr, *Nay-Saying in Concord,* p. 66.

68. Ralph Waldo Emerson, "Thoreau," in *The Selected Writings of Ralph Waldo Emerson* (New York: Modern Library, 1968), p. 897.

69. Ibid., p. 910.

70. Ibid., p. 911.

71. As an illustration of the contrast between Emerson's "insider" social status and Thoreau's critical distance from the mainstream of American society, see Leonard Neufeldt's interesting discussion of Emerson's admiration for, and Thoreau's unflagging distrust of, Daniel Webster. Neufeldt, "Emerson, Thoreau, and Daniel Webster," p. 35 and passim.

72. "'A people is the association of a multitude of rational beings united by a common agreement on the objects of their love.'. . . And, obviously, the better the

objects of this agreement, the better the people; the worse the objects of this love, the worse the people." Augustine, *City of God* (New York: Penguin, 1981), p. 890.

Chapter 2. Founding

1. Ralph Waldo Emerson, *Essays and Lectures* (New York: Library of America, 1983), p. 88.

2. Emerson, "Literary Ethics," in ibid., p. 101.

3. Emerson, *Nature,* in ibid., p. 48.

4. Emerson, "Self-Reliance," in ibid., p. 262.

5. Henry David Thoreau, *Excursions* (Boston: Houghton Mifflin, 1893), p. 301.

6. Henry D. Thoreau, *The Journal of Henry D. Thoreau*, vol. 9, ed. Bradford Torrey and Francis H. Allen (Boston: Houghton Mifflin, 1949), p. 208.

7. Jane Bennett, *Thoreau's Nature* (Thousand Oaks, Calif.: Sage, 1994), p. 132.

8. John Patrick Diggins, "Thoreau, Marx, and the 'Riddle' of Alienation," *Social Research* 39 (Winter 1972): 581.

9. C. Roland Wagner, "Lucky Fox at Walden," in *Thoreau in Our Season*, ed. John H. Hicks (Amherst: University of Massachusetts Press, 1967), pp. 130–31.

10. Walter Harding, *The Days of Henry Thoreau* (New York: Alfred A. Knopf, 1966), p. 253.

11. Henry S. Salt, *The Life of Henry David Thoreau*, ed. George Hendrick, Willene Hendrick, and Fritz Oehlschlaeger (Urbana: University of Illinois Press, 1993), p. 68.

12. "*A Week* is his [Thoreau's] attempt to immerse himself in the river of time in order to recover from time his greatest loss." H. Daniel Peck, *Thoreau's Morning Work* (New Haven, Conn.: Yale University Press, 1990), p. 11; ". . . the central concerns of *A Week*—death and a brotherhood that transcends death." Linck C. Johnson, *Thoreau's Complex Weave* (Charlottesville: University Press of Virginia, 1986), p. 52; "The toughest, most disturbing problem with which Thoreau struggled to come to terms in *A Week*—frequently in an indirect, subterranean, unconscious manner—centered around the painful loss of his brother." Richard Lebeaux, *Thoreau's Seasons* (Amherst: University of Massachusetts Press, 1984), p. 4.

13. Robert D. Richardson, *Henry Thoreau* (Berkeley and Los Angeles: University of California Press, 1986), p. 171.

14. Henry David Thoreau, *A Week on the Concord and Merrimack Rivers*, in *A Week on the Concord and Merrimack Rivers; Walden, or, Life in the Woods; The Maine Woods; Cape Cod* (New York: Library of America, 1985), p. 7.

15. Thoreau follows a similar strategy in his "Huckleberries" lecture, when he argues for the use of the Indian rather than the Latin names for huckleberries, out of respect for those who knew them first and best. "I think that it would be well if the Indian names, were as far as possible restored and applied to the numerous

species of huckleberries, by our botanists—instead of the very inadequate—Greek and Latin or English ones at present used." Henry David Thoreau, *Huckleberries,* ed. Leo Stoller (Iowa City: The Windhover Press of the University of Iowa and the New York Public Library, 1970), pp. 5, 20.

16. "To an extinct race it was grass-ground, where they hunted and fished, and it is still perennial grass-ground to Concord farmers, who own the Great Meadows, and get the hay from year to year." *A Week,* p. 7.

17. Linck Johnson, one of the foremost students of Thoreau's composition of *A Week,* points out Thoreau's deepening interest in the conflict between Indian and colonist as the book evolved. Johnson, *Thoreau's Complex Weave,* p. 135.

18. Joan Burbick, *Thoreau's Alternative History* (Philadelphia: University of Pennsylvania Press, 1987), p. 33.

19. H. Daniel Peck writes, "He [Thoreau] is sensitive to the way in which the historical record, through self-serving distortion and omission, can destroy vital elements of the past. He feels this with special force in relation to the American settlers' treatment of the Indians." *Thoreau's Morning Work,* p. 17.

20. *A Week,* p. 15.

21. Ibid.

22. Peck observes that Thoreau appears to be reluctant to cast off on this journey and that it is with some difficulty that he floats beyond the "familiar meadows" of Concord. This is not surprising, since the "unusual enterprise" upon which he is embarking will take him far from the safe and comforting moral ground of the histories we tell in our everyday lives. *Thoreau's Morning Work,* p. 12.

23. *A Week,* p. 16.

24. Ibid., p. 37.

25. Ibid., p. 41. Thoreau later notes that this "howling wilderness" was experienced quite differently by the native inhabitants: ". . . the primeval forest . . . ; to the white man a drear and howling wilderness, but to the Indian a home, adapted to his nature, and cheerful as the smile of the Great Spirit." Ibid., p. 264.

26. Ibid., p. 41.

27. Ibid., p. 42.

28. Ibid., p. 44.

29. As Peck writes, "lacking a written history of their own, the Indians have in effect fallen out of human memory." *Thoreau's Morning Work,* p. 18.

30. *A Week,* p. 44.

31. Ibid., p. 46.

32. Ibid., p. 47.

33. William Cronon, *Changes in the Land: Indians, Colonists, and the Ecology of New England* (New York: Hill and Wang, 1983), p. 81. Cronon has much to say about the incompatibility of the European and Native American understandings of property, wealth, and production in this brilliant study; see esp. chap. 4.

34. *Journal*, 1: 445. Robert Sattelmeyer points out that while writing *A Week*, Thoreau "conceived of the Indians largely as a race either extinct or on its way to extirpation." Robert Sattelmeyer, *Thoreau's Reading* (Princeton, N.J.: Princeton University Press, 1988), p. 102. Historian Robert Wiebe writes that it was common in the early nineteenth century for white Americans to think of the Indian as already vanished: "In the white mind's eye, which saw the future in the present, Native Americans slipped out of focus. 'Yet they have vanished from the face of the earth,' one eastern gentleman sighed as early as 1825, '—their very names are blotted from the pages of history.' Fated to die, dying, soon to die, already dead blurred into a single vision of Native American elimination not just as inevitable but as natural." Thoreau certainly believed that the Indian stood very little chance against the onslaught of white society, but it is precisely the blotting of "their very names . . . from the pages of history" that he protests in this work. Robert H. Wiebe, *Self-Rule* (Chicago: University of Chicago Press, 1995), p. 87.

35. *A Week*, pp. 66–67.

36. Ibid., p. 68.

37. Ibid., p. 90.

38. In "Wednesday," ibid., p. 206.

39. It is interesting to note that Tyng's legacy fails to clarify the proper ownership of Wicasuck Island. Thoreau comments that as they sail by the island on their return down the river, a boatman asks them about it, explains that it is currently disputed property, and suspects that Thoreau and his brother have a claim upon it. Ibid., p. 291. Apparently the history of the island will not allow for an unambiguously just claim to it. As Thoreau observes in *Cape Cod*, "I know that if you hold a thing unjustly, there will surely be the devil to pay at last." Henry David Thoreau, *Cape Cod*, in *A Week, Etc.*, p. 878.

40. *A Week*, pp. 96–97. See page 129 for a slightly different biographical sketch.

41. Ibid., p. 97.

42. A revisionist poet denies this abandonment, and, as Thoreau says, "assigned him company in his last hours." Ibid., p. 98.

43. *Journal*, 12: 124.

44. *A Week*, p. 99.

45. Ibid.

46. Ibid., p. 97.

47. Discussing the passage in "Civil Disobedience" in which Thoreau says he does "not wish to be regarded as a member of any incorporated society which I have not joined," Stanley Cavell makes the following observation: "The joke very quickly went sour. In particular, he could not name society or the government as such, because he knows he has somehow signed on." Even though Thoreau finds association with the government shameful, he nevertheless "recognizes that *he* is associated with it, that his withdrawal has not 'dissolved the Union' between our-

selves and the state, and hence that he is disgraced. Apparently, as things stand, one cannot but choose to serve the state; so he will 'serve the state with [his conscience] also, and so necessarily resist it for the most part.'" Stanley Cavell, *The Senses of Walden* (San Francisco: North Point Press, 1981), pp. 83–84.

48. *A Week*, p. 129.

49. Ibid.

50. Ibid., p. 130.

51. Ibid., pp. 134–35.

52. Ibid., p. 136.

53. Ibid., p. 161; see also p. 179.

54. Ibid., p. 193.

55. Ibid., p. 206.

56. Thoreau also mentions open warfare between Penacooks and Mohawks on ibid., p. 201.

57. Ibid., p. 206.

58. Ibid., pp. 178–79.

59. Ibid., p. 224. Henry's story is quite extraordinary. As he tells it, he escaped death in a massacre of English by Chipeway Indians at Michilimackinac, partly through his own efforts and good luck, and partly through the efforts of his friend Wawatam. Henry says that the Indians cooked a broth from their victims, from which they believed they would gain courage. After saving Henry, Wawatam eats, in Henry's presence, a bowl of human broth containing a hand and a large piece of flesh—from men Henry had just been held captive with. For a full account of this relationship, see Alexander Henry, *Travels and Adventures* (Rutland, Vt.: Charles E. Tuttle, 1969), pp. 73–152.

60. *A Week*, pp. 262–64.

61. Ibid., p. 290.

62. Ibid., p. 319.

63. *Journal*, 3: 95.

64. Quentin Anderson, *Making Americans* (New York: Harcourt Brace Jovanovich, 1992), pp. 182, 230.

65. *A Week*, p. 215.

66. See Robert F. Sayer, *Thoreau and the American Indians* (Princeton, N.J.: Princeton University Press, 1977), p. 52. Hawthorne tells the Dustan story in "The Duston Family," first published in 1836 and reprinted in Nathaniel Hawthorne, *Hawthorne as Editor*, ed. Arlin Turner (Port Washington, N.Y.: Kennikat Press, 1941), pp. 131–37; see esp. pp. 136–37.

67. Diggins, "Thoreau, Marx, and the 'Riddle' of Alienation," p. 582.

68. Bennett, *Thoreau's Nature*, p. 89.

69. *A Week*, p. 75. The *Iliad* is the only book that Thoreau keeps on his table at Walden. See Henry David Thoreau, *Walden*, in *A Week, Etc.*, p. 402.

70. Thoreau notes in his *Journal* that the Indian measures time by winters and moons, while whites measure summers and days, suggesting significant differences in the thought and experience of these two cultures. *Journal*, 4: 400.

71. Alexander Henry's account of his friendship with Wawatam suggests that even in this ideal relationship, a friendship seemingly sanctioned by the gods (Wawatam was told of Henry by the Great Spirit in a dream), there is a fair amount of room for ambiguity and inequality. For example, Henry notes that Wawatam assumed the roles of both brother and father to him. Thoreau, therefore, was well aware of both the possibilities for overcoming social barriers in discovering a common humanity and the complexities (even ignoring intrusions by other individuals or groups) of any such relationship. See Henry, *Travels and Adventures*, pp. 73–76, 152.

72. *A Week*, p. 49. Consider this more negative formulation of the same idea that nature is an equalizer across cultures and history: "There might be seen here on the bank of the Merrimack, near Goff's Falls, in what is now the town of Bedford, famous 'for hops and for its fine domestic manufactures,' some graves of the aborigines. The land still bears this scar here, and time is slowly crumbling the bones of a race. Yet, without fail, every spring, since they first fished and hunted here, the brown thrasher has heralded the morning from a birch or alder spray, and the undying race of reed-birds still rustles through the withering grass. But these bones rustle not. These mouldering elements are slowly preparing for another metamorphosis, to serve new masters, and what was the Indian's will erelong be the white man's sinew." Ibid., pp. 193–94.

73. Ibid., p. 60.

74. "Must the citizen ever for a moment, or in the least degree, resign his conscience to the legislator? Why has every man a conscience, then? I think that we should be men first, and subjects afterward." Henry D. Thoreau, *Reform Papers*, ed. Wendell Glick (Princeton, N.J.: Princeton University Press, 1973), p. 65.

75. Robert Sayre suggests that Thoreau's discussion of reformers, and how they annoy him so, is based upon what he takes to be their ignorance of "the true state of things." (See *A Week*, pp. 102–4, for Thoreau's comments.) At least part of their ignorance is of the "uncivil history" presented in this book, and its implications for meaningful reform. Sayre, *Thoreau and the American Indians*, p. 38.

76. *A Week*, p. 60.

77. Ibid., p. 105.

78. Ibid., p. 106.

79. Ibid., p. 256.

80. Ibid., p. 208.

81. "The mass of men serve the state thus, not as men mainly, but as machines, with their bodies. . . . In most cases there is no free exercise whatever of the judgment or of the moral sense; but they put themselves on a level with wood and earth and stones, and wooden men can perhaps be manufactured that will serve the pur-

pose as well. Such command no more respect than men of straw, or a lump of dirt." "Civil Disobedience," in *Reform Papers*, p. 66.

82. "There is nothing to redeem the bigotry and moral cowardice of New-Englanders in my eyes." *Journal*, 11: 326.

83. *A Week*, p. 9.

84. Ibid., p. 204.

85. "There are nine hundred and ninety-nine patrons of virtue to one virtuous man." "Civil Disobedience" p. 69.

86. *A Week*, p. 238.

87. Nancy L. Rosenblum, "Thoreau's Militant Conscience," *Political Theory* 9 (February 1981): 92.

Chapter 3. Frontier

1. Henry David Thoreau, "Natural History of Massachusetts," in *Excursions* (Boston: Houghton Mifflin, 1893), p. 161.

2. Joan Burbick writes: "Above all, Thoreau wrote the natural history of where he lived and journeyed, a history of the American landscape that was committed to the story of redemption." *Thoreau's Alternative History* (Philadelphia: University of Pennsylvania Press, 1987), p. 10.

3. Biocentrism is the view that all living beings, rather than humans alone, are primary bearers of moral value. From this perspective, the biosphere, rather than the human world, is the source of moral life and the proper context for moral analysis. For a discussion of biocentric environmental ethics, see my book *Our Limits Transgressed: Environmental Political Thought in America* (Lawrence: University Press of Kansas, 1992), chap. 5.

4. Donald Worster, *Nature's Economy* (San Francisco: Sierra Club Books, 1977), pp. 75, 85.

5. Max Oelschlaeger, *The Idea of Wilderness* (New Haven, Conn.: Yale University Press, 1991), p. 139.

6. Lawrence Buell, *The Environmental Imagination* (Cambridge, Mass.: Harvard University Press, 1995), p. 125.

7. Ibid., pp. 384, 138.

8. Buell's analysis is, of course, remarkably patronizing toward Thoreau as a thinker. The unargued presumption is that our (Buell's) ideas are correct, and that the task is to legitimate these ideas by tracing them back to Thoreau, even though the fit is certainly less than perfect. In the process, Thoreau is made to look like little more than an immature, imperfect version of ourselves. There is no recognition that Thoreau's ideas might have coherence, consistency, and integrity on their own terms, or that we might consider the possibility that Thoreau knows something that we do not, or has good reason to believe something that does not fit neatly with

our own convictions. Buell gives away the game at the end of his book: "Thoreau's importance as an environmental saint lies in being remembered, in the affectionate simplicity of public mythmaking, as helping to make the space of nature ethically resonant" (ibid., p. 394). Instead of discovering in Thoreau a powerful thinker, Buell instead finds only an "environmental saint," a symbol we can exploit in promoting our own views and fighting our own battles. Here Thoreau has been completely drained of his critical and philosophical power.

9. Buell criticizes those who think "Thoreau was not really *that* interested in nature as such; nature was a screen for something else." Ibid., p. 11.

10. Henry Seidel Canby, *Classic Americans* (New York: Harcourt, Brace, 1931), p. 212.

11. Ralph Waldo Emerson, "Thoreau," in *The Selected Writings of Ralph Waldo Emerson* (New York: Modern Library, 1968), p. 907.

12. One of the nastiest versions of this claim is implied in Oliver Wendell Holmes's snide comment that Thoreau "told the story of Nature in undress as only one who had hidden in her bedroom could have told it." Oliver Wendell Holmes, *Ralph Waldo Emerson* (Boston: Houghton, Mifflin, 1886), p. 72. More respectfully but to the same point, see Walter Harding, *The Days of Henry Thoreau* (New York: Alfred A. Knopf, 1966), p. 104; Richard Bridgman, *Dark Thoreau* (Lincoln: University of Nebraska Press, 1982), p. 271.

13. Sherman Paul, *The Shores of America* (Urbana: University of Illinois Press, 1958), p. 143.

14. Ibid., p. 305.

15. Leo Stoller, *After Walden* (Sanford, Calif.: Stanford University Press, 1957), p. 91.

16. Henry David Thoreau, *The Maine Woods*, in *A Week on the Concord and Merrimack Rivers; Walden, or, Life in the Woods; The Maine Woods; Cape Cod* (New York: Library of America, 1985), p. 603.

17. Ibid., p. 594.

18. Ibid., p. 655.

19. Ibid., p. 652.

20. Ibid., p. 654.

21. Thoreau's interest in the "natural" foundation of American society is, of course, not in the least unique or unusual. Henry Golemba points out, "By the time Thoreau went to college, it had become a stock slogan for Americans to refer to their country as 'Nature's Nation.'" Henry Golemba, *Thoreau's Wild Rhetoric* (New York: New York University Press, 1990), p. 62.

22. Remember that in *A Week* Thoreau had written, "The Indian's intercourse with Nature is at least such as admits of the greatest independence of each." *A Week on the Concord and Merrimack Rivers*, in *A Week, Etc.*, p. 46.

23. Henry David Thoreau, "Walking," in *Excursions*, p. 273.

24. *Maine Woods*, p. 609.

25. Ibid., p. 602.

26. Ibid., p. 653.

27. Ibid., p. 654.

28. Ibid., p. 685. This last sentence is the famous line that was censored by Lowell, causing Thoreau to withdraw the remainder of the Maine essays from publication in the *Atlantic Monthly,* which in turn encouraged Lowell's future bitterness toward Thoreau.

29. *A Week,* p. 238.

30. Perry Miller once wrote that Thoreau "was not a lover of nature itself: as he said, he ever sought the 'raw materials of tropes and figures.' For him these metaphors . . . were the rewards of an exploitation of natural resources, as self-centered, as profit-seeking, as that of any railroad-builder or lumber-baron, as that of any John Jacob Astor." Perry Miller, *Consciousness in Concord* (Boston: Houghton Mifflin, 1958), p. 33.

31. *Maine Woods,* p. 653.

32. Ibid., p. 640.

33. Ibid.

34. Ibid., p. 645.

35. Ibid., p. 731.

36. Ibid., p. 685.

37. Ibid., p. 710.

38. Ibid., p. 711.

39. Ibid., p. 712. Thoreau, of course, also supported the protection of local forests through the creation of town parks. See, for example, Henry David Thoreau, *Huckleberries,* ed. Leo Stoller (Iowa City: The Windhover Press of the University of Iowa and the New York Public Library, 1970), p. 35; and Henry D. Thoreau, *The Journal of Henry D. Thoreau,* vol. 3, ed. Bradford Torrey and Francis H. Allen (Boston: Houghton Mifflin, 1949), p. 216.

40. *Maine Woods,* p. 710.

41. The development of Thoreau's understanding of the significance of nature in *The Maine Woods* is paralleled by the development of Thoreau's views on this topic over the course of his life. The claim that Thoreau developed an increasingly biocentric view as time went on (see Buell, note 6 above) is not supported by the evidence of the *Journal.* It is in the early volumes (2–5) that we find the most vigorous biocentric sentiments, interspersed with clearly humanist or anthropocentric views—he is obviously arguing with himself about these matters during these years. In the later volumes the humanist/anthropocentric view emerges almost unopposed. For representative passages, see *Journal,* 1: 323; 2: 421, 474; 3: 381, 400; 4: 163, 258–59, 445; 5: 472; 9: 43, 121; 10: 168; 13: 154–55.

42. *Maine Woods,* p. 595.

43. Ibid., p. 596.

44. Ibid., p. 615.

45. Ibid., p. 651.

46. Ibid., p. 665.

47. Ibid., p. 674.

48. See ibid., pp. 677–78, 681.

49. Ibid., p. 683.

50. Ibid.

51. Ibid., p. 684.

52. Ibid., pp. 798, 800.

53. Ibid., p. 695.

54. Ibid., p. 696.

55. Ibid., p. 697.

56. Ibid., p. 704.

57. Ibid., p. 724–25.

58. Ibid., p. 730.

59. See his comments, ibid., p. 742.

60. Ibid., p. 817.

61. Ibid., p. 735.

62. Ibid., pp. 774, 775.

63. Ibid., p. 821.

64. Ibid., p. 797.

65. Ibid., p. 821.

66. Ibid., pp. 713–14, 778.

67. Ibid., pp. 793–95.

68. This is, incidentally, a nice illustration of Thoreau's humanity, for all those who have doubts about it.

69. *Maine Woods*, p. 813.

70. Ibid., p. 747. In this case, the technology mentioned is transportation.

71. Ibid.

72. Ibid., p. 717.

73. Ibid., pp. 787–88.

74. Ibid., p. 706; see also p. 819.

75. Ibid., pp. 819–20.

76. Ibid., p. 820.

77. Ibid., p. 819.

78. Ibid., p. 781.

79. Ibid., p. 602.

80. Ibid., p. 608.

81. Ibid., p. 617; emphasis in original.

82. Again, see ibid., p. 615.

83. Ibid., p. 629.

84. Henry David Thoreau, "Wild Apples," in *Excursions*, pp. 369–70. This image is very similar to that of Thoreau's bean field in *Walden*.

85. Ibid., p. 372. Steven Fink argues that "Wild Apples," not "Life without Principle," is Thoreau's greatest late jeremiad and autobiography. Steven Fink, *Prophet in the Marketplace* (Princeton, N.J.: Princeton University Press, 1992), pp. 275–77.

86. *Maine Woods*, p. 595.

87. Thoreau says he, too, "is semi-civilized." *Excursions*, p. 393.

88. *Maine Woods*, p. 687.

89. Ibid., p. 692.

90. Ibid., p. 708.

91. Ibid., p. 710.

92. Ibid., p. 595.

93. Ibid., p. 769.

94. Ibid., pp. 769–70. In *Huckleberries*, Thoreau writes, "Such is the inevitable tendency of our civilization, to reduce huckleberries to a level with beef-steaks—that is to blot out four fifths of it, or the going a-huckleberrying, and leave only a pudding, that part which is the fittest accompaniment to a beef-steak." *Huckleberries*, p. 28.

95. *Excursions*, pp. 282–83.

96. "Nowadays almost all man's improvements, so called, as the building of houses, and the cutting down of the forest and of all large trees, simply deform the landscape, and make it more and more tame and cheap." Ibid., p. 259.

97. Fink, *Prophet in the Marketplace*, p. 283.

98. *Maine Woods*, p. 712.

99. *Excursions*, p. 275.

Chapter 4. Fraternity

1. Henry David Thoreau, *Cape Cod*, in *A Week on the Concord and Merrimack Rivers; Walden, or Life in the Woods; The Maine Woods; Cape Cod* (New York: Library of America, 1985), p. 1027.

2. Ibid., p. 1039.

3. Ibid., p. 851.

4. Ibid., p. 1028.

5. *Cape Cod* has only in recent years been taken seriously as a philosophical work. For representative examples of scholarship that has portrayed *Cape Cod* (like many of the other travel narratives) as just a light travelogue with no serious substance, see Walter Harding, *The Days of Henry Thoreau* (New York: Alfred A. Knopf, 1966), p. 361, and Robert Louis Stevenson, *Familiar Studies of Men and Books* (London: Chatto and Windus, 1924), p. 150. Harding, the dean of Thoreau studies, says *Cape Cod* is "Thoreau's sunniest, happiest book," that it "bubbles over with jokes, puns, tall tales, and genial good humor. . . . Except for a few digressions on the history of the Cape, it is purely and simply a report on his various excursions to the

peninsula." This view is bizarre, considering that the book opens with handbills screaming "Death!" and Thoreau's description of the carnage of a shipwreck. More recent scholarship has pointed out that the book is much gloomier than Harding would have it (see, for example, Richard Bridgman, *Dark Thoreau* [Lincoln: University of Nebraska Press, 1982], p. 161), and that it deals with serious topics, but it remains the least studied of Thoreau's major works.

6. Sam Baskett refers to *Cape Cod* as both Thoreau's "Pilgrim's Progress" and a meditation on death. Robert D. Richardson calls it "Thoreau's exploration of salvation, of how, if at all, man is (to be) saved." See Sam S. Baskett, "Fronting the Atlantic: *Cape Cod* and 'The Dry Salvages,'" *New England Quarterly* 56 (1983): 210, 214; Robert D. Richardson, *Henry Thoreau* (Berkeley and Los Angeles: University of California Press, 1986), p. 201.

7. *Cape Cod*, p. 979.

8. "Instead of harmony with nature, Thoreau found at Cape Cod an eternal battle between man, the land animal, and the sea, the bottomless wilderness." Richard J. Schneider, "*Cape Cod*: Thoreau's Wilderness of Illusion," *ESQ* 26 (1980): 193.

9. *Cape Cod*, p. 939.

10. Ibid., p. 963.

11. Ibid., p. 893.

12. "The sense of being alone, the fate of bare unaccommodated man, the bleak emptiness of death is strongest in *Cape Cod* of all Thoreau's writings. It is the book in which, even more than *The Maine Woods*, he confronts not only a cold and unfriendly nature, but the cessation of life itself." Richardson, *Henry Thoreau*, p. 215. Mario D'Avanzo notes that, in *Cape Cod*, "Nature's provision is death, not transcendence and rebirth, as in *Walden*." Mario L. D'Avanzo, "Fortitude and Nature in Thoreau's *Cape Cod*," *ESQ* 20 (1974): 132.

13. *Cape Cod*, pp. 853–54.

14. Ibid., p. 854.

15. Ibid., p. 855.

16. Ibid., p. 853.

17. In the light of this passage, it is difficult to understand why some, including Robert Louis Stevenson and more recently Richard Bridgman, insist that Thoreau lacks compassion and pity for others. See Stevenson, *Familiar Studies*, p. 160; Bridgman, *Dark Thoreau*, p. xi.

18. *Cape Cod*, p. 857.

19. See ibid., pp. 913–14.

20. Ibid., p. 857.

21. Ibid., p. 860.

22. Ibid., p. 861.

23. Ibid., p. 901.

24. Ibid., p. 902.

25. Ibid.

26. Ibid., p. 900.

27. Ibid., pp. 967–68.

28. Ibid., p. 903.

29. Ibid.

30. Ibid., p. 922.

31. Ibid., p. 914.

32. Henry D. Thoreau, *The Journal of Henry D. Thoreau*, vol. 3, ed. Bradford Torrey and Francis H. Allen (Boston: Houghton Mifflin, 1949), p. 242.

33. *Cape Cod*, pp. 1007–10.

34. Ibid., p. 1011. John Lowney writes: "Although often skeptical about earlier discovery and exploratory narratives, Thoreau most harshly questions the settlement narratives that center the origins of American history in New England and, more specifically, in the New England village." John Lowney, "Thoreau's *Cape Cod*: The Unsettling Art of the Wrecker," *American Literature* 64 (June 1992): 241.

35. *Cape Cod*, pp. 1011–12.

36. See ibid., pp. 983, 1021.

37. Ibid., p. 1023.

38. Ibid.

39. "... how much blood and cruelty lie at the bottom of all 'good things'!" Friedrich Nietzsche, *On the Genealogy of Morals*, in *Basic Writings of Nietzsche*, ed. Walter Kaufmann (New York: Modern Library, 1968), p. 498.

40. Henry David Thoreau, *Walden, or, Life in the Woods* in *A Week, Etc.*, p. 384.

41. John C. Broderick, "Thoreau's Proposals for Legislation," *American Quarterly* 7 (1955): 289.

42. Philip Abbott has seriously misunderstood Thoreau's attack on charity. He writes, "It is clear that acts of charity ... are for Thoreau, at best, spent in wasted time, and are not unlike the wasted labor that he saw in the economic system in general." As we have seen, Thoreau's complaint is not that it is a "waste of time" to care for others, but rather that our charity is cruel and sometimes serves to reinforce injustices. Philip Abbott, *States of Perfect Freedom* (Amherst: University of Massachusetts Press, 1987), p. 88.

43. *Cape Cod*, p. 1000.

44. "I think that there is nothing, not even crime, more opposed to poetry, to philosophy, ay, to life itself, than this incessant business." "Life without Principle," in Henry D. Thoreau, *Reform Papers*, ed. Wendell Glick (Princeton, N.J.: Princeton University Press, 1973), p. 156.

45. *Journal*, 1: 239.

46. *Cape Cod*, p. 933.

47. Ibid., p. 877.

48. See ibid., p. 880.

49. Ibid., p. 881.

50. Ibid., p. 884.

51. Ibid., pp. 884–85.

52. Ibid., p. 886.

53. Ibid.

54. Ibid., p. 887.

55. Of early New England authors in general, Thoreau writes, "Certainly that generation stood nearer to nature, nearer to the facts, than this, and hence their books have more life in them." *Journal*, 7: 109.

56. "Like clergymen generally, with or without the gown, they made on us the impression of effeminacy." He describes the nuns as having "cadaverous faces," "their complexions parboiled with scalding tears," and looking as if they "have been dead and buried for a year, and then untombed, with the life's grief upon them, and yet, for some unaccountable reason, the process of decay arrested." *A Yankee in Canada*, in Henry David Thoreau, *Excursions* (Boston: Houghton Mifflin, 1893), pp. 18–19.

57. "We saw one school-house in our walk, and listened to the sounds which issued from it; but it appeared like a place where the process, not of enlightening, but of obfuscating the mind was going on, and the pupils received only so much light as could penetrate the shadow of the Catholic Church." Ibid., p. 57.

58. Ibid., p. 64.

59. Ibid., pp. 15–16.

60. Ibid., p. 84.

61. Ibid., pp. 58–59.

62. *Journal*, 13: 20.

63. *Yankee*, p. 103.

64. Ibid., p. 33.

65. Ibid., p. 32.

66. Ibid., p. 19.

67. Ibid., p. 32.

68. Ibid., p. 94.

69. Ibid., p. 99.

70. Ibid., pp. 20–21.

71. *Journal*, 3: 195.

72. Nancy L. Rosenblum, "Thoreau's Militant Conscience," *Political Theory* 9 (February 1981): 89.

73. It is puzzling why Joel Porte finds this position so unacceptably self-indulgent. Porte writes, "Because no actual society is ever good enough for our American hero [i.e., Thoreau], we are led to suspect that his act [of moving to Walden Pond] is a selfish, not a social, one." Porte seems to think that to believe, as Thoreau does, that all known and possible political communities fail to live up to their professed ideals is to also hold that all are equally illegitimate. This is clearly false, as is the assumption that to understand a community's vices is to be blinded to its virtues. Thoreau's point is simply that a citizen should admire the virtues and loath the

vices. Such a position seems to me very "social," to say nothing of sensible, and the only alternatives appear to be uselessly utopian or uncritically chauvinistic. Joel Porte, "Henry Thoreau: Society and Solitude," *ESQ* 19 (1973): 133.

74. *Cape Cod*, p. 1028.

75. Ibid., p. 912.

76. Ibid., p. 918.

77. Ibid., p. 912.

78. Ibid., p. 913.

79. Ibid., p. 905.

80. Ibid., p. 916.

81. Ibid., p. 919.

82. When John Patrick Diggins writes that Thoreau preferred "solitary existence to social solidarity," he mistakes Thoreau's criticism of the American political community with a rejection of political community per se. Richard Ellis makes the same error, writing, "Cooperation no less than competition, Thoreau believed, would subject the individual to coercion and manipulation by others," as does Irving Howe when he says that "Thoreau's vision of freedom did not depend upon or require communal experience." See John Patrick Diggins, "Thoreau, Marx, and the 'Riddle' of Alienation," *Social Research* 39 (Winter 1972): 580; Richard J. Ellis, *American Political Cultures* (New York: Oxford University Press, 1993), p. 142; Irving Howe, *The American Newness* (Cambridge, Mass.: Harvard University Press, 1986), p. 35.

83. Sherman Paul's comment, that "one of the most persistent errors concerning Thoreau that has never been sufficiently dispelled is that Thoreau was an anarchical individualist," is as true today as it was when he wrote it in 1958. Jane Bennett is just one of the most recent scholars to repeat this conventional wisdom when she writes of Thoreau's "rejection of politics," his fundamental anarchism. Sherman Paul, *The Shores of America* (Urbana: University of Illinois Press, 1958), p. 75; Jane Bennett, *Thoreau's Nature* (Thousand Oaks, Calif.: Sage 1994), p. xxiv.

Perhaps this mistake grows out of the assumption by so many interpreters that Thoreau is only an echo of Emerson. George Kateb rightly explains that "Emerson would be an anarchist if he could," but we must be careful not to allow this fact to influence our evaluation of Thoreau's politics. George Kateb, *Emerson and Self-Reliance* (Thousand Oaks, Calif.: Sage, 1995), p. 189.

84. *Walden*, p. 410.

85. Wilson Carey McWilliams, *The Idea of Fraternity in America* (Berkeley and Los Angeles: University of California Press, 1973), p. 296. John C. Broderick points out, "If Thoreau's journal is read aright, Thoreau himself had specific notions about what sort of government he would respect, one that provided for human welfare and enabled the individual person to realize his highest aspirations." Broderick, "Thoreau's Proposals for Legislation," p. 290.

86. Henry David Thoreau, *The Correspondence of Henry David Thoreau*, ed. Walter

Harding and Carl Bode (New York: New York University Press, 1958), pp. 435–36 (20 October 1856).

87. *Walden*, p. 583.

Chapter 5. Independence

1. Joyce Appleby, *Liberalism and Republicanism in the Historical Imagination* (Cambridge, Mass.: Harvard University Press, 1992), p. 4.

2. "Instead of creating a new order of benevolence and selflessness, enlightened republicanism was breeding social competitiveness and individualism; and there seemed no easy way of stopping it. Since at the outset most revolutionary leaders had conceded primacy to society over government, to modern social virtue over classical public virtue, they found it difficult to resist people's absorption in their private lives and interests. The Revolution was the source of its own contradictions. . . . In many respects this new democratic society was the very opposite of the one the revolutionary leaders had envisaged." Gordon S. Wood, *The Radicalism of the American Revolution* (New York: Alfred A. Knopf, 1992), p. 230.

3. Henry David Thoreau, *Cape Cod*, in *A Week on the Concord and Merrimack Rivers; Walden, or, Life in the Woods; The Maine Woods; Cape Cod* (New York: Library of America, 1985), p. 1033.

4. Ibid., p. 1036.

5. "I confess I was surprised to find that so many men spent their whole day, ay, their whole lives almost, a-fishing. It is remarkable what a serious business men make of getting their dinners, and how universally shiftlessness and a grovelling taste take refuge in a merely ant-like industry. Better go without your dinner, I thought, than be thus everlastingly fishing for it like a cormorant. Of course, *viewed from the shore*, our pursuits in the country appear not a whit less frivolous." Ibid., p. 976.

6. This quarrel goes at least as far back as Thoreau's graduation address at Harvard, which carried the title "The Commercial Spirit of Modern Times, Considered in Its Influence on the Political, Moral, and Literary Character of a Nation." Walter Harding, *The Days of Henry Thoreau* (New York: Alfred A. Knopf, 1966), p. 49.

7. Nahman of Bratslav, *The Tales* (New York: Paulist Press, 1978), p. 224.

8. Ibid., p. 225.

9. "He has only one thing to consider in performing any action—that is, whether he is acting rightly or wrongly, like a good man or a bad one." Plato, "The Apology," in *The Collected Dialogues of Plato*, ed. Edith Hamilton and Huntington Cairns (New York: Bollingen Foundation, 1966), p. 14.

10. "Perhaps when I say this I may give you the impression, as I did in my remarks about exciting sympathy and making passionate appeals, that I am showing a deliberate perversity. That is not so, gentlemen.The real position is this. I am

convinced that I never wrong anyone intentionally, but I cannot convince you of this, because we have had so little time for discussion." Ibid., p. 22.

11. Henry David Thoreau, *Walden*, in *A Week, Etc.*, p. 585.

12. Ibid., pp. 325–26. Sherman Paul claims, "No one in his generation had such a hunger for place—unless it was Hawthorne—or knew its values in an age when mobility was becoming a marked characteristic of American life." Henry Seidel Canby writes, "Like Socrates in this respect if in no other, he talked always of his townsmen and of himself, who were real people in a real environment." Most recently, Simon Schama notes that "although we generally think of Thoreau as the guardian of wilderness, one of his most powerful passions was for the local and the intimate." Sherman Paul, *The Shores of America* (Urbana: University of Illinois Press, 1958), p. 145; Henry Seidel Canby, *Thoreau* (Boston: Houghton Mifflin, 1939), p. 450; Simon Schama, *Landscape and Memory* (New York: Alfred A. Knopf, 1995), p. 576.

It is interesting that one of the sources of tension between Thoreau and Emerson was Thoreau's disapproval of Emerson's European travels. See Robert D. Richardson, Emerson: *The Mind on Fire* (Berkeley and Los Angeles: University of California Press, 1995), p. 462.

13. *Walden*, p. 330. For the whole passage, see pages 330–31.

14. Referring to his conflict with the state over his refusal to pay his taxes, Thoreau writes, "It is true, I might have resisted forcibly with more or less effect, might have run 'amok' against society; but I preferred that society should run 'amok' against me, it being the desperate party." Ibid., p. 459.

15. Ibid., p. 377.

16. Ibid., p. 334.

17. Ibid., pp. 398–99.

18. "Be it life or death, we crave only reality." Ibid., p. 400.

19. Telling how one "inoffensive, simple-minded pauper," whom others frequently abused, said to him simply that he was "deficient in intellect," Thoreau comments, "It seemed that from such a basis of truth and frankness as the poor weak-headed pauper had laid, our intercourse might go forward to something better than the intercourse of sages." Ibid., pp. 442–43.

20. Ibid., p. 427.

21. Ibid., p. 499.

22. Ibid., p. 361.

23. In what is perhaps the most lovely, thoughtful, and insightful essay in all the secondary Thoreau literature, E. B. White says that one of the reasons *Walden* is "the best youth's companion yet written by an American" is because "it steadfastly refuses to record bad news." E. B. White, "Walden—1954," *Yale Review* 44 (1954): 14.

24. *Walden*, p. 389.

25. Ibid., p. 586.

26. Ibid., p. 329.

27. This is true, despite the doubts that are raised from time to time, such as when Thoreau writes, "I confess, that practically speaking, when I have learned a man's real disposition, I have no hopes of changing it for the better or worse in this state of existence." Ibid., p. 418.

28. Steven Fink points out that even Thoreau's prose style is democratic and populist, in comparison with the impossibly obscure and elitist language of other transcendentalists. Steven Fink, *Prophet in the Marketplace* (Princeton, N.J.: Princeton University Press, 1992), p. 64.

29. *Walden*, p. 335. Taylor Stoehr insightfully observes of the transcendentalists in general, "They were among the first to confront the world as we know it—a world of *too much*." Taylor Stoehr, *Nay-Saying in Concord* (Hamden, Conn.: Archon Books, 1979), p. 155.

30. *Walden*, p. 394.

31. Ibid., pp. 526–32. F. B. Sanborn is only slightly overdramatic when he says the area around Walden Pond "was anciently a place of dark repute, the home of pariahs and lawless characters, such as fringed the sober garment of many a New England village in Puritanic times." F. B. Sanborn, *Henry D. Thoreau* (Boston: Houghton Mifflin, 1910), p. 202.

32. *Walden*, p. 434.

33. "Like the *Leviathan*, and the *Second Treatise of Government*, and the *Discourse on the Origin of Inequality*—which we perhaps regard as more or less prescientific studies of existing societies—*Walden* is, among other things, a tract of political education, education for membership in the polis. It locates authority in the citizens and it identifies citizens—those with whom one is in membership—as 'neighbors.'" Stanley Cavell, *The Senses of Walden* (San Francisco: North Point Press, 1981), p. 85.

34. Richard Ellis is only one of the most recent interpreters to misunderstand this point by describing Thoreau as a "voluntary recluse or hermit." Richard J. Ellis, *American Political Cultures* (New York: Oxford University Press, 1993), p. 141.

35. *Walden*, p. 394.

36. One of the few astute observations Emerson makes about Thoreau is when he calls him a "born protestant." Ralph Waldo Emerson, "Thoreau," in *The Selected Writings of Ralph Waldo Emerson* (New York: Modern Library, 1968), p. 896.

37. Robert Richardson writes, "When Thoreau presents himself as economic man, he does so not to isolate himself, but to speak as a typical, a representative individual." Michael Fischer claims that Thoreau "speaks for others because he speaks for himself, not despite it." Robert D. Richardson, "The Social Ethics of *Walden*," in *Critical Essays on Henry David Thoreau's Walden*, ed. Joel Myerson, (Boston: G. K. Hall, 1988), p. 240; Michael R. Fischer, "*Walden* and the Politics of Contemporary Literary Theory," in *New Essays on Walden*, ed. Robert F. Sayer (New York: Cambridge University Press, 1992), p. 99.

38. *Walden*, p. 336. When asked what the hound, horse, and turtledove symbolize, Thoreau simply responded, "Well, Sir, I suppose we have all had our losses." Harding, *Days of Henry Thoreau*, p. 383.

39. "My actual life is a fact in view of which I have no occasion to congratulate myself, but for my faith and aspiration I have respect. It is from these that I speak." Henry David Thoreau, *The Correspondence of Henry David Thoreau*, ed. Walter Harding and Carl Bode (New York: New York University Press, 1958), p. 216 (27 March 1848).

If we fail to recognize the egalitarian and self-critical presuppositions of Thoreau's "sermon," we will be misled to believe, like so many interpreters, that Thoreau was haughty and conceited toward his audience. See, for example, George Hochfield (Thoreau feels "scorn for ordinary human weakness") and Nancy Rosenblum ("He simply could not abide other men"). George Hochfield, "Anti-Thoreau," *Sewanee Review* 96 (Summer 1988): 433; Nancy L. Rosenblum, "Thoreau's Militant Conscience," *Political Theory* 9 (February 1981): 96.

40. *Walden*, p. 326.

41. Ibid., p. 327.

42. Ibid., p. 335. In "Life without Principle" he puts it like this: "There is no more fatal blunderer than he who consumes the greater part of his life getting his living." Henry D. Thoreau, *Reform Papers*, ed. Wendell Glick (Princeton, N.J.: Princeton University Press, 1973), p. 160.

43. *Walden*, p. 349.

44. Ibid., p. 352.

45. Ibid., p. 396.

46. Ibid., p. 453.

47. "This world is a place of business. What an infinite bustle! I am awakened almost every night by the panting of the locomotive. It interrupts my dreams. There is no sabbath. It would be glorious to see mankind at leisure for once." "Life without Principle," in *Reform Papers*, p. 156.

48. "The ways by which you may get money almost without exception lead downward." Ibid., p. 158.

49. *Walden*, pp. 343–44.

50. Ibid., p. 359.

51. *Correspondence*, p. 496 (16 November 1857).

52. *Walden*, p. 454. Writing about those who treat wild berries as private property, Thoreau says: "It is true, we have as good a right to make berries private property, as to make wild grass and trees such—it is not worse than a thousand other practices which custom has sanctioned—but that is the worst of it, for it suggests how bad the rest are, and to what result our civilization and division of labor naturally tend, to make all things venal." "Thus we behave like oxen in a flower garden. The true fruit of Nature can only be plucked with a fluttering heart and a

delicate hand, not bribed by any earthly reward." Henry David Thoreau, *Huckle-berries*, ed. Leo Stoller (Iowa City: The Windhover Press of the University of Iowa and the New York Public Library, 1970), pp. 28–29, 30.

53. *Walden*, p. 482.

54. ". . . the woodcutters, and the railroad, and I myself have profaned Walden." Ibid., p. 480.

55. Ibid., p. 365.

56. Ibid., p. 460.

57. Ibid., p. 350.

58. Ibid., p. 368.

59. "As for the Pyramids, there is nothing to wonder at in them so much as the fact that so many men could be found degraded enough to spend their lives constructing a tomb for some ambitious booby, whom it would have been wiser and manlier to have drowned in the Nile, and then given his body to the dogs." Ibid.

60. Ibid., p. 329.

61. Ibid., p. 327; Henry D. Thoreau, *The Journal of Henry D. Thoreau*, vol. 12, ed. Bradford Torrey and Francis H. Allen (Boston: Houghton Mifflin, 1949), p. 331.

62. *Walden*, p. 331.

63. It is significant that Thoreau does not think of his own experiment at Walden as radically unique or unprecedented among his contemporaries. In his *Journal* he discusses neighbors whom he admires and considers as role models, men perhaps even more experienced than himself in living independently. He describes his friend Minot as a farmer who loves his life and lives it well, who (along with his friends) actually improves nature by his presence, mainly because he is an "old-fashioned man" who "has not scrubbed up and improved his land" in the modern sense (3: 41–43; 10: 168; 14: 67); Rice and his son live life as vigorously and enthusiastically as if it were a sport to be played (8: 26–27); Hosmer is equated with virtuous Roman farmers (8: 245). Thoreau has the deepest admiration for these neighbors, and clearly thinks of himself as indebted to their examples. Thoreau is not the only, or even the most virtuous, "representative man."

64. *Walden*, p. 586.

65. Ibid., p. 367.

66. Martin Bickman, *Walden: Volatile Truths* (New York: Twayne, 1992), p. 5. Sacvan Bercovitch makes the same point: "Like a biblical prophet, he [Thoreau] hoped to wake his countrymen up to the fact that they were desecrating their own beliefs." Sacvan Bercovitch, *The American Jeremiad* (Madison: University of Wisconsin Press, 1978), p. 187.

67. Henry Seidel Canby writes, "His [Thoreau's] dilemma is the true subsistence problem of the industrial revolution, which gave us control of nature without control of ourselves." Henry Seidel Canby, *Classic Americans* (New York: Harcourt, Brace, 1931), p. 202.

68. See note 30 above.

69. There is confusion about this issue in the secondary literature. Philip Abbott, for example, writes scornfully, "If *Walden* has any single clear message as to how to achieve happiness, it is in the doctrine of self-improvement." Less critically but to a similar point, Jane Bennett writes that Thoreau's "dissent is more a means toward self-refashioning than toward societal reform." Lumping Thoreau with Emerson and Whitman, Quentin Anderson comes to the same conclusion: "This sounds rather more like a demand that everybody take care of his own salvation than a preparation for civic life." These commentators, and many others like them, observe that Thoreau encourages his readers to take an active role in establishing their independence, and conclude that the message of the book is private, apolitical, and personal. There is no reason to believe this is so. Yes, Thoreau is speaking to individual citizens about the way they will understand and practice their freedom. This project, however, has profound civic implications, since it goes to the heart of American political culture. As Stanley Cavell writes, "As against the usual views about Thoreau's hatred of society and his fancied private declaration of independence from it, it is worth hearing him from the outset publicly accept a nation's promise."

See Philip Abbott, *States of Perfect Freedom* (Amherst: University of Massachusetts Press, 1987), p. 79; Jane Bennett, *Thoreau's Nature* (Thousand Oaks, Calif: Sage, 1994), p. 8; Quentin Anderson, *Making Americans* (New York: Harcourt Brace Jovanovich, 1992), p. 38; Cavell, *Senses of Walden*, p. 6.

70. *Walden*, p. 403.

71. Ibid., p. 402.

72. Ibid., p. 406.

73. Ibid., p. 408.

74. Ibid., pp. 409–10.

75. Ibid., p. 409.

76. Ibid., p. 410. See chap. 4, n. 84.

77. Ibid., p. 405.

78. See ibid., pp. 437–42, for Thoreau's realistic and respectful portrait of Theron.

79. Ibid., p. 411.

80. Ibid., p. 448. See chap. 3, n. 84.

81. Ibid., p. 432.

82. Ibid., p. 583. In "Autumnal Tints" Thoreau writes, "Wealth indoors may be the inheritance of few, but it is equally distributed on the Common. All children alike can revel in this golden harvest." Henry David Thoreau, *Excursions* (Boston: Houghton Mifflin, 1893), p. 334.

83. *Walden*, p. 429.

84. Ibid., p. 456.

85. Ibid., p. 459.

86. Ibid., p. 349.

87. Ibid., p. 330.

88. "How can you expect the birds to sing when their groves are cut down?" Ibid., p. 476.

89. "Nature, the earth herself, is the only panacea." *Journal*, 12: 350.

90. *Walden*, p. 575.

91. Ibid., p. 584.

92. "Before we can adorn our houses with beautiful objects the walls must be stripped, and our lives must be stripped, and beautiful housekeeping and beautiful living be laid for a foundation: now, a taste for the beautiful is most cultivated out of doors, where there is no house and no housekeeper." Ibid., p. 353.

93. Ibid., p. 551.

94. Ibid., p. 581.

95. "Moral reform is the effort to throw off sleep. . . . I have never yet met a man who was quite awake. How could I look him in the face?" Ibid., p. 394.

96. "The earth is not a mere fragment of dead history, stratum upon stratum like the leaves of a book, to be studied by geologists and antiquaries chiefly, but living poetry like the leaves of a tree, which precede flowers and fruit,—not a fossil earth, but a living earth; compared with whose great central life all animal and vegetable life is merely parasitic." Ibid., p. 568.

97. Ibid., p. 570.

98. Ibid., p. 567.

99. Ibid., p. 573.

100. Ibid., p. 576.

101. Thoreau is obviously a key figure in what Michael Rogin calls the "division at the center of American politics between a nature become commodities which separates men in civil society, and a virgin land which purifies and unites them." Michael Rogin, "Nature as Politics and Nature as Romance in America," *Political Theory* 5 (February 1977): 13.

102. *Walden*, p. 575.

103. Bradley P. Dean and Gary Scharnhorst, "The Contemporary Reception of Walden," in *Studies in the American Renaissance, 1990*, ed. Joel Myerson (Charlottesville: University Press of Virginia, 1990), p. 312.

104. In "Life without Principle" Thoreau writes: "Lieutenant Herndon, whom our Government sent to explore the Amazon, and, it is said, to extend the area of Slavery, observed that there was wanting there 'an industrious and active population, who know what the comforts of life are, and who have artificial wants to draw out the great resources of the country.' But what are the 'artificial wants' to be encouraged? Not the love of luxuries, like the tobacco and slaves of, I believe, his native Virginia, nor the ice and granite and other material wealth of our native New England; nor are 'the great resources of a country' that fertility or barrenness of soil which produces these. . . . When we want culture more than potatoes, and illumination more than sugar-plums, then the great resources of a world are taxed and drawn out, and the result, or staple production, is, not slaves, nor operatives, but

men,—those rare fruits called heroes, saints, poets, philosophers, and redeemers."
Reform Papers, pp. 176–77.

105. *Walden*, p. 378.

106. Ibid., p. 387.

107. Ibid., p. 479.

108. Ibid., p. 395.

109. "In proportion as he simplifies his life, the laws of the universe will appear less complex, and solitude will not be solitude, nor poverty poverty, nor weakness weakness." Ibid., p. 580.

110. "We should be blessed if we lived in the present always, and took advantage of every accident that befell us, like the grass which confesses the influence of the slightest dew that falls on it; and did not spend our time in atoning for the neglect of past opportunities, which we call doing our duty." Ibid., pp. 572–73.

111. Ibid., p. 355.

112. Ibid., p. 366.

113. Ibid., p. 358.

114. Ibid.

115. Irving Howe is therefore unpersuasive in his claim that "Thoreau's vision of freedom did not depend upon or require communal experience." For what is probably the most biting portrayal of Thoreau as entirely isolated from society, see Melville's satire of *Walden*, "Cock-A-Doodle-Do." Irving Howe, *The American Newness* (Cambridge, Mass.: Harvard University Press, 1986), p. 35; Herman Melville, *The Apple-Tree Table and Other Sketches* (New York: Greenwood, 1969), pp. 211–56.

116. *Walden*, p. 379.

117. Ibid; emphasis in original.

118. Ibid., p. 583. See chap. 4, n. 87.

119. Misunderstanding this point has led some critics to become almost hysterical in their denunciations of Thoreau. Oliver Wendell Holmes calls him "the nullifier of civilization," and Vincent Buranelli screams that "Thoreau is actually calling for an end to organized, civilized life, for a scattering of us all, each to his own Walden." Oliver Wendell Holmes, *Ralph Waldo Emerson* (Boston: Houghton, Mifflin, 1886), p. 86; Vincent Buranelli, "The Case against Thoreau," *Ethics* 67 (1957): 265.

120. *Walden*, p. 380.

121. "If I knew for a certainty that a man was coming to my house with the conscious design of doing me good, I should run for my life." Ibid., p. 381.

122. Ibid., p. 384.

123. "The human race is interested in these experiments, though a few old women who are incapacitated for them, or who own their thirds in mills, may be alarmed." Ibid., p. 374. Sherman Paul observes, "Intent on erecting a 'higher society,' Thoreau did not go to the woods for himself alone, but to serve mankind." Paul, *Shores of America*, p. 76

124. Thoreau never mentions in *Walden* that he held an antislavery society meeting at his cabin. The focus of the book is independence, but this does not mean that Thoreau was opposed to political activity or participating in necessary communal tasks. Those activities are simply not what the book is about, and Thoreau obviously believes that encouraging independent citizens is the more important issue for him to address for the sake of the long-term health of the nation. For a reference to the antislavery meeting, see Henry Golemba, *Thoreau's Wild Rhetoric* (New York: New York University Press, 1990), p. 181.

125. *Walden*, p. 490. This passage is only one illustration of how imperceptive Emerson is when he says that Thoreau "had no temptations to fight against—no appetites, no passions, no taste for elegant trifles." Emerson, "Thoreau" p. 897.

126. *Walden*, p. 490.

127. Ibid., p. 492.

128. Ibid., pp. 494, 495, 496.

129. Ibid., p. 497.

130. Ibid., p. 498.

131. Ibid., pp. 497–98.

132. Robert D. Richardson, *Henry Thoreau* (Berkeley and Los Angeles: University of California Press, 1986), p. 310.

133. *Walden*, p. 532.

134. Ibid., p. 580.

135. For a reading of Thoreau as a champion of precapitalist subsistence agriculture, see Carolyn Merchant, *Ecological Revolutions* (Chapel Hill: University of North Carolina Press, 1989), p. 260.

136. *Walden*, p. 417.

137. Ibid., p. 354.

138. It is hard not to sympathize with Stanley Edgar Hyman's exasperation over Emerson's "obtuse tribute" to Thoreau in his eulogy. As we saw in chapter 1 Emerson says, "I cannot help counting it a fault in him that he had no ambition. Wanting this, instead of engineering for all America, he was the captain of a huckleberry-party." Either Emerson was honestly unaware of Thoreau's intensely ambitious project, in which case we must seriously doubt his perceptiveness, or he was being disingenuous, in which case we must question his faith and sincerity. Stanley Edgar Hyman, "Henry Thoreau Once More," *Massachusetts Review* 4 (1962): 167; Emerson, *Selected Writings*, p. 911.

139. Andrew Delbanco observes that "the instillation of ambition as the one common good was the great transformation of nineteenth-century American life. By 1850, Americans found themselves both liberated and imprisoned by the enormously compelling idea—once decried as pride—of the striving self." In his own way, Thoreau was as much a part of this development as any capitalist. Andrew Delbanco, *The Death of Satan* (New York: Farrar, Straus and Giroux, 1995), pp. 105–6.

140. "But the only true America is that country where you are at liberty to pursue such a mode of life as may enable you to do without these [luxuries], and where the state does not endeavor to compel you to sustain the slavery and war and other superfluous expenses which directly or indirectly result from the use of such things." *Walden*, p. 486.

141. "The civilized man is a more experienced and wiser savage." Ibid., p. 354.

142. "It is not for a man to put himself in such an attitude to society, but to maintain himself in whatever attitude he find himself through obedience to the laws of his being, which will never be one of opposition to a just government, if he should chance to meet with such." Ibid., p. 579.

143. Ibid., pp. 516–17. Thoreau betrays his old New England sensibilities in his description of the architecture of this dream house. Rather than imagining an ornate and luxurious castle, he conjures something closer to a magnificent, oversized, rude, and perhaps even incomplete Congregational meetinghouse. Thanks to Pat Neal for this observation.

144. Stanley Cavell observes that *Walden*'s "central action" of Thoreau's construction of his own house "is the general prophecy: the nation, and the nation's people, have yet to be well made." Cavell, *Senses of Walden*, p. 116.

Chapter 6. Resistance

1. Henry D. Thoreau, "Civil Disobedience," in *Reform Papers*, ed. Wendell Glick (Princeton, N.J.: Princeton University Press, 1973), p. 66.

2. "I have never declined paying the highway tax, because I am as desirous of being a good neighbor as I am of being a bad subject." Ibid., p. 84.

3. Ibid., p. 86.

4. "Slavery in Massachusetts," in *Reform Papers*, p. 108.

5. "A Plea for Captain John Brown," in *Reform Papers*, p. 133.

6. *Walden*, in *A Week on the Concord and Merrimack Rivers; Walden, or, Life in the Woods; The Maine Woods; Cape Cod* (New York: Library of America, 1985), p. 384.

7. Vincent Buranelli intends his comment to be a devastating criticism when he says, "He [Thoreau] is not a philosopher, but a prophet and a preacher." It is obvious, however, that Thoreau never intended to be a philosopher in the sense Buranelli has in mind. In these polemical essays he cultivates the role of a "prophet and a preacher" quite knowingly and appropriately. Vincent Buranelli, "The Case against Thoreau," *Ethics* 67 (1957): 262.

8. "Slavery," p. 91.

9. "Civil Disobedience," p. 68.

10. Ibid., p. 63.

11. Ibid., p. 64.

12. Ibid.

13. Taylor Stoehr is one of the few commentators on "Civil Disobedience" to emphasize the implicit acceptance of (just) government in Thoreau's argument. Taylor Stoehr, *Nay-Saying in Concord* (Hamden, Conn.: Archon Books, 1979), p. 54.

14. "Civil Disobedience," p. 78.

15. Ibid., p. 65.

16. Ibid., p. 66.

17. Ibid., p. 70.

18. Ibid., p. 67.

19. Ibid., p. 72.

20. Ibid., p. 89.

21. Ibid.

22. John Patrick Diggins could not be further from the truth when he writes, "No other social philosopher asked so much of man and demanded he do so little." John Patrick Diggins, "Thoreau, Marx, and the 'Riddle' of Alienation," *Social Research* 39 (Winter 1972): 571.

23. "Civil Disobedience," p. 86.

24. Jane Bennett, "On Being a Native: Thoreau's Hermeneutics of Self," *Polity* 22 (Summer 1990): 560.

25. "Slavery," p. 94.

26. Ibid., pp. 96–97.

27. Ibid., p. 92.

28. Ibid., p. 97.

29. Ibid., p. 107.

30. Ibid., p. 98.

31. Ibid., p. 99.

32. Ibid.

33. Ibid., p. 102.

34. Ibid.

35. "A Plea," p. 115.

36. Ibid., p. 125.

37. Ibid., p. 113.

38. Ibid., p. 127

39. Ibid., p. 135. In "The Last Days of John Brown," Thoreau writes of Brown's career, "I know of nothing so miraculous in our history." "The Last Days of John Brown," in *Reform Papers*, p. 145.

40. "A Plea," p. 112. Walter Harding, defending a pacifist reading of Thoreau, writes, "Had Thoreau known of Brown's perpetration of the bloodthirsty Pottawatomie massacre in Kansas, he might never have endorsed him and might have been convinced of his insanity." Michael Meyer convincingly demonstrates, however, that Thoreau must have been aware of the reports from Pottawatomie. Wal-

ter Harding, *The Days of Henry Thoreau* (New York: Alfred A. Knopf, 1966), p. 418; Michael Meyer, "Thoreau's Rescue of John Brown from History," in *Studies in the American Renaissance, 1980,* ed. Joel Myerson (Boston: Twayne, 1980), pp. 301–16.

41. "A Plea," p. 134.

42. Jane Bennett is therefore unpersuasive when she claims that Thoreau "loudly rejects all collective ideals." Jane Bennett, *Thoreau's Nature* (Thousand Oaks, Calif: Sage, 1994), p. 132.

43. In "The Last Days of John Brown," Thoreau is optimistic that the north, inspired by Brown, is becoming "all transcendental." "The Last Days of John Brown," p. 147.

44. "A Plea," p. 119.

45. Ibid., p. 135.

46. Ibid., p. 137.

47. Ibid., p. 124.

48. In his *Journal* Thoreau exclaims, "Better that the British Empire be destroyed" than that Canada return an escaped slave to the American South. Henry D. Thoreau, *The Journal of Henry D. Thoreau,* vol. 14, ed. Bradford Torrey and Francis H. Allen (Boston: Houghton Mifflin, 1949), p. 293.

49. "A Plea," p. 130.

50. Ibid., p. 131.

51. Ibid., pp. 130–31.

52. Ibid., p. 133.

53. Ibid., pp. 132–33.

54. Frederick Douglass, *The Life and Writings of Frederick Douglass,* vol 2, ed. Philip S. Foner (New York: International Publishers, 1950), p. 460. Foner points out (p. 87) that Brown, in the 1840s, was the first to make Douglass doubt the strategy of moral suasion.

55. Douglass's November 1859 editorial was entitled "Captain John Brown Not Insane." Douglass argues as follows: "His entire procedure in this matter disproves the charge that he was prompted by an impulse of mad revenge, and shows that he was moved by the highest principles of philanthropy. His carefulness of the lives of unarmed persons—his humane and courteous treatment of his prisoners—his cool self-possession all through his trial—and especially his calm, dignified speech on receiving his sentence, all conspire to show that he was neither insane nor actuated by vengeful passion; and we hope the country has heard the last of John Brown's madness." Ibid., p. 459.

56. "This age is too gross and sensual to appreciate his deeds, and so calls him mad." Ibid., p. 460.

57. Ibid., p. 459.

58. "We Abolitionists profess to propagate no new doctrines in politics or morals, but to urge all men to practice the old well-defined and immutable principles 'of

the fatherhood of God and the universal brotherhood of man.'" Benjamin Quarles, *Blacks on John Brown* (Urbana: University of Illinois Press, 1972), pp. 14, 11–15 generally.

59. Ibid., p. 23.

60. Ibid., p. 29. In "A Plea for Captain John Brown," Thoreau writes: "It seems as if no man had ever died in America before, for in order to die you must first have lived." "A Plea," p. 134.

61. It is also interesting to compare Thoreau's rhetoric with Emerson's, who wrote favorably of the following claim by Brown: "Better that a whole generation of men, women and children should pass away by a violent death than that one word of either [the Golden Rule or the Declaration of Independence] should be violated in this country." Maurice Gonnaud points out that this language is more extreme and immoderate than that used by Thoreau. This should make us very wary of those who attempt, like Irving Howe, to contrast what they take to be Emerson's good sense with Thoreau's political irresponsibility: "Thoreau could fall into the rigidity of the fanatic, perhaps the crank. Emerson never did." Ralph Waldo Emerson, "John Brown," in *The Selected Writings of Ralph Waldo Emerson* (New York: Modern Library, 1968), p. 880; Maurice Gonnaud, *An Uneasy Solitude* (Princeton, N.J.: Princeton University Press, 1987), p. 401; Irving Howe, *The American Newness* (Cambridge, Mass.: Harvard University Press, 1986), p. 35.

62. Quarles, *Blacks on John Brown*, pp. 57, 66.

63. Quoted in Benjamin Quarles, *Allies for Freedom* (New York: Oxford University Press, 1974), p. 154.

64. Quarles, *Blacks on John Brown*, p. 67.

65. Ibid., pp. 79, 81.

66. W. E. B. Du Bois, *John Brown* (New York: International Publishers, 1969), p. 8.

67. Quarles, *Blacks on John Brown*, p. 123.

68. Ibid., p. 139.

69. Quarles, *Allies for Freedom,* pp. 118–19.

70. For example, see C. Vann Woodward, "John Brown's Private War," in *America in Crisis,* ed. Daniel Aaron (New York: Alfred A. Knopf, 1952), pp. 109–30.

71. Stephen B. Oates, *Our Fiery Trial* (Amherst: University of Massachusetts Press, 1979), p. 40.

72. Roland Wagner may be more blunt than most critics, but many share his suspicion that the support for Brown says more about Thoreau's private obsessions than about the events themselves. Wagner writes: "Thoreau was not insane and Brown probably was, yet Thoreau grasped Brown's character well enough to understand how Brown could justify violence in the name of absolute principle. But it was an unconscious understanding. Thoreau sensed that Brown killed the representatives of civilized authority in part because they were simply authorities and had to be destroyed." "Brown was a monstrous mirror of Thoreau's inner life." Roland C. Wagner, "Lucky Fox at Walden," in *Thoreau in Our Season,* ed. John H.

Hicks (Amherst: University of Massachusetts Press, 1967), pp. 132, 133. See also Nancy L. Rosenblum, "Thoreau's Militant Conscience," *Political Theory* 9 (February 1981): 93: "The three pieces on John Brown have virtually nothing to say about slavery at all. Thoreau's emphasis is not neither the justice of abolition nor the efficacy of Brown's raids. He was principally interested in Brown as a representative of antagonism as a way of life."

73. "Civil Disobedience," p. 77.
74. "Slavery," p. 104.
75. Ibid., p. 108.
76. Ibid.
77. Thoreau rages against the hypocrisy of our praise of the "easy exploit of the Boston tea party," but our silence "about the braver and more disinterestedly heroic attack on the Boston Court-House, simply because it was unsuccessful!" In his *Journal* Thoreau discusses a Canadian case in which the courts were deciding whether to return an escaped slave to servitude. Thoreau notes that if the fugitive is returned, his best hope for freedom lies with threatened mob action in New York. "There, then, is the only resort of justice,—not where the judges are, but where the mob is, where human hearts are beating, and hands move in obedience to their impulses." Ibid., p. 105; *Journal*, 14: 293.
78. "A Plea," p. 133.
79. Some interpreters have insisted on a contradiction or at least an important conceptual and political discontinuity between "Civil Disobedience" and the John Brown essays. This position rests upon either a much more pacific reading of "Civil Disobedience" than I think the text will bear, or a much more critical assessment of the merits of Thoreau's rhetorical support for Brown than I believe is warranted, or both. See James Duban, "Conscience and Consciousness: The Liberal Christian Context of Thoreau's Political Ethics," *New England Quarterly* 60 (June 1987): 219, 221; Joseph Wood Krutch, *Henry David Thoreau* (New York: William Sloan Associates, 1948), p. 133; most importantly, see Wilson Carey McWilliams, *The Idea of Fraternity in America* (Berkeley and Los Angeles: University of California Press, 1973), p. 300.
For critics who argue (unpersuasively) for other discontinuities between "Civil Disobedience" and the John Brown essays, see Heinz Eulau, "Wayside Challenger: Some Remarks on the Politics of Henry David Thoreau," in *Thoreau: A Collection of Critical Essays* (Englewood Cliffs, N.J.: Prentice-Hall, 1962), pp. 117–30; Truman Nelson, "Thoreau and the Paralysis of Individualism," *Ramparts* 4 (March 1966): 17–26. Eulau argues that "Civil Disobedience" is a radically antidemocratic document, in contradiction with Thoreau's (grudging) approval of democracy in "A Plea for Captain John Brown," and Nelson insists that in the John Brown essays Thoreau finally overcomes the "individualism" that characterizes the rest of his writings.
80. "Slavery," p. 106.

81. Ibid. Compare this with Martin Luther King's formulation: "Any law that uplifts human personality is just. Any law that degrades human personality is unjust." Martin Luther King Jr., "Letter from Birmingham Jail," in his *Why We Can't Wait* (New York: Penguin, 1964), p. 82.

82. "A Plea," p. 112.

83. There are higher laws than the Constitution, of course, but Thoreau appears to hold the view that, properly understood, the principles of the Constitution conform to these higher laws. See "Slavery," p. 104.

84. "A Plea," p. 129.

85. "Life without Principle," in *Reform Papers*, pp. 175–76.

86. When Thoreau makes statements like "I feel that my connections with and obligations to society are at present very slight and transient," or "I am never invited by the community to do anything quite worth the while to do," it is important to understand them in the context of Thoreau's alienation from American politics. These comments are critical and explicitly addressed to the immediate political context, and are not commentaries on the relationship of individuals to politics generally. Even the famous comment from "Natural History of Massachusetts ("The merely political aspect of the land is never very cheering; men are degraded when considered as the members of a political organization") is followed by sentences that clearly modify these seemingly general anarchist sentiments by directing our attention to specific corruptions in American society: "On this side all lands present only the symptoms of decay. I see but Bunker Hill and Sing-Sing, the District of Columbia and Sullivan's Island, with a few avenues connecting them." *Journal*, 2: 141, 4: 252; Henry David Thoreau, *Excursions* (Boston: Houghton Mifflin, 1893), p. 129.

87. "Civil Disobedience," pp. 89–90.

88. Ibid., p. 84.

89. "Slavery," pp. 108–9.

90. Lawrence Buell misses this point when he claims that the water lily passage suggests that Thoreau abandoned his radicalism by escaping to nature. Lawrence Buell, *The Environmental Imagination* (Cambridge, Mass.: Harvard University Press, 1995), p. 37. On the role of the water lily as a symbol of virtue for Thoreau, see Stephen Railton, "Thoreau's 'Resurrection of Virtue,'" *American Quarterly* 24 (1972): 210–27.

91. Hubert Hoeltje argues that in the very first volume of the *Journal* we can see Thoreau withdrawing from human affairs to the world of nature—a withdrawal that was more or less complete and lifelong. As we saw in chapter 1, Hoeltje's conclusion is that this disqualifies Thoreau as a serious political writer. This view, common in one form or another in the secondary literature, is built upon the false premise that Thoreau's interest in nature is radically separate from his interest in the human community, and the false conclusion from this premise that his love of

nature transcended his concern for humanity. Hubert H. Hoeltje, "Misconceptions in Current Thoreau Criticism," *Philological Quarterly* 47 (October 1968): 565–67.

92. Barry Kritzberg, "Thoreau, Slavery, and Resistance to Civil Government," *Massachusetts Review* 30 (Winter 1989): 537. Robert Louis Stevenson makes a similar but even more general criticism of Thoreau when he writes, "Marcus Aurelius found time to study virtue, and between whiles to conduct the imperial affairs of Rome; but Thoreau is so busy improving himself, that he must think twice about a morning call." Robert Louis Stevenson, *Familiar Studies of Men and Books* (London: Chatto and Windus, 1924), p. 131.

93. "Life without Principle," pp. 162–63.

Chapter 7. Conclusion

1. Henry D. Thoreau, "Civil Disobedience," in *Reform Papers*, ed. Wendell Glick (Princeton, N.J.: Princeton University Press, 1973), p. 67.

2. Henry David Thoreau, *Walden*, in *A Week on the Concord and Merrimack Rivers; Walden, or, Life in the Woods; The Maine Woods, Cape Cod* (New York: Library of America, 1985), p. 335.

3. Hannah Arendt, *The Human Condition* (Chicago: University of Chicago Press, 1958), p. 5.

4. Ibid., p. 322.

5. Robert Coles, "Remembering Christopher Lasch," *New Oxford Review* 61 (September 1994): 18.

6. Andrew Delbanco has recently observed, "Arendt's most frightening implication was that the concept of evil might actually be incompatible with the very nature of modern life. She confirmed how hard it had become to find the place (as Henry David Thoreau had described a hundred years earlier) where one can 'no longer accuse institutions and society, but must front the true source of evil'—the self." Andrew Delbanco, *The Death of Satan* (New York: Farrar, Straus and Giroux, 1995), pp. 7–8.

7. *Walden*, p. 450.

8. Ibid.

9. "Slavery in Massachusetts," in *Reform Papers*, p. 102.

10. "An essential concomitant of guerrilla politics—which initially this [i.e., a democratic politics] would be—is a healthy [political] disrespect." Robert H. Wiebe, *Self-Rule* (Chicago: University of Chicago Press, 1995), p. 259.

11. "Civil Disobedience," p. 66. We should not, however, confuse Thoreau's ornery assertion of independence with a postmodern irony and relativism as Jane Bennett has recently done. Thoreau's morality is ultimately foundationalist, and his language is too accessible and democratic to have much in common with the

postmodern sensibility. See Jane Bennett, *Thoreau's Nature* (Thousand Oaks, Calif: Sage, 1994).

12. *Walden,* p. 486. Compare with Rousseau's attack on luxury: "Luxury is a remedy far worse than the evil it means to cure; or rather it is itself the worst of all evils in any state, however large or small it may be, and which, in order to feed the hoards of lackeys and wretches it has produced, crushes and ruins the laborer and the citizen—like those scorching south winds that, by covering grass and greenery with devouring insects, take sustenance away from useful animals, and bring scarcity and death to all the places where they make themselves felt." Jean-Jacques Rousseau, "Discourse on the Origin of Inequality," in *Basic Political Writings* (Indianapolis, Ind.: Hackett Publishing, 1987), p. 93.

13. *Walden,* p. 395.

14. Ibid., p. 578.

15. Ibid., p. 349.

16. Ibid., p. 352.

17. On this issue, as many others, Thoreau differs from Emerson. For example, Emerson writes of commerce: "It is easy to see that the existing generation are conspiring with a beneficence, which, in its working for coming generations, sacrifices the passing one, which infatuates the most selfish men to act against their private interest for the public welfare. The history of commerce, is the record of this beneficent tendency." Ralph Waldo Emerson, "The Young American," in *Essays and Lectures* (New York: Library of America, 1983), p. 219.

For an alternative (but I think unconvincing) reading of Emerson as an opponent of modern conceptions of progress, see Christopher Lasch, *The True and Only Heaven* (New York: Norton, 1991), chap. 6.

18. *Walden,* p. 580.

19. While it is well known, particularly among environmentalists, that Thoreau believed that "in Wildness is the preservation of the World," the sentence preceding this declaration is often overlooked: "I felt that *this was the heroic age itself,* though we know it not, for the hero is commonly the simplest and obscurest of men." The importance of nature is that it provides an environment in which we can become "wild" and "heroic," less restrained and inhibited by society, more independent and free. Henry David Thoreau, "Walking," in *Excursions* (Boston: Houghton Mifflin, 1893), p. 275.

20. In his *Journal,* Thoreau once wrote: "I can remember that when I was very young I used to have a dream night after night, over and over again, which might have been named Rough and Smooth. All existence, all satisfaction and dissatisfaction, all event was symbolized in this way. Now I seemed to be lying and tossing, perchance, on a horrible, a fatal rough surface, which must soon, indeed, put an end to my existence, though even in the dream I knew it to be the symbol merely of my misery; and then again, suddenly I was lying on a delicious smooth surface, as of a summer sea, as of gossamer or down or softest plush, and life was such a

luxury to live. My waking experience always has been and is such an alternate Rough and Smooth. In other words it is Insanity and Sanity." Henry D. Thoreau, *The Journal of Henry D. Thoreau*, vol. 9, ed. Bradford Torrey and Francis H. Allen, (Boston: Houghton Mifflin, 1949), pp. 210–11.

As this poignant moment of self-analysis suggests, Thoreau suffered a tumultuous psychic life, although he was remarkably successful overall in overcoming his sorrows and fears. His writings exhibit, not surprisingly, changes in mood and disposition corresponding to his "Rough" and "Smooth." Thoreau struggled throughout his life with swings from optimism to pessimism, from hope to despair, from respect to contempt for others, from feelings of social integration to isolation. Although there are passages in Thoreau's writings that can be used to support an anarchist reading, these passages often represent Thoreau's darkest moments, and should not be taken to represent the core and primary thrust of his views; or, as we have seen, they are confined to an expression of Thoreau's disgust with contemporary affairs and are wrongly generalized to politics as a whole, or are rhetorically inflated for the purpose of jarring the reader.

21. "I saw that the State was half-witted, that it was timid as a lone woman with her silver spoons, and that it did not know its friends from its foes, and I lost all my remaining respect for it, and pitied it." "Civil Disobedience," p. 80.

22. C. Carroll Hollis, "Thoreau and the State," *Commonweal*, 9 September 1949, p. 531. In an interesting rejoinder, Robert Ludlow, a radical Catholic, defends Thoreau from Hollis's attack in "Communications: Thoreau and the State," *Commonweal*, 27 September 1949, pp. 581–82.

23. See chap. 1, n. 34.

24. Laraine Fergenson, "Thoreau, Daniel Berrigan, and the Problem of Transcendental Politics," *Soundings* 65 (Spring 1982): 119. Fergenson is appalled by Daniel Berrigan's attack on Israel, and is concerned in this article to criticize not only his policy position but the type of political reasoning that can lead to what she believes is such wrongheaded self-righteousness.

25. Heinze Eulau, "Wayside Challenger: Some Remarks on the Politics of Henry David Thoreau," in *Thoreau: A Collection of Critical Essays*, ed. Sherman Paul (Englewood Cliffs, N.J.: Prentice-Hall, 1962), p. 125; Fergenson, "Thoreau, Daniel Berrigan, and the Problem of Transcendental Politics," p. 115.

26. *Journal*, 1: 233.

27. "Reason is what engenders egocentrism, and reflection strengthens it. Reason is what turns man in upon himself. Reason is what separates him from all that troubles him and afflicts him. Philosophy is what isolates him and what moves him to say in secret, at the sight of a suffering man, 'Perish if you will; I am safe and sound.' No longer can anything but danger to the entire society trouble the tranquil slumber of the philosopher and yank him from his bed. His fellow man can be killed with impunity underneath his window. He has merely to place his hands over his ears and argue with himself a little in order to prevent nature, which rebels

within him, from identifying him with the man being assassinated. Savage man does not have this admirable talent, and for lack of wisdom and reason he is always seen thoughtlessly giving in to the first sentiment of humanity. When there is a riot or a street brawl, the populace gathers together; the prudent man withdraws from the scene. It is the rabble, the women of the marketplace, who separate the combatants and prevent decent people from killing one another." Rousseau, "Discourse on the Origin of Inequality," pp. 54–55.

28. "I have never yet met a man who was quite awake. How could I have looked him in the face?" *Walden*, p. 394.

29. Perry Miller argues that "*Walden* is not the transcript of an adventure in primitive living, but a highly schematized pattern of words, designed not so much to make a sociological point as to become a thing of beauty, to translate facts into form." Perry Miller, *Consciousness in Concord* (Boston: Houghton Mifflin, 1958), p. 27. Also see Stanley Edgar Hyman, "Henry Thoreau Once More," *Massachusetts Review* 4 (1962): 169; Henry Golemba, *Thoreau's Wild Rhetoric* (New York: New York University Press, 1990), pp. 5, 17, and passim.

30. "To be a philosopher is not merely to have subtle thoughts, nor even to found a school, but so to love wisdom as to live according to its dictates, a life of simplicity, independence, magnanimity, and trust. It is to solve some of the problems of life, not only theoretically, but practically." *Walden*, p. 334.

31. The classic case here is Nancy Rosenblum, for whom, as we have seen, Thoreau is the champion of a belligerent and irresolvable antagonism toward others and society at large. Nancy L. Rosenblum, "Thoreau's Militant Conscience," *Political Theory* 9 (February 1981): 81–110, and *Another Liberalism* (Cambridge, Mass.: Harvard University Press, 1987), pp. 103–18.

32. In Michael Walzer's striking imagery, Thoreau is assuming the role of a democratic "prophet," as opposed to an elitist "priest." See his contrast between these types of moral leadership in *Exodus and Revolution* (New York: Basic Books, 1985), esp. chap. 4.

33. "If the injustice is part of the necessary friction of the machine of government, let it go, let it go: perchance it will wear smooth,—certainly the machine will wear out ... but if it is of such a nature that it requires you to be the agent of injustice to another, then, I say, break the law. Let your life be a counter friction to stop the machine." "Civil Disobedience," pp. 73–74.

34. Leo Marx, "The Two Thoreaus," *New York Review of Books*, 26 October 1978, p. 42.

35. Truman Nelson, "Thoreau and the Paralysis of Individualism," *Ramparts* 4 (March 1966): p. 21.

36. Milan Kundera, *The Unbearable Lightness of Being* (New York: HarperCollins, 1984), p. 251. Kundera explains: "Since the days of the French Revolution, one half of Europe has been referred to as the left, the other half as the right. Yet to define one or the other by means of the theoretical principles it professes is all but impos-

sible. And no wonder: political movements rest not so much on rational attitudes as on the fantasies, images, words, and archetypes that come together to make up this or that *political kitsch*." Ibid., p. 257.

37. Ibid., p. 257.

38. "There is no odor so bad as that which arises from goodness tainted." *Walden*, p. 381.

39. Ibid., p. 575.

40. Henry Thoreau, *Collected Poems of Henry Thoreau*, ed. Carl Bode (Baltimore, Md.: Johns Hopkins University Press, 1970), p. 195.

REFERENCES

Aaron, Daniel, ed. *America in Crisis*. New York: Alfred A. Knopf, 1952.

Abbott, Philip. *States of Perfect Freedom*. Amherst: University of Massachusetts Press, 1987.

Anderson, Quentin. *Making Americans*. New York: Harcourt Brace Jovanovich, 1992.

Appleby, Joyce. *Liberalism and Republicanism in the Historical Imagination*. Cambridge, Mass.: Harvard University Press, 1992.

Arendt, Hannah. *The Human Condition*. Chicago: University of Chicago Press, 1958.

Augustine. *City of God*. New York: Penguin, 1981.

Baskett, Sam. "Fronting the Atlantic: *Cape Cod* and 'The Dry Salvages.'" *New England Quarterly* 56 (1983): 200–219.

Bennett, Jane. "On Being a Native: Thoreau's Hermeneutics of Self." *Polity* 22 (Summer 1990): 559–80.

———. *Thoreau's Nature*. Thousand Oaks, Calif.: Sage, 1994.

Bercovitch, Sacvan. *The American Jeremiad*. Madison: University of Wisconsin Press, 1978.

Bickman, Martin. *Walden: Volatile Truths*. New York: Twayne, 1992.

Bridgman, Richard. *Dark Thoreau*. Lincoln: University of Nebraska Press, 1982.

Broderick, John C. "Thoreau's Proposals for Legislation." *American Quarterly* 7 (1955): 285–90.

Buell, Lawrence. *The Environmental Imagination*. Cambridge, Mass.: Harvard University Press, 1995.

———. "The Thoreauvian Pilgrimage: The Structure of an American Cult." *American Literature* 61 (May 1989): 175–199.

Buranelli, Vincent. "The Case against Thoreau." *Ethics* 67 (1957): 257–68.

Burbick, Joan. *Thoreau's Alternative History*. Philadelphia: University of Pennsylvania Press, 1987.

Canby, Henry Seidel. *Classic Americans*. New York: Harcourt, Brace, 1931.

_____ . *Thoreau*. Boston: Houghton Mifflin, 1939.

Cavell, Stanley. *The Senses of Walden*. San Francisco: North Point Press, 1981.

Coles, Robert. "Remembering Christopher Lasch." *New Oxford Review* 61 (September 1994): 16–19.

Cronon, William. *Changes in the Land: Indians, Colonists, and the Ecology of New England*. New York: Hill and Wang, 1983.

D'Avanzo, Mario. "Fortitude and Nature in Thoreau's *Cape Cod*." *ESQ* 20 (1974): 131–38.

Dedmond, Francis B. "Thoreau and the Ethical Concept of Government." *The Personalist* 36 (1955): 36–46.

Delbanco, Andrew. *The Death of Satan*. New York: Farrar, Straus and Giroux, 1995.

Diggins, John Patrick. "Thoreau, Marx, and the 'Riddle' of Alienation." *Social Research* 39 (Winter 1972): 571–98.

Douglass, Frederick. *The Life and Writings of Frederick Douglass*. 5 vols. Edited by Philip S. Foner. New York: International Publishers, 1950.

Duban, James. "Conscience and Consciousness: The Liberal Christian Context of Thoreau's Political Ethics." *New England Quarterly* 60 (June 1987): 208–22.

Du Bois, W. E. B. *John Brown*. New York: International Publishers, 1969.

Ellis, Richard J. *American Political Cultures*. New York: Oxford University Press, 1993.

Emerson, Ralph Waldo. *Essays and Lectures*. New York: Library of America, 1983.

_____ . *The Selected Writings of Ralph Waldo Emerson*. New York: Modern Library, 1968.

Fergenson, Laraine. "Thoreau, Daniel Berrigan, and the Problem of Transcendental Politics." *Soundings* 65 (Spring 1982): 103–22.

Fink, Steven. *Prophet in the Marketplace*. Princeton, N.J.: Princeton University Press, 1992.

Goldman, Emma. *Anarchism and Other Essays*. Port Washington, N.Y.: Kennikat Press, 1969.

Golemba, Henry. *Thoreau's Wild Rhetoric*. New York: New York University Press, 1990.

Gonnaud, Maurice. *An Uneasy Solitude*. Princeton, N.J.: Princeton University Press, 1987.

Harding, Walter. *The Days of Henry Thoreau*. New York: Alfred A. Knopf, 1966.

_____ , ed. *Thoreau: A Century of Criticism*. Dallas: Southern Methodist University Press, 1954.

_____ . ed. *Thoreau, Man of Concord*. New York: Holt, Rinehart and Winston, 1960.

Hawthorne, Nathaniel. *Hawthorne as Editor*. Edited by Arlin Turner. Port Washington, N.Y.: Kennikat Press, 1941.

Henry, Alexander. *Travels and Adventures*. Rutland, Vt.: Charles E. Tuttle, 1969.

Hicks, John H., ed. *Thoreau in Our Season*. Amherst: University of Massachusetts Press, 1967.

Hochfield, George. "Anti-Thoreau." *Sewanee Review* 96 (Summer 1988): 433–43.

Hoeltje, Hubert H. "Misconceptions in Current Thoreau Criticism." *Philological Quarterly* 47 (October 1968): 563–70.

Hollis, C. Carroll. "Thoreau and the State." *Commonweal*, 9 September 1949, 530–33.

Holmes, Oliver Wendell. *Ralph Waldo Emerson.* Boston: Houghton, Mifflin, 1886.

Howe, Irving. *The American Newness.* Cambridge, Mass.: Harvard University Press, 1986.

Hyman, Stanley Edgar. "Henry Thoreau Once More." *Massachusetts Review* 4 (1962): 163–70.

Johnson, Linck C. *Thoreau's Complex Weave.* Charlottesville: University Press of Virginia, 1986.

Kateb, George. *Emerson and Self-Reliance.* Thousand Oaks, Calif.: Sage, 1995.

King, Martin Luther, Jr. *Why We Can't Wait.* New York: Penguin, 1964.

Kritzberg, Barry. "Thoreau, Slavery, and Resistance to Civil Government." *Massachusetts Review* 30 (Winter 1989): 535–65.

Krutch, Joseph Wood. *Henry David Thoreau.* New York: William Sloan Associates, 1948.

Kundera, Milan. *The Unbearable Lightness of Being.* New York: HarperCollins, 1984.

Lasch, Christopher. *The True and Only Heaven.* New York: Norton, 1991.

Lebeaux, Richard. *Thoreau's Seasons.* Amherst: University of Massachusetts Press, 1984.

Lowney, John. "Thoreau's *Cape Cod:* The Unsettling Art of the Wrecker." *American Literature* 64 (June 1992): 239–54.

Ludlow, Robert. "Communications: Thoreau and the State." *Commonweal*, 27 September 1949, 581–82.

Marx, Leo. "The Two Thoreaus." *New York Review of Books*, 26 October 1978, 37–44.

Matthiessen, F. O. *American Renaissance.* New York: Oxford University Press, 1941.

McWilliams, Wilson Carey. *The Idea of Fraternity in America.* Berkeley and Los Angeles: University of California Press, 1973.

Melville, Herman. *The Apple-Tree Table and Other Stories.* New York: Greenwood, 1969.

Merchant, Carolyn. *Ecological Revolutions.* Chapel Hill: University of North Carolina Press, 1989.

Miller, Perry. *Consciousness in Concord.* Boston: Houghton Mifflin, 1958.

Moller, Mary Elkins. *Thoreau in the Human Community.* Amherst: University of Massachusetts Press, 1980.

Myerson, Joel, ed. *Critical Essays on Henry David Thoreau's Walden.* Boston: G. K. Hall, 1988.

———, ed. *Studies in the American Renaissance, 1980.* Boston: Twayne, 1980.

———, ed. *Studies in the American Renaissance, 1990.* Charlottesville: University Press of Virginia, 1990.

Nahman of Bratslav. *The Tales.* New York: Paulist Press, 1978.

Nelson, Truman. "Thoreau and the Paralysis of Individualism." *Ramparts* 4 (March 1966): 17–26.

Neufeldt, Leonard N. "Emerson, Thoreau, and Daniel Webster." *ESQ* 26 (1980): 26–37.

Nietzsche, Friedrich. *Basic Writings of Nietzsche.* Edited by Walter Kaufmann. New York: Modern Library, 1968.

Oates, Joyce Carol. "The Mysterious Mr. Thoreau." *New York Times Book Review,* 1 May 1988, 1, 31–33.

Oates, Stephen B. *Our Fiery Trial.* Amherst: University of Massachusetts Press, 1979.

Oelschlaeger, Max. *The Idea of Wilderness.* New Haven, Conn.: Yale University Press, 1991.

Parrington, Vernon L. *Main Currents of American Thought.* New York: Harcourt, Brace, 1927.

Paul, Sherman. *The Shores of America.* Urbana: University of Illinois Press, 1958.

_____ , ed. *Thoreau: A Collection of Critical Essays.* Englewood Cliffs, N.J.: Prentice-Hall, 1962.

Peck, H. Daniel. *Thoreau's Morning Work.* New Haven, Conn.: Yale University Press, 1990.

Plato. *The Collected Dialogues of Plato.* Edited by Edith Hamilton and Huntington Cairns. New York: Bollingen Foundation, 1966.

Porte, Joel. "Henry Thoreau: Society and Solitude." *ESQ* 19 (1973): 131–40.

Quarles, Benjamin. *Allies for Freedom.* New York: Oxford University Press, 1974.

_____ . *Blacks on John Brown.* Urbana: University of Illinois Press, 1972.

Railton, Stephen. "Thoreau's 'Resurrection of Virtue.'" *American Quarterly* 24 (1972): 210–27.

Richardson, Robert D. *Emerson: The Mind on Fire.* Berkeley and Los Angeles: University of California Press, 1995.

_____ . *Henry Thoreau.* Berkeley and Los Angeles: University of California Press, 1986.

Rogin, Michael. "Nature as Politics and Nature as Romance in America." *Political Theory* 5 (February 1977): 5–30.

Rosenblum, Nancy L. *Another Liberalism.* Cambridge, Mass.: Harvard University Press, 1987.

_____ . "Thoreau's Militant Conscience." *Political Theory* 9 (February 1981): 81–110.

Rousseau, Jean-Jacques. *Basic Political Writings.* Indianapolis, Ind.: Hackett Publishing, 1987.

Salt, Henry S. *The Life of Henry David Thoreau.* Edited by George Hendrick, Willene Hendrick, and Fritz Oehlschlaeger. Urbana: University of Illinois Press, 1993.

Sanborn, F. B. *Henry D. Thoreau.* Boston: Houghton Mifflin, 1910.

Sanders, Frederick K. "Mr. Thoreau's Timebomb." *National Review* 4 (June 1968): 541–47.

Sattelmeyer, Robert. *Thoreau's Reading.* Princeton, N.J.: Princeton University Press, 1988.

References

Sayre, Robert F. *New Essays on Walden*. New York: Cambridge University Press, 1992.

_____ . *Thoreau and the American Indians*. Princeton, N.J.: Princeton University Press, 1977.

Schama, Simon. *Landscape and Memory*. New York: Alfred A. Knopf, 1995.

Schneider, Richard J. "*Cape Cod:* Thoreau's Wilderness of Illusion." *ESQ* 26 (1980): 184–96.

Stevenson, Robert Louis. *Familiar Studies of Men and Books*. London: Chatto and Windus, 1924.

Stoehr, Taylor. *Nay-Saying in Concord*. Hamden, Conn.: Archon Books, 1979.

Stoller, Leo. *After Walden*. Stanford, Calif.: Stanford University Press, 1957.

Taylor, Bob Pepperman. *Our Limits Transgressed: Environmental Political Thought in America*. Lawrence: University Press of Kansas, 1992.

Thoreau, Henry David. *Collected Poems of Henry David Thoreau*. Edited by Carl Bode. Baltimore, Md.: Johns Hopkins University Press, 1970.

_____ . *The Correspondence of Henry David Thoreau*. Edited by Walter Harding and Carl Bode. New York: New York University Press, 1958.

_____ . *Early Essays and Miscellanies*. Edited by Joseph J. Moldenhauer and Edwin Moser. Princeton, N.J.: Princeton University Press, 1975.

_____ . *Excursions*. Boston: Houghton Mifflin, 1893.

_____ . *Huckleberries*. Edited by Leo Stoller. Iowa City: The Windhover Press of the University of Iowa and the New York Public Library, 1970.

_____ . *The Journal of Henry D. Thoreau*. 14 vols. Edited by Bradford Torrey and Francis H. Allen. Boston: Houghton Mifflin, 1949.

_____ . *Reform Papers*. Edited by Wendell Glick. Princeton, N.J.: Princeton University Press, 1973.

_____ . *A Week on the Concord and Merrimack Rivers; Walden, or, Life in the Woods; The Maine Woods; Cape Cod*. New York: Library of America, 1985.

Walzer, Michael. *The Company of Critics*. New York: Basic Books, 1988.

_____ . *Exodus and Revolution*. New York: Basic Books, 1985.

White, E. B. "Walden—1954." *Yale Review* 44 (1954): 13–22.

Wiebe, Robert H. *Self-Rule*. Chicago: University of Chicago Press, 1995.

Wood, Gordon. *The Radicalism of the American Revolution*. New York: Alfred A. Knopf, 1992.

Worster, Donald. *Nature's Economy*. San Francisco: Sierra Club Books, 1977.

INDEX

Abbott, Philip, 1, 5, 147n42, 155n69
Agassez, Louis, 12
Aitteon, Joe, 42–43
American Revolution, 19, 20, 28, 71, 108
Anderson, Quentin, 29, 155n69
Appleby, Joyce, 75
Arendt, Hannah, 120, 121
Aristotle, 122
Augustine, 13
"Autumnal Tints," 155n82

Baskett, Sam, 146n6
Bennett, Jane
  on Thoreau and anarchism, 16, 30, 149n69, 161n42
  on Thoreau and conditions for civil disobedience, 105
  on Thoreau and post modernism, 165n6
  on Thoreau as "artist of the self," 5, 155n69
Bercovitch, Sacvan, 154n66
Blake, H. G. O., 83
Brickman, Martin, 86
Bridgman, Richard, 142n12, 146nn5,17
Broderick, John C., 134n49, 149n85

Brown, John, 44, 99, 126
  African American views of, 110–12
  as American hero/patriot, 101, 107–8, 114, 117, 161n43
  and insanity, 110, 111–12, 161n55, 162n72
  Thoreau's defensiveness about, 100, 115
  and violence, 109–10, 113, 162nn61,72
Buell, Lawrence
  on Thoreau and literary studies, 134n49
  on Thoreau as radical environmentalist, 36, 37, 141n8, 142n9, 164n90
Buranelli, Vincent, 3, 6, 7, 157n119, 159n7
Burbick, Joan, 18, 141n2
Burns, Anthony, 99, 105, 106, 113, 115

Canby, Henry Seidel, 4, 36, 132n21, 151n12, 154n67
Cavell, Stanley, 80, 138n47, 155n69, 159n144
Channing, William Ellery, 70, 71
Cholmondeley, Thomas, 72
Coles, Robert, 120

177

11/97   O 7/97